Contributions to Economics

The series *Contributions to Economics* provides an outlet for innovative research in all areas of economics. Books published in the series are primarily monographs and multiple author works that present new research results on a clearly defined topic, but contributed volumes and conference proceedings are also considered. All books are published in print and ebook and disseminated and promoted globally. The series and the volumes published in it are indexed by Scopus and ISI (selected volumes).

More information about this series at https://link.springer.com/bookseries/1262

Maurizio Bovi

Why and How Humans Trade, Predict, Aggregate, and Innovate

An Economist's Lessons on the Role of Human Behavior and Economic Systems

Springer

Maurizio Bovi
Italian National Institute of Statistics
Roma, Italy

ISSN 1431-1933 ISSN 2197-7178 (electronic)
Contributions to Economics
ISBN 978-3-030-93884-0 ISBN 978-3-030-93885-7 (eBook)
https://doi.org/10.1007/978-3-030-93885-7

This Springer imprint is published by the registered company Springer Nature Switzerland AG
The registered company address is: Gewerbestrasse 11, 6330 Cham, Switzerland

To Debbina, Vale, and Robino

Contents

1 Prologue

1.1 Introducing the *Four*: Trading, Forecasting, Aggregating, Innovating

Trading, forecasting, aggregating, and innovating are activities that people have engaged in since the beginning of our race. They are part of the human fabric because they stem from mankind's peculiarities—heterogeneity, inclination to forecast, sociality, and inventiveness. Trading, forecasting, aggregating, and innovating activities, referred to from here on out as the *Four*, are key social interactions in human life at both the individual and aggregate levels.

In 2019, the value of worldwide global exports amounted to approximately US $19 trillion. The majority of humans live together in urban areas, while an even larger share belongs to social groups such as families and nations. Virtually everyone, finally, has very often to deal with forecasts and innovations. In a nutshell, the *Four* are ancestral, vital social interactions that each of us face not in only special moments but, rather, every day. It is therefore unsurprising that several books have been written on each of these essential human endeavors.

As such, the view that inspired me to write this book on how humans address the *Four* is both narrow and wide. It is narrow because I have preferred synthesis to analysis. Hence, I have organized the book as a short tour, touching upon only some of the topics regarding the *Four*. On the other hand, the view is wide because the bird's-eye view offered by the proposed tour involves a combination of trading, forecasting, aggregating, and innovating efforts.

Of course, a book this wide-ranging inevitably leaves unexplored many interesting themes, hints, and viewpoints. Generality, coupled with brevity, leads to a lack of details. This said, there are benefits in focusing on the big picture, and I hope that the balance for the traveler will be strictly positive. A first advantage of addressing the *Four* all together is the description of existing ideas in a novel way—as far as I know, this is the first attempt to do that. The inclusive approach, then, affords to frame several important themes in a coherent picture. In one single short trip, the traveler will wander across the significant gains realized from trade, the critical

M. Bovi, *Why and How Humans Trade, Predict, Aggregate, and Innovate*,
Contributions to Economics, https://doi.org/10.1007/978-3-030-93885-7_1

advantages of effective forecasting at both the individual and system-wide levels, the rewards of living together in various social clusters, and the accumulated enhancements achieved through innovation. Several notions will be cleared and even more connections among them emerge. These notions and connections magnify the importance of the four businesses under scrutiny and might be appreciated by the traveler.

In addition, the inclusive view is justified by the fact that the *Four* share a number of commonalities. Among them, all the four human interactions under scrutiny are performed by humans for humans; thus, the same behavioral attitudes of humans are behind all of the *Four*. Trading, forecasting, aggregating, and innovating can then reinforce each other, and all have a dark side. Another common thread pops up considering that these activities are all endeavors unavoidably inserted in an economic system featured by specific rules of the game. During the tour, I will repeatedly emphasize that the result of trading, forecasting, aggregating, and innovating is a joint product of behaviors and rules of the game, which is one of the several takeaways of the proposed journey.

All told, the main idea of this book is to include in a single tour a collection of insights on why and how humans implement the *Four*. The narrative highlights several connections as well as how key these businesses are as the traveler is escorted through some *Four*-related behavioral problems and institutional solutions that humans have been, respectively, facing and elaborating over time.

Even though the behaviors represented by the *Four* have been analyzed through different scientific disciplines, I offer insights mainly from economics. Economists are thus the travel guides of the tour. Economics students may exploit this book by both inserting what they are learning from textbooks into a wider framework and enjoying some of the hints revealed by the grand social theorizing of giants such as A. Smith and J. Schumpeter. But the proposed tour may also attract outsiders to economics who are curious about disparate economic themes linked to the *Four* but who wish to gain an overview without engaging in longer readings.

Given the intended readership, some word on the travel guide seems necessary. Some readers hear that economics celebrates selfishness and greed, ignoring environmental issues, fairness, social cohesion, and our sense of what it is to be human. Our tour should make clear that this is a limited view that disregards many major achievements of economics. Also, some readers consider—or are aware that many people consider—economics as mainly forecasting exercises that, more often than not, record very poor scores. In Chap. 2, I argue that economists can be partly blamed for this situation, but by the end of the journey, travelers should be aware that this opinion is inaccurate, too.

Although economists are the official guides of the tour, I also consider ideas stemming from other sciences. It should not come as a surprise that many disciplines address the four activities under scrutiny, and I believe that no science has the monopoly on good ideas. F. Hayek once said: "an economist who is only an economist cannot be a good economist [1]."[1] Further, some of the guides that I have selected for this tour are Nobel Prize laureates in Economics who are mathematicians, political scientists, and psychologists. Finally, it is worth recalling that the economist T.R. Malthus's *Essay on the Principle of Population* influenced the biologist Charles Darwin's theory of evolution; that the concept of "reciprocal altruism" was independently elaborated by the biologist R. Trivers and, several years earlier, by the economist R. Aumann; and that the economist F.Y. Edgeworth tried to ground his economics on the psychophysics developed in Germany by the sociologist M. Weber [2].

The foregoing suggests putting forward a general cautionary note on definitions. Due to the huge complexity and dynamic nature of human societies, it is difficult to achieve ultimate all-encompassing definitions in social sciences [3]. Despite its usefulness, digging into definitions is outside the scope of this book. Deep exploration of even a limited number of the definitions that we will encounter in our journey would easily fill very many pages, possibly leading the reader astray. Moreover, it neither matches with my bird's-eye approach nor, I imagine, the main interest of the intended readership. But readers and the author need to establish some minimal common understanding of a term to eliminate, as far as possible, misunderstandings stemming from definitions with imprecise boundaries. Hence, I will focus on definitions which I think are most suitable for this tour. For example, social capital is a key, yet vague, concept that could be identified with the willingness to respect the rules of the game, the level of trust and trustworthiness inside human aggregations, or thought of as a cluster of norms, such as cooperation and civic engagement or as social networks/relationships, or as a combination of them all. In this tour, this last inclusive definition is valid. Given the role of economics in this tour, I will often refer to the definitions reported in sources such as the OECD glossary or economic literature. The given definition is only one of the possible choices, and it might not be the preferred one for some readers. That said, here it only aims to make explicit to the reader that it is the definition I follow throughout the book. Henceforth, I will refer to this guide as the "definitory *caveat*."

The trip proceeds as follows. In the remainder of this Prologue, I introduce the cited commonalities behind the trading, forecasting, aggregating, and innovating affairs. In the first two sections, specifically, I give the traveler an overall idea of the behavioral features and economic systems that necessarily accompany humans in undertaking all of the businesses under scrutiny. In these excursions, some links between behaviors and systems materialize. In the third and last section of this Prologue, I focus more directly on the *Four*, presenting to the traveler the instruments that humans use to accomplish these activities as well as the goals and other common features of these affairs. From Chapter 2 to Chapter 5, the outings

[1] Clearly this raises the question of defining who economists are, but I do not want to engage in definitory issues. In the tour I will use the term *economist* to refer, admittedly roughly, also to people like K. Marx, J.N. Nash, and R.D. Putnam. In my defense, there is the fact that this tour's aim is economic issues, not economists. Not to mention that an oft-quoted sentence by J. Viner (a prominent economist) "clarifies" that "economics is what economists do."

concentrate on each of the four endeavors separately and, specifically, on why and how humans implement the *Four*. The logic is that besides having several commonalities, the *Four* are different activities, derive from specific skills and attitudes, and as observed, offer unique gains. In the Epilogue, finally, I return to scout the *Four* all together to provide the traveler further considerations. In particular, I stress the possibility that the *Four* can reinforce each other, I outline the problems that arise from these activities and the solutions found by humans, and I offer some speculations on the future of these four key social interactions.

1.2 Behavioral Commonalities Behind the *Four*: Cooperation, Symbolic Language, Multifaceted Behavior, Adaptability

Since this tour deals with why and how humans trade, forecast, aggregate, and innovate, an excursion on human behavior is essential. Accordingly, our journey starts introducing behavioral commonalities behind the *Four*: specifically, cooperation, symbolic language, multifaceted behavior, and adaptability. In the first part of this stage, we will see that these elements are very special behavioral traits that have always accompanied human actions. The exploration then examines how these behavioral factors influence the *Four* as considered together. Insight from our guides highlights that cooperation, symbolic language, and mixed behavior introduce opposite forces and lead to disparate outcomes when adaptive humans put in place the four businesses that frame our trip.

Humans have cooperative and communicative skills unique in the animal world. To show how ancestral and special these traits are, I start from the very beginning, wondering what made us humans. Needless to say, it is a hard-to-answer question. Conclusions are disparate and depend on which standpoint one takes. As a general matter, humans are seen as animals equipped with unique physical, intellectual, social, biological, and emotional traits such as self-awareness, imagination, morality, bipedalism, soul, and introspection. With this in mind, I narrow my attention to conclusions from paleoanthropologists, whose suggestions turn out to be fruitful in light of our tour. Scientific evidence from paleoanthropology shows that the physical traits that make us humans are bipedalism and a large brain, while our behavioral peculiarities lie in how we cooperate as well as communicate via symbolic language. Clearly, physical and behavioral traits are connected (e.g., a large brain helps in understanding symbolic language). Because of our tour's aim, however, I will focus on the behavioral traits. Scientists argue that these two attributes originated from apelike ancestors approximately six million years ago—a "starting moment" that for future reference I label the socioeconomic Big Bang.[2] What is important in terms of

[2]Obviously, humankind did not emerge all of a sudden on planet Earth. Indeed, scientists argue that million years ago there were about twenty different species of early humans, called hominins. Other branches of humans died out, but that leading to the modern human, Homo Sapiens, continued to evolve. I put forward the idea of an explosion to emphasize the somehow common dynamic aftermath of the astrophysical and socioeconomic Big Bang. As the Universe Mankind is

our tour is not the precise date of this Big Bang but the examination of why Sapiens began to cooperate and communicate.

Some authors have argued that cooperative behavior was caused by evolution [4], while others point to the environment. Focusing on the latter, the so-called savannah hypothesis [5] suggests that proto hominins, perhaps voluntarily, abandoned forested or wooded habitats and gradually adapted to survive in the open and dangerous world of the savannah. In this new environment, there were few fruits and other foods, but large herbivores could furnish an abundant source of protein. However, hunting in the savannah was extremely difficult and dangerous. Cooperation then emerged as a functioning strategy to address the new situation, giving rise to the socioeconomic Big Bang. Similarly, other paleoanthropologists have emphasized that the nocturnal ancestors of today's primates became more active during the day. The conclusion is that while it is easier to capture and avoid being captured at night, during the day, prey and predators can more easily spot you. Again, humans soon learned that unity is strength, and cooperation emerged as a fruitful exit strategy. While this cooperative choice may have individualistic motives, sharing food, caring for infants, and building social networks helped our ancestors meet the daily challenges of their environments. As I shall stress throughout the tour, Sapiens are adaptive animals, which, indeed, is a very useful quality because human history looks like a never-ending sequence of the "new normal."

There are different theories about the evolution of language in humans. One view is that language is what is known in biology as a *spandrel*, i.e., a characteristic that is a by-product of the evolution of some other characteristic. For instance, language may be the by-product of the larger brain of Sapiens. However, the most common explanation is *social*, and since cooperation and symbolic language are closely related, they likely emerged contextually during the socioeconomic Big Bang. In fact, as cooperative, social animals, we need to communicate with each other, and language is a clear example of our effort to coordinate and cooperate. Here again emerges the adaptability of humans: language was an adaptation linked to the need to operate in groups and, in general, to face the increasing complexity of the environment surrounding us.

In summary, for our tour, the basic message from paleoanthropology is that humans have cooperated and communicated since almost the inception of our species as an adaptive, perhaps at least partly individualistically based, response to tackle new necessities. This paves the way for the next question: in what sense are these two behavioral characteristics unique to humankind? In fact, it is easy to find cooperative behaviors in other species; we are not the only living beings that

"expanding" through time and space because of the continuous execution of the *Four*. The expansion involves the world population, the life expectancy, the size of human aggregations (from family to clan up to the UN), the average IQ, and lifelong distance covered. Even time goes "faster"—our forefathers' life flowed less frantically than ours. According to the latest trend in space exploration, lastly, it might be that in the next future the planet Earth will no longer constitute a physical limit to the expansion of our species.

communicate. More importantly for our aim, the answer highlights further aspects of human behavior.

As for cooperation, small fish swim in schools because there is safety in numbers. Ants, bees, and other insects live in even more organized colonies where cooperation has additional goals besides safety. The distinctive feature of humans is that we do not have—and, more importantly, we do not need—a queen bee to live together in large numbers. We are able to cooperate in huge groups involving very many members with no genetic link. A striking thing is that this special ability was not present in early humans. Robust evidence shows that the early humans' society was similar to that of other social primates [6]. Thus, the unique way in which humans cooperate follows a process of learning to adapt to the increasingly complex environment we have been facing over time, a process which is long lasting, if not endless. Starting with the socioeconomic Big Bang, only an increasing ability to cooperate in larger and larger numbers has afforded us the ability to live and operate in our modern social aggregations, clustering together very many individuals with no genetic relationship.[3] As I will emphasize during our journey, human behavior and human societies are tightly intertwined, and both are a constant presence when humans implement each of the *Four*.

As for communication, a cat may communicate that it is hungry, ants use sounds to indicate social status and distress, bees dance to tell one another where to find honey, and chimpanzees can learn sign language. Our uniqueness lies in the fact that we can communicate in ways that no other animal can because we are able to use abstractions, ideas, and symbols. In short, humans and only humans communicate via symbolic language. Below, I offer definitions of abstraction and symbol that highlight a number of nice elements about symbolic language. On one hand, they seem to suggest that humans have unique communicative skills to compensate for their inferior senses. On the other hand, their message seems to be that humans need symbolic language because they are complex, heterogeneous animals operating in complex social systems that, in turn, can be developed only thanks to symbolic language. Whatever the case, the definitions show the uniqueness of the communication skills of humans, which, of course, humans exploit to implement the *Four*.

J. Locke gave a magisterial definition of abstraction, one which also stresses the skill of humans in addressing complexity (p. 76): [7] "[…] if every particular idea that we take in had its own special name, there would be no end to names. To prevent this, the mind makes particular ideas, received from particular objects, to become general; which it does by considering them as they are in the mind—mental appearances—separate from all other existences, and from the circumstances of real existence, such as time, place, and other concomitant ideas." Centuries later, A. Einstein, surprised by the practical power of an abstract language such as math, wondered (p. 28) [8] "How can it be that mathematics, a product of human thought that is independent of experience, is so admirably appropriate to the objects of

[3]For instance, Bowles S and Gintis H (2011) A Cooperative Species: Human Reciprocity and Its Evolution. Princeton University Press.

reality?" Non-physical things are hard to figure out using our senses. But humans are clever problem solvers. To represent something non-physical, they have concocted the symbol, which is a physical thing. The national flag, for example, is a symbol of the concept of "nation." While abstractions let humans understand concepts such as "nation," symbols offer humans a reason to stand united. Because within a certain group, we share the same ideology, religion, flag, or beliefs, we behave in ways to protect each other. This happens even if we have no genetic link and we do not know each other.

The symbolic language is then "the pact which links subjects together in one action." [9] In other words, symbolic language acts as a strong unique social glue that allows both cooperation and the ability to address human endeavors such as the *Four*.

So far so good. At the core of our species, we have two powerful complementary instruments for accomplishing the *Four*. But this is only part of the story. The four activities we are traveling through are unavoidably affected by the multifaceted behavior of humans—we are individualistic, social animals. The distribution of human behaviors, both by individuals and as a species, looks like a bell. Very few humans behave totally and constantly selfishly; very few behave totally and constantly as good Samaritans. Most people show a significant persistent share of individualism and collectivism (the tendency to give more weight to, respectively, either personal or collective rights and interests). Child psychologists claim that it is a perfectly normal part of development for toddlers to believe that everything is "mine." The egocentric nature of a child is his natural behavior. But psychologists also posit that as time passes, children understand others' perspective too. The typical human being is not a sociopath; he is able to feel empathy and, as noticed, humans learnt the importance to socialize since the inception of our race. Further insights on the compound nature of the human behavior can be drawn by looking at some prominent scholars. Confucius assumed that the ethical life of responsibility to others and individual flourishing are inextricably intertwined.[4] Plato asserted that virtue consists in living in harmony with the others, but he was also an advocate of individual liberty. Aristotle emphasized that we need others; we benefit from our social interactions, but altruism should always be accompanied by self-interested motives. According to Hobbes, despite their selfish, violent tendencies from taking over, humans are nonetheless able to form social contracts and governments. J. Locke thought that humans are inherently tolerant and reasonable, though he acknowledged humanity's capacity for selfishness. In Rousseau's state of nature solitary individuals act according to their basic urges (for instance, hunger) as well as their natural desire for self-preservation. This latter instinct, however, is tempered by an equally natural sense of compassion. A. Smith's two most famous works highlight the multifold aspect of the behavioral nature of humans [10, 11]. In

[4]Shun, K (2003) Conception of the Person in Early Confucian Thought, in Confucian Ethics: A Comparative Study of Self, Autonomy, and Community, ed. Shun K and Wong D B, New York: Cambridge University Press. pp. 183–199.

his book on moral sentiments, he argues that humans show *sympathy*; that is, they have a natural inclination to care about the well-being of others for no other reason than the pleasure one gets from seeing someone else happy. Years later, inquiring into the nature and causes of the wealth of nations he famously said that we should expect our dinner not from the benevolence of the butcher, the brewer, or the baker, but from their regard to their own interest. A balanced view is also sustained by the consideration that, as we shall see, multifaceted behavior may be a powerful feature of individuals and a winning strategy for our race. Holding a compound behavior permits individuals to be flexible in facing disparate situations. Extreme individualism brings strong (not necessarily material) incentives to improve but also weak social responsibility and cooperation. With diffuse collectivism, the situation is typically the opposite. The good of belonging to and contributing to a community must be compared to the good of respect for the individual apart from any potential contribution to community. No extreme standpoint by itself provides the best opportunity for the economy and individuals to flourish and would not allow the human race to be as successful as it is. More cooperative groups have more chances to prevail over groups that are not so good at internal group solidarity which, over time, propagate various form of altruism. But this cannot avoid that self-oriented people survive and thrive within a group through deception, free riding, manipulation and overpowering. As Latin wisely adverted, *in medio stat Virtus,* when tackling humans' affairs, avoiding extreme positions is usually advisable.[5] Data support the variety in human behavior. According to a recent survey data set from 80,000 people in 76 countries there is substantial heterogeneity in the degree of reciprocity, altruism, and trust across countries, and even larger within-country heterogeneity.[6] A more immediate confirmation comes from our own experience. As we all know well, this complex behavioral heterogeneity is still with us. Modern humans apply norms of good behavior only to a narrow group of relatives or friends. Dealing with a stranger, especially one who we think that we will not interact with again, may lead us to behave more selfishly. We are capable of having contradictory impulses toward one another, integrating and disintegrating as well as cooperating and dominating, and behaving prosocially and anti-socially. If, on one hand, the foregoing points out the multifaceted adaptive nature of humans, on the other hand, it supports the stability of this behavioral feature—despite thousands of years and several sociocultural-economic transformations that have passed since Plato's description of how ordinary people typically behave, it still substantially holds these days.[7]

The situation is so mixed that even a quick look at the nuances of the concepts allows progress (and avoids possible misunderstandings). It is not true that "self-

[5] This indication often pops up during our tour. Needless to say, it gives only a very vague indication, but in the huge uncertainty of humans' world it may be nonetheless useful.

[6] Falk A et al. (2018). Global evidence on economic preferences. Quarterly Journal of Economics, 133 (4), 1645–1692.

[7] A.N. Whitehead famously said that all of philosophy is just footnotes to Plato. I believe this is especially true for Plato's insights on human behavior.

interested" and "altruistic" are totally opposite notions. If a single motive cannot be characterized in both ways, a single act can nonetheless be undertaken from both motives. A collaborative spirit may have individualistic pushes and vice versa. Pure altruism materializes when in someone's behavior, self-interested motives are entirely absent, but scientists distinguish between two more realistic kinds of altruism—weak and strong. The former can be defined as behavior that benefits another individual rather than the individual carrying out the behavior; the latter is behavior that benefits others but at one's own cost [12]. Then, there is reciprocal altruism, which consists of acting altruistically because of the expected related reward of the altruistic act. A significant number of humans behave altruistically, even when it is costly for them. There are voluntary associations and nonprofit organizations where very many people offer their time for free, even in dangerous environments such as those experienced by the members of *Medecins sans frontieres*. But the view that the majority of humans are altruistic in the sense of being capable of valuing and pursuing another person's welfare as an ultimate goal is untenable. Looking at the individualistic part of humans' behavioral distribution, behavioral nuances may be revealed by contrasting, e.g., self-interest and opportunism. A self-interested individual seeks to maximize her own welfare. But in doing so, she may behave either honestly (i.e., never breaking her word or misrepresenting what she knows) or opportunistically (i.e., she would break her word, engage in misrepresentation, or refuse to divulge information under the right circumstances). As recently recalled,[8] then, there are two ways for humans to behave selfishly, one wise and the other foolish. According to the latter, one pursues her own interest in a narrow, shortsighted way. According to the former, one recognizes that her own long-term individual interest lies in the welfare of everyone.

The multiform behavioral disposition of humans is a natural trait, but individual behavior also depends on culture and changes according to the context. In our wandering across the *Four*, we shall see that individual behavior may be affected by family and society, but it is an adaptation that, as such, is destined to be reversed in other contexts (cf., for example, Chap. 4). Moreover, it hardly pushes the majority of humans toward complete persistent independence or interdependence; that is, it hardly obscures their innate behavioral complexity. This is also because, as we shall see, human clusters tend to be contextually integrated and heterogeneous; thus, they always maintain some cultural dispersion. As for behavioral adaptability, according to the context, behavioral economists[9] have performed several experiments [13]. Humans may act selfishly in some cases, but they also engage in deliberative processes that produce moral and other-regarding judgments and behaviors. Deliberation can also evoke a such a strong concern for fairness that we disregard material

---

[8]Dalai Lama on Facebook: https://www.facebook.com/DalaiLama/posts/foolish-selfish-people-are-always-thinking-of-themselves-and-the-result-is-alway/10150176894272616/

[9]I find the term behavioral economics potentially misleading. As this book hopefully makes clear, *all* economics deals with behavior. After all, even the Walrasians that we will meet in Chap. 2 have their own behavior. This kind of ambiguity is diffuse (cf. Chap. 3) and surely does not help non-professional economists in taking advantage of the economists' job.

gain. Behavioral economists have been arguing, inter alia, that human behavior depends not only on the amount of money gained but also on the way in which the money is earned. A point in case is the dictator game. In these games—where a monetary endowment is given to one player (the dictator) who has to split it with the other player—robust findings point out that no dictator holds 100% power despite the fact he can be never punished by the other. Empirical results also suggest that humans frequently are willing to reduce their own material well-being not only to improve that of others but also to penalize others who have harmed them, or others, or violated an ethical norm.

For our goal, this excursion reveals that humans are adaptive, individualistic social animals driven by emotions and rationality who act in complex environments using a changing mix of cooperative and exploitative strategies, foolish and wise self-interest, pure and reciprocal altruism, and opportunism. In a nutshell, humans always maintain a significant share of individualism and collectivism. Using the names of our guides, in our roaming, we will meet humans behaving as Walrasians, Keynesians, Ostromians, etc. To be sure, all these Sapiens are different representations of the same entity—the human being—but they highlight the importance of addressing the *Four* with due flexibility.

The next step is to look at how nice behavioral features such as cooperation and communication can introduce opposite forces that can lead to disparate outcomes in the human interactions we are traveling across. The multifaceted behavior is not the only factor that keeps us contextually integrated and separated and that makes the results of our actions mixed. In fact, these are elements often resurfacing when dealing with the *Four* and introduces the next section on economic systems and institutions which, as we shall see, are key tools to tackle interactions among mixed-behavior agents.

Let us start with the communicative skill of humans. The phenomenon that our guides label *homophily* [14] is an example of how symbolic language can be contextually both an inclusive and a discriminating factor in social interactions. It is the widespread persistent tendency of humans to form sub-networks made by similar people, whereby the inner social glue is based on symbolic language. In fact, members of subgroups are similar by age, gender, ethnicity, religion, and so forth. Basically, humans like likeness because it is easier to be empathic to a peer than to an alien—*better wed over the mixen than over the moor*, as an old saying goes. As easily imaginable, the presence of these subgroups may strongly affect the execution of the *Four* within and between human clusters (cf. Chap. 4). Among important products of symbolic language, then, there is the language in the strict sense of a system of words and grammatical rules such as English, Italian, and Spanish. As humans know from the Tower of Babel, language may both unify and divide, again influencing all of the *Four*. Today, researchers have counted nearly 7000 languages across the globe. As a counter example, the language of mathematics is a much stronger unifier than plain language: we all agree that $1 + 1 = 2$ whatever the ideology, norms, nationality, age, or period. There is neither need to interpret nor to question, which helps to focus cooperatively on targets and to obtain better and quicker results. This peculiar communicative skill positively impinges on the innovating efforts that we will visit in Chap. 5. Apart from the fact that technological regression is much less probable than socioeconomic regression, social progress proceeds slower than technological progress because of the unifying use of mathematics that enhances cooperation and diffusion of knowledge in scientific circles.[10] Science is a social process wherein communication and understanding are vital. To the extent that scientific communication involves ordinary language, it unavoidably suffers from its trappings and ambiguities. It is perhaps worth recalling what is said in the paragraph devoted to the definitory *caveat*.

Problems may become even bigger when mixed-behavior humans need to cooperate in order to execute the *Four*. The potentially disruptive factor is coordination because the final result of cooperation depends on the behavior of several interconnected individuals. The likelihood of negative results is then further magnified by the (ineluctable) presence of scarcity because the latter imposes constraints to humans' desires, generates frustration, and may push partners toward individualism in that exacerbating social conflicts. As I mentioned, these behavioral issues are key elements often resurfacing throughout our tour; thus, I shall focus on them.

It is easy to figure out that game theory is a strong analytical tool to study cooperation and coordination in social interactions, which, indeed, can be conceived as games. In the following, I outline two famous cases that shed further light on the connections of behavioral attitudes and social outcomes.

The so-called prisoner's dilemma (PD) deals with two selfish rational prisoners, *A* and *B*. They can either confess—thereby implicating the other—or deny committing a crime. To deny implies cooperation in the sense of remaining silent; to confess means to defect. Of course, their cooperation would be negative for society at large, but here, the "society" is only made up by these two prisoners. Table 1 shows the payoffs faced by these two humans; outcomes are negative because numbers indicate years of prison (e.g., a payoff of 0 means to be free).

		B	
	Table 1	Confess	Deny
A	Confess	*−3*, **−3**	*0*, **−6**
	Deny	*−6*, **0**	*−1*, **−1**

The payoffs are calibrated in order to generate and study the dilemma faced by the selfish prisoners. It is easy to see that the strategy (deny, deny) is in a sense "efficient"—there is no other strategy choice that makes any one player better off without making the other individual worse off. The traveler is advised that we will often see this kind of efficiency. It sounds like the Hippocratic precept *primum nil nocere* (first do no harm)[11] and in economics is a paramount concept labeled Pareto

[10] Mathematics helps scientific progress also imposing internal coherence and making errors more easily detectable.

[11] The prudence is dictated by the difficulty of making reliable cardinal comparisons of "happiness" among humans. How can we compare the subjective happiness (utility, satisfaction, pleasure, etc.)

efficiency[12] (from V. Pareto). The solution of this PD, however, is not (deny, deny) but (confess, confess) that is evidently Pareto inefficient. In spite of its inefficiency, it is nonetheless the solution of the game because *whatever B* decides, *A* prefers to confess.

Since the game is symmetric (as the reader can see by looking at the payoffs), the same logic leads *B* to confess to whatever *A* does. The dilemma is that mutual cooperation would yield a better outcome than mutual defection, but the latter is the best response because, from a selfish perspective, it is rational while the choice to cooperate is irrational. The prisoner's dilemma structure, where individual interest and common interest are misaligned, applies to a wide range of real-life social interactions.[13] But if most social interactions among humans were adequately modeled, played, and solved as in the above-mentioned PD, humans would not have evolved as social animals and, possibly, they would have [illegible]. What often happens is that the need to cooperate overcomes individualism and compromising becomes a working strategy. Facing necessity, humans adapt and cooperate.[14] Our ancestors had necessarily to channel all their efforts to secure food, water, and shelter. To live longer and better they could not afford to spend energy in conflicts so very early on humans began to develop and improve their social skills. Without cooperation, early Sapiens would have starved. Thus, like other pack hunters, they possibly formed circles, sang, and danced to give themselves strength and courage, and then cooperatively hunted even the most dangerous prey.

On 9 March 2020, Italy's 60 million citizens were confined to their homes to halt the spread of COVID-19. People responded by taking to their balconies, windows, and rooftops to sing to one another, to play music, and to lift one another's spirits. Similar reactions were reported in other countries sharing the same dramatic situation. In football stadiums, modern Sapiens face the PD to stand upright all the time in order to better watch particular moments of the game. Experience shows that often the solution is to agree to sit down. In our journey, we will encounter several examples of cooperation among humans, which gives ground for the success of our species in implementing all of the *Four*.

---

stemming from consuming a good? Trivially, if I like an apple "4" and you like it "2" does it make any sense to say that I prefer the apple the double of you?

[12]Pareto efficiency deals with allocative efficiency—it is a state where resources cannot be reallocated to make one individual better off without making at least one individual worse off. In economics, there are other kinds of efficiency such as productive efficiency which concerns with the optimal (lowest cost) method of producing goods (cf. Chap. 5). For the sake of example, a system producing at the lowest costs only left gloves is efficient from the productive standpoint but inefficient from the allocative one.

[13]For instance, this kind of dilemma may emerge in fighting tax heavens, arms races, and divorce. Regarding firms, dilemmas emerge in cartels or in price choices of two big competitors such as Coca-Cola vs PepsiCo, or Apple vs Samsung. The prisoner's dilemma may then explain why mafia-type organizations are particularly attentive to establish the conspiracy of silence among their affiliates and why the state tries to break the conspiracy (e.g., via witness protection).

[14]Bowles S and Gintis H (2011) op. cit.

The second case from game theory shows further indications of the behavioral nature of humans and of how they may successfully address potentially dangerous interactions. In a famous experiment, R. Axelrod held a tournament of various strategies for the PD to show how cooperation could emerge in a world of self-interest without a central authority. He invited a number of well-known game theorists to submit strategies to be run by computers. In the tournament, programs played games against each other and themselves repeatedly. Each strategy specified whether to cooperate or defect based on the previous moves of both the strategy and its opponent. Intriguingly, the strategy that obtained the highest overall payoff turned out to be the simplest strategy, one which led to a better social outcome than the one-shot PD. It is called tit-for-tat and goes like this. In the first round, the goal is to cooperate. In all subsequent rounds, the goal is to replicate whatever the other player did in the last round. The tit-for-tat strategy has a number of nice features that are worth discussing in our journey. First, this strategy emerges as the winning strategy even if the number of players who select it is less than that of the selfish players. Then, if it sends the message that humans who do not cooperate will be punished immediately, it also limits the number of punishments to one for each defection. In other words, punish quickly but do not hold a grudge. A sense of "fair justice" is at work, and humans like that [15].

Thanks to symbolic language, indeed, many humans agree to depict justice as a woman who is blind (impartial) and holding a pair of balance scales (fair) in one hand and a sword (enforcement power) in the other. Moreover, the tit-for-tat strategy suggests not to be nasty first; thus, an improved social outcome is achieved by following a very simple strategy that promotes cooperation. Again, the tit-for-tat strategy shows its "human nature"—humans appreciate simplicity (W. Occam *docet*) and the fruits of cooperation (Paleoanthropology *docet*) [17].[15] All told, with respect to the one-shot PD solution the tit-for-tat strategy solution is closer to the typical behavior, multifaceted and adaptive, of humans. As observed for the PD, however the tit-for-tat strategy cannot fit all social interactions among humans [18].[16] In light of the compound nature of human behavior and the heterogeneity of human affairs, the lack of one-size-fits-all solutions is unsurprising. This will accompany us during the whole tour, which looks like a never-ending spiral of problems and solutions.

In their attempt to understand human activities and societies, economists have addressed the connections of behavior and performances in social relations such as the *Four* from other standpoints, too. Among them, there is the *invisible hand*

[15]The tit-for-tat strategy is used in practice by BitTorrent peers to optimize their download speed, and there are instances of cartels of real firms employing this kind of strategy. A point in case is the Joint Executive Committee was a famous cartel that set the price of railroad freight in the USA in the late 1800s (at the time it was perfectly legal). Their tit-for-tat strategy was apparently able to support the cartel arrangement, but only for some time [16, 17].

[16]Researchers have shown that the generality of the findings and the policy implications drawn from the tit-for-tat strategy are contingent on the design of the tournament, the criterion used to determine success, and the particular values chosen for the prisoner's dilemma payoff matrix [18].

mechanism theorized by A. Smith. Specifically, he examined system-wide cooperation among self-regarding individuals and famously wrote (p. 593): [19] "[. . .] every individual [. . .] intends only his own gain, and he is in this, as in many other cases, led by an invisible hand to promote an end which was no part of his intention. [. . .] By pursuing his own interest he frequently promotes that of the society more effectually than when he really intends to promote it." In view of this stopover—and of the whole tour—three major takeaways materialize from this short passage. First, interactions among self-interested humans do not necessarily end up in a PD. Although under some conditions (that we shall see below), even these kinds of humans may achieve good social outcomes when individual targets and system-wide targets are aligned. Second, the happy ending is achieved via unintended coordination; the cited alignment is fortuitous. Third, the invisible hand coordination mechanism functions even without communication. This invisible mechanism deserves to be made more visible. Basically, even seemingly simple operations of production and distribution of goods can require contributions by many people, most of whom never meet or directly communicate with each other. Take a moment to figure out how many people are involved in projecting, assembling, and selling a computer or a car or a bank service, i.e., how many disperse heterogeneous decision makers must coordinate their efforts to achieve the intended outcome. Also, consider that coordination must be achieved to create each of the many components that make up a computer, a car, or even a bank service and that, in modern societies, there are millions of goods and services permanently available. The size of the required coordinating efforts is really huge.

L. Walras [20] addressed this coordination problem mathematically. In particular, he wondered how economic systems can coordinate productive efforts and adjust them so that demand equals supply in all markets at the same time despite the presence of a virtually infinite number of small, self-regarding agents, each of which requires separate decisions. Under some conditions (such as perfect competition and no externalities[17]), he was able to formally determine the general equilibrium of economic systems (henceforth labeled "Walrasian") populated by behavioral entities that I call "Walrasians [21]."[18] This sort of human being is assumed to be rational, emotionless, fully informed, optimizing, self-interested, and equipped with exogenously determined stable preferences.[19] Any Walrasian also believes that all others in the system are Walrasians. In fact, these traits do not necessarily refer to each and every individual, but rather to the "average" decision maker emerging when consid-

[17]In fact, there are other conditions but for our tour's aim these two are the most important and we will explore them in the Epilogue.

[18]Under "Walrasian" conditions this equilibrium is also Pareto efficient. Cf. [21]

[19]Rational means that agents' choices are coherent. Basically, if X is preferred to Y, and Y is preferred to Z, then X must be preferred to Z. Exogenously determined stable preferences mean that preferences stay fixed from *cradle to grave*, i.e., they are natural traits not social traits and do not change according to the context (cf. Chap. 2).

ering a large group (cf. also Chap. 3).[20] Besides assuming that humans are on average very specific individuals, Walrasian systems left unexplored some crucial elements of humans' social life and, in particular, the rules of the game (the institutions, as I shall discuss in the next section). As D. Heymann ironically puts it, Walras "seems to describe the behavior of incredibly smart people in unbelievably simple situations [22]."[21] But as I will recurrently point out in our tour, the efficiency of humans' way of tackling the *Four* is a joint product of the rules of the game and behaviors. This is why both rules and behaviors are commonalities found behind all of the *Four*, which naturally steers us to the next stop of the tour.

1.3 Background Commonalities Behind the *Four*: Economic Systems and Institutions

As seen, the *Four* are social interactions in need of an efficient way to coordinate the efforts of participants who, despite their behavioral complexity, must act all together as a working system—as social animals equipped with mixed behavior, humans need to organize themselves in order to maintain, improve, and extend their social interactions as well as a safe and ordered life within and between any kind of human aggregation. Once human affairs get large enough that anonymous acts are possible, somehow something pops up in order to manage the mixed behavior of humans. To this end, economic systems, institutions, and social capital are key notions. In this sojourn, therefore, I will shift the attention from common behavioral elements to the common operating system behind the *Four*, which, for illustrative reasons, I split into economic systems and institutions (I shall discuss social capital in Chap. 4).

For our purposes, the economic system may be defined as the way in which humans arrange their scarce resources and their multifaceted behavior to achieve their goals via the *Four*. Consider anarchy (featured by the absence of the rule of law or of settled government) or feudalism (where a lord divided portions of his land among his vassals in exchange for certain services). In our tour we will explore a more widespread system, namely capitalism, also referred to as the market system. Because of our tour's aim, I do not try to define it (which, in fact, would be really hard), but I describe this system via its main ingredients—private property rights,

[20] Most standard economic models are interested in the aggregate behavior of many individuals, not in the behavior of a single individual. The Walrasian is the "representative individual" whose choices coincide with the aggregate choices of the individuals in the economy.

[21] This phrase is reported in [22]. Walras was aware of imposing simplifying assumptions, yet he did so to keep manageable his general equilibrium analysis. A model necessarily needs simplifying assumptions: economic systems are immensely complex, and nobody knows how they work. Starting from the declared hypotheses what a good model does is to obtain reliable and useful knowledge using preferably, although not necessarily, the unifying language of math. The issue with a good economic model deals rather with its users. On the one hand, the enthusiasts tend to generalize its indications beyond the assumptions and, on the other, the critics tend to be not constructive: if one is disappointed with the model, then (s)he should elaborate a new model and coherently derive new indications from new assumptions.

private firms, markets, and state. On the positive side, this permits to achieve the main intended takeaway of this tour stop—to stress the role of the economic system in supporting the *Four*.

In market systems, private property rights and private firms are widely diffuse and goods—especially private goods—are mostly and preferably allocated via markets. Though also present in other economic systems, these first three components are substantially more widespread in market systems than elsewhere. It is perhaps worth noticing that private property was established well before capitalism and that, although one can easily find markets even in non-capitalistic systems, as we shall see soon in capitalism markets carry out a peculiar function. Let us explore a bit closer how these four ingredients constitute a common background for the *Four*.

In economics, private goods are rivalrous—if someone consumes more of it others must consume less—and excludable in that their owner can exercise private property rights, i.e., someone can prevent others from consuming her good. Classical instances of rival goods are food and beverage—if I drink a glass of wine, you cannot drink it. An example of excludable good is a show in a theater—not everyone can go to a theater as they please. Satisfying Walrasian conditions, markets are a suitable tool for managing economic activities dealing with private goods. In Walrasian systems, markets are socially useful coordination tools with nice allocative properties.

I have already touched upon how disperse, heterogeneous decision-making units must be coordinated to project, produce, and sell goods and services. Nonetheless, this does not completely summarize what markets do. Markets, of course, also have a demand side. Therefore, economic systems need some mechanism for the transmission of information to the agents acting as producers about the agents acting as consumers. In capitalism, specifically, consumer demand embodies this mechanism because, while trying to satisfy consumers' preferences, producers have a clear indication of what to produce, how much, and at what price to sell. At least in the mid-long run, basically any commodity that cannot be sold at a profitable price will not be produced by private firms. Note that this avoids wasting useful resources to produce unwanted stuff. By the same token, any commodity that is valued (so that it can be sold at a profit) is probably going to be produced by someone sooner or later (more on the market mechanism in Chap. 2).

The importance of consumer demand in market systems is reflected in an oft-quoted expression—the consumer is sovereign. The rationale is that if sellers have some power in shifting humans to buy a good from them rather than from one of their competitors, they cannot persuade a significant share of consumers to persistently consume goods that consumers do not desire. Marketers follow consumers much more than vice versa. It is hard to believe that most of the goods that we consume these days derive from artificially induced wants. Cars and cellular phones, for example, are widely consumed because, compared to horses and fixed-line phones, they make our life better. The fact that we only see "successful" items may induce us overestimate the firms' power over consumers. But data tells us that the firms' willingness to sell is necessary but not sufficient to sell. Analyzing large firms' intensive advertising campaigns, researchers have recorded 160 product flops (e.g., New Coke, Amazon Fire Phone, and Google Glass).[22] In Chap. 5, we then shall see that a very small percentage of ideas actually achieve commercial success.

Competition is key both for economic systems and for our tour across the *Four*, which calls for stressing three things about it. First, competition sustains widespread incentives and opportunities that are vital for the dynamism of economic systems. Second, competition penalizes dullness and rewards alertness and initiative—in competitive market systems, losers are the less efficient, not the weaker. Accordingly, the greater the competition, the more efficiently goods are allocated toward reducing the waste of scarce and valuable resources. Someone will suffer, but eliminating the incentives to be efficient and penalizing the most efficient is evidently costly for the system. These costs are typically larger than allowing the less efficient to remain in the market. Third, competition is a general feature of human life rather than an element of a specific economic system. Competition would occur even in non-capitalistic systems with no money, no prices, and no markets. Again, definitions matter: interpreting competition as the interpersonal striving for more of what is scarce and desired, it stems from human wants outweighing the number of available resources, not from a specific economic system.

The issue with economic systems as common background behind the *Four* is how they manage the multifold behavioral nature of humans. According to A. Smith, market systems may lead profit-seeking behaviors to efficiently improve the collective well-being from below. A similar message comes from Mandeville, who, earlier than Smith, pointed out that "private vices" (profit-seeking behavior) lead to "public benefits" (orderly social structures like language and markets) [23]. One may think that the system may affect behaviors. But this is true only to a limited extent because, as remarked, humans are naturally equipped with multifaceted behavior. It seems more likely that the system reflects the degree of collectivism or individualism of the participants than vice versa.

Possibly surprising, saying capitalism generates egoism and greed is thus a clear case of non sequitur. History teaches that the typical humans living in pre-capitalistic systems such as feudalism did not systematically behave as good Samaritans. If Gordon Gekko—the famous character of two films on Wall Street—is often taken as the example of the intrinsic greed of capitalistic systems, what about the greedy moneylender Shylock in Shakespeare's *The Merchant of Venice*? The same can be said for profit-seeking behaviors. Just think about Babylonians merchants. On the other hand, history teaches that collapsed Soviet-like command economic systems led individuals to shrink trust, trustworthiness, cooperation, and all those similar prosocial attitudes that constitute social capital. If capitalism may lead humans to be stuck in self-regarding behaviors, it may nonetheless enhance pro-sociality when people execute the *Four*. Instead of inducing or exacerbating selfishness, for example, the diffusion of property rights might promote sharing because humans are secure in their ownership and that they can always get their goods back. To the extent

[22] Available at https://www.cbinsights.com/research/corporate-innovation-product-fails/

that individualism and opportunism are present in social interactions, without enforceable private property rights, the result is chaos, not order (cf. Chap. 2).

Likewise, executing the *Four* in market systems may stimulate the search for reputation and the enlargement of social capital. As observed, suppliers in competitive markets must take care of customers. Word of mouth is a powerful tool for customers. This is the reason why, for example, sellers often write on their shop windows "Since. . . ." or "Est. . . ." or the like; they are telling their potential new customers that they are worthy of trust. The same logic is behind the five-star review system put in place by Amazon and other virtual platforms. The basic point is that in market systems consumers can (and do) punish sellers that behave selfishly and lose sight of the needs of their customers. Somewhat ironically, it is individuals' selfish rationality that pushes them to avoid close relationships with those who do not reciprocate. In social interactions performed in working capitalistic systems, opportunism often results in more costs than benefits. As our guides highlight, trust and being trustworthy facilitates the extension of anonymous market exchanges, reduces the need for external enforcement of contractual agreements, and even affects the cost of transactions [24].

This is not to say that markets and social capital are sufficient for capitalism to be a well-functioning framework in which to implement the *Four*. Even if them are major elements in social interactions such as the *Four*, these latter activities, even when reiterated, must nonetheless be assisted by enforceable rules. Efficiency is a joint product of behavior and rules. This is why the state—here intended as government (local, central, federal) and independent authorities (e.g., the Federal Reserve, the Federal Trade Commission, etc.)—is a key ingredient of capitalism. In this sense, wild privatization and deregulation, dark web, black market, shadow banking, and underground economy are suggestive instances of what is *not* capitalism as intended in our tour.

It is frequently overlooked that even A. Smith highlighted the importance of both behaviors and formal institutions for capitalism to function well (p. 1227) [19]: "Commerce and manufacturers can seldom flourish long in any state which does not enjoy a regular administration of justice, in which the people do not feel themselves secure in the possession of their property, in which the faith of contracts is not supported by law, and in which the authority of the state is not supposed to be regularly employed in enforcing the payment of debts from all those who are able to pay."

If under some conditions, property rights, competitive markets, and private firms can efficiently maximize the "pie," the state must realize these conditions, supporting (via enforcement and regulation) and complementing (via public goods[23]) the other three ingredients. As we shall see during the tour, for instance, the state must address externalities and ensure fair competition. In terms of the *Four*, inter alia, trading needs laws protecting customers and enforceable contracts,

[23] At the opposite of private goods, public goods are non-rivalrous and non-excludable. Examples are national defense, atmosphere, etc.

aggregating in family needs family law, aggregating in firms calls for antitrust laws, and innovating needs a mix of competition and patent system.

More specifically, the state must ensure that individuals have equal opportunities and an harmless but adequate social safety net. It must let markets and enterprises function well, neither inhibit nor substitute them; it should, preferably, regulate more than produce; and it must offer insurance and support to proactive or blameless unhealthy people, not charity to lazy and opportunistic individuals. The state must make economic inequality a fair and efficiency-enhancing element of the system. The state also plays a role in fostering social capital; easing the connections between public agencies, firms, and other social aggregations; and facilitating the alignment of the interests of the various economic agents. In doing all that, of course, the state must be efficient, honest, and not invasive, otherwise it ends up weakening the social capital and worsening the performances of the system. The state, in fact, must neither exceed its role nor reduce opportunities and incentives for private agents—providing ex ante equal opportunities must not lead to guarantee ex post equality.

The state needs the other three ingredients of capitalism, and these latter need the state. If economic systems placing too much trust in markets hardly flourish, for instance, the same can be said for economic systems placing too much trust in the state. If both markets (because of externalities, public goods, etc.) and the state (because of corruption, rent-seeking, state capture, etc.)[24] often fail, they can work together to achieve better social outcomes (cf. Epilogue). All considered, capitalism as a common background of the Four may be considered as a system placed somewhere between anarchy and pure command economies. Somewhere because, as we shall learn during our journey, it is an evolving entity as its main ingredients are so that it is always in a "beta" (testing learning) situation.

The fact that the economic system should aim to arrange scarce resources managing mixed behaviors suggests that behaviors "precede" systems—earlier arrangements were instituted by humans, for humans and, hence, came after the inception of our race. Systems, then, should not try to, in fact, they cannot, change human behaviors. The state, for instance, may appeal to civic responsibility and use "moral suasion" but humans, typically, need more. We are naturally equipped with multifaceted behavior thus, on the one side, adapting the system to human behavior is easier and faster than vice versa and, on the other, the system may affect behaviors only to a limited extent.

We are now in a position to introduce the notion of institution. In short, institutions are the (framework of) rules that govern human behavior. In Latin, indeed, the term institution sounds like "setup." This suggests that institution-free

[24]State capture happens when private interests significantly influence a state's decision-making processes to their own advantage. Rent-seeking implies extraction of uncompensated value from others without making any contribution to productivity. All these are problems stemming from behaviors rather than from particular economic systems. Russian oligarchs bring to mind that these issues are not an exclusive of Western countries. As we shall see in the Epilogue, then, in China large tech companies are bargaining with the state on regulations.

economic systems simply do not exist. Just to mention, capitalism strictly needs property rights. Institutions and economic systems, then, constitute the necessary (practically indissoluble) common substrate to perform the *Four*—these latter are never implemented in an institutional vacuum.[25]

Institutions are very human entities; no other animal has the institutional complexity of humans. Institutions stem from our unique behavioral skills in communicating and cooperating. Recalling what we said about abstractions and symbols, symbolic language may be thought of as the institution of institutions—no symbolic language, no institutions. As observed, then, virtually every social interaction needs the more-or-less conscious cooperation of great numbers of humans and, as we shall see, the institutions' help to solve the problems of cooperation. In a nutshell, institutions modify the rewards and penalties associated with particular behaviors and typically aim to ease the adoption of cooperative actions so that even the self-regarding are often induced to act in the interest of the collectivity. In game theory jargon, effective institutions raise the benefits of cooperative solutions or the costs of defection. Throughout the tour, we shall see examples of how well-designed institutions may manage behaviors in such a way to pilot potentially devastating social interactions toward socially good solutions. The tour guides that I have selected—D. North, D. Acemoglu, and J. Robinson—broadly design the scope of the institutional setting operating in the background of the *Four* through their different, but complementary, perspectives [25, 26].

D. North (p. 3) claims that: "Institutions are the rules of the game in a society or, more formally, are the humanly devised constraints that shape human interaction."

The more formal part of North's definition points out that institutions work as constraints in the interactions among humans. Why do humans need constraints when dealing with interactions such as the *Four*? The short answer is that, due to the natural eagerness and multifaceted behavioral nature of humans, their social interactions may lead to unwanted outcomes and need to be managed. If most humans were omniscient Samaritans, then possibly anarchy would be a much more widespread economic system these days. In our tour, we shall see that the need to manage our behavior applies even in the "social relations" with ourselves—knowing our weakness, we constraint our multifaceted behavior by elaborating some sort of pre-commitment. As noticed, a sequence "behavior-hence-institution" is continuously at work—we have seen, and we shall see several examples during our journey.

The first part of North's definition stresses how the notion of institution is related to that of social interactions seen as games played by the humans populating an economic system. Interpreting institutions as rules of the game instructively suggests

[25] Anarchy is the exception to the rule. It is perhaps worth noticing that to function peacefully and efficiently humans aggregating via anarchy should behave with a degree of collectivism that seems at odds with their natural insatiability and multifaceted behavior. Of course, then, the more numerous the aggregation, the higher the possibility of conflicts. Centuries ago, J.S. Mill posited that with respect to monarchy and aristocracy, democracy has an advantage because it forces decision-makers to take into account the interests, rights and opinions of most people in society.

looking at economic systems as playing fields which, in turn, brings to mind an illuminating question—how is it possible to understand and appreciate a game as well as the participants' behavior without knowing the rules of that game? Consider, for example, the different incentives faced by humans living in economies in which private property rights are diffused in dramatically different degrees, say South Korea vs North Korea. Assuming that the representative South Korean and the representative North Korean do not have dramatically dissimilar behavioral attitudes, while carrying out the *Four*, they will behave differently, as the institutional frameworks in which they operate are dramatically different.

Characterizing institutions as rules of the games, finally, leads us to think that institutions deal with the connections among humans rather than the human being himself. For our purposes, institutions are rules that help to guide behaviors and reduce uncertainty when humans tackle trading, forecasting, aggregating, and innovating affairs. In the case of trading, for example, standards of politeness or obligations to buyers and sellers give humans some hints on what to do. More insights can be drawn by noticing that North emphasizes that in guiding/constraining behaviors and reducing uncertainty, institutions may be formal or informal.

Formal institutions are written rules that are established by the government—laws, constitutions, contracts, and form of government. Humans have relied on these kinds of institutions for millennia: the Babylonian king Hammurabi's Code being a good example.[26] In the 1500s, N. Machiavelli [27] emphasized the importance of written rules as a tool for managing the multifold nature of human behavior. For him, the law provides incentives and constraints to harness self-interest to public ends (recall the danger of having individual and collective interests misaligned), and at the same time maintains the good customs on which the effectiveness of the laws depends. The importance of some formal rules for establishing, maintaining, and developing economic systems—hence for sustaining the *Four*—can be inferred by the names that humans have given to them (e.g., Magna Carta and Constitution). This said, formal institutions may impact badly on the *Four* because they may hamper social capital. A system with large social capital does not need to rely on diffuse formal institutions, and, in turn, individuals learn how to manage their interactions by themselves. On the other hand, a system typically resorting to formal institutions lowers the possibility of individuals forming trust, which, in turn, calls for even more formal institutions because this is what individuals expect.

Informal institutions are not written rules, conventions, taboos, customs, and social norms. They are not less important than formal ones in executing the *Four*—they are so widespread in human societies that virtually every form of interaction is governed to some degree by informal institutions. Moreover, on the one hand, not all social relations need or can be managed by formal institutions (think about neighbourly relations) and, on the other hand, while formal institutions

[26]The presence of written norms dates back to Sumerians. Hammurabi's Code, a collection of rules that established standards for commercial interactions and set fines and punishments to meet the requirements of justice, was written about two millennia later, around 1772 B.C.

are relatively easy to change, informal institutions die hard. In Chap. 3, we shall consider how informal institutions emerge, how they are enforced, and how they relate to expectations. What is more important to stress here is their coordinating function when humans interact. In a nutshell, informal institutions coordinate behavior, giving a durable structure to social interactions.

Conventions establish the way in which something is *usually* done, and this naturally coordinates behaviors. They are so common that one must not even think before applying them, such as which hand to extend in greeting or the idea of "ladies first." Norms coordinate life inside human aggregations, shaping our sense of obligation to family, communities, and higher-level social aggregations (Chap. 4). Norms of reciprocity suggest how to behave in, for example, trading affairs based on gift-giving. Norms also coordinate communications, determining the meanings we attach to words. As formal institutions may shrink social capital, informal ones have a flip side, too. If informal institutions help humans to coordinate, yet they also create tensions among them. Social glues, such as norms and languages, guide humans to be contextually integrated as well as differentiated. Homophily is a point in case, but we will meet several similar contingencies during our trip. Although distinct, informal and formal institutions are linked. As we shall see during the journey, usually economic systems became more and more formalized and, occasionally, some informal institutions evolve into formal ones. Time standards or traffic rules are points in case, but one may also imagine the "codification process" of property rights in passing from prehistoric economic systems to modern economic systems.

Acemoglu and Robinson add further insights. In particular, they have proposed a fourfold taxonomy of institutions that emerges from comparing economic vs political and inclusive vs extractive institutions. Their view leads to think that to distinguish well-functioning economic systems from poor ones, what is really crucial is not whether the system is, say, communist or capitalist, but whether it has extractive or inclusive institutions. Acemoglu and Robinson note that centrally planned economies are by their nature extractive and so are many capitalist economies. Trying to discern well-functioning institutions from others has the big advantage of reducing the ideological content of the definitions. Not to mention that defining inclusive and extractive institutions turns out to be less challenging than defining capitalism.

Economic institutions—such as private property and competition—shape the opportunities and incentives in the economic sphere, affecting human activities. They are key in determining production costs (i.e., the cost of inputs such as labor and capital) and transaction costs (costs of searching and bringing buyers and sellers together, of bargaining, of drawing up a contract, of contract enforcement, and the like). Accordingly, economic institutions are essential for the profitability and feasibility of engaging in the *Four*. Political institutions do the same thing, but in the political sphere. They are political rules of the game, such as democracy, electoral laws, constraints on politicians and elites, and separation of powers.

Extractive institutions remove most agents from participation in economic and political affairs. They are pro-elite (rentiers, monopolists, groups of power, and the like) and aim to keep most people out of the game and/or to assure the elites on the winning side of social interactions. The discriminating word is *most*—inclusive institutions are those that allow most individuals to exploit opportunities and incentives.[27] Inclusive institutions are what make an economic system a favorable free-entry and equal-opportunity playing field in which to perform the *Four*.

As our guides argue, for economic institutions to be inclusive they (p. 74) [28] "must feature secure private property, an unbiased system of law, and a provision of public services that provides a level playing field in which people can exchange and contract; it also must permit the entry of new businesses and allow people to choose their careers." Acemoglu and Robinson yet posit that inclusive political institutions are what is necessary for any non-transitory economic success. This is so because although economic institutions shape economic opportunities and incentives, allowing humans to improve individual and system-wide conditions, they are ultimately determined by political institutions.

Although this break is aimed to outline the common framework shared by the *Four*, it seems fruitful to present the economists' views on the causes that allow the creation of economic systems and institutions.

In their long-term research on "why nations fail," Acemoglu and Robinson conclude that economic systems seem to end up with good or bad institutional settings accidentally, driven by a chain of uncertain (rather than risky[28]) events and/or by small differences in initial circumstances. For instance, they note that it is possible to effect meaningful change to extractive institutions on the heels of particularly disruptive or revolutionary random events (that they label "critical junctures") such as the Black Death. Of course, uncertainty and luck also imply that prosperity may come and go. Actually, history teaches that once-successful systems are falling behind. Finally, Acemoglu and Robinson emphasize that while inclusive political institutions are resilient, they are also not always robust enough to resist turning into extractive institutions if there is a lack of good leaders, the wrong kind of leadership exists, and/or a set of negative circumstances comes along.

F.A. Hayek, [29] underlined that capitalism developed as "spontaneous order." He noticed that the emergence of capitalism can be compared to other systems such as the language or the common law—no one individual or committee created them. Though this may be seen as too extreme a view, one may recall that systems without central control are ubiquitous in nature—Darwin's theory of evolution explains how complex biological systems may coordinate spontaneously. This said, however, humans are as insatiable as stubborn—since the socioeconomic Big Bang, when they face difficulties, they typically react actively.

---

[27] Centuries ago, J.S. Mill posited that with respect to monarchy and aristocracy, democracy has an advantage because it forces decision-makers to take into account the interests, rights and opinions of most people in society.

[28] In our guides' jargon, uncertainty (or, equivalently, ambiguity) is unmeasurable risk and risk is measurable uncertainty. Trivially, for example, in the classic lottery game one number is drawn out of 90. Though none can know for sure which number will be drawn, we can say that each number has a probability of 1/90 to be drawn. This is a risky situation. If one does not even know how many numbers are in play, then we are in a state of uncertainty.

We have then already seen that, in fact, North thinks that institutions are "humanly devised." According to O.E. Williamson, likewise, institutions of governance are often partly the result of human design, reflecting "an effort to craft order" so as "to mitigate conflict and realize mutual gains" (p. 599) [30]. Another hint comes from K. Marx who put forward the idea that in capitalism operate both firms, whose hierarchical structure and behavior are deliberate planning, and the spontaneous forces of the market. We will see other examples throughout the tour.

To recap, regardless of how economic systems and institutions develop, they constitute critical habitats for the *Four*. But they are just that, that is, they are only instrumental for assessing the *Four*. Therefore, they must aim to help humans manage behaviors, and they must do that taking into account that human behavior is by nature multifold. They must not—in fact, they cannot—try to modify the very essence of human behavior (the "Communist Man" ideal) [31].[29] Thus, since the inception of our species, we are animals contextually exhibiting both individualism and collectivism, and I believe that we will behave this way for the foreseeable future at least. In order to establish a working economic system, it is therefore better to manage our behavioral complexity via institutions rather than attempt to change it (cf. Chap. 6).

1.4 Common Traits of the *Four*: Goals, Instruments, Importance, Uniqueness, Immanence

So far, we have sojourned in the common behavioral and institutional settings behind the *Four*, delineating some basic features of human behavior and capitalism. This frame of reference will accompany us throughout the entire journey on why and how humans address the *Four*. But trading, forecasting, aggregating, and innovating efforts are also stitched together by their own commonalities. This layover is thus devoted to these common traits and, specifically, to the goals pursued; the instruments used; and the importance, uniqueness, and immanence of the *Four*.

Humans are purposeful animals. Why then do they trade, forecast, aggregate, and innovate? In the chapters devoted to the *Four*, I will highlight that each of these businesses has some peculiar gain which stimulates humans to exert these efforts. Here, I focus on a more general motive that, as such, constitutes yet another common thread behind these businesses—humans implement the *Four* to fulfill their basic wishes.

But the main aim of this short halt is to explore the *Four*, not to burrow into what humans' basic wants are (which would open a Pandora's box). Exploiting the definitory *caveat*, thus, I merely assume that humans' basic wants can be synthetized by the following mantra—"we want to live together, longer, and better." Though this mantra is not exhaustive of humans' ultimate goals, it is nonetheless central in our

[29] According to Trotsky "Under Socialism, solidarity will be the basis of society. (. . .). The average human type will rise to the heights of an Aristotle, a Goethe, or a Marx [31]".

tour because it can be connected to the *Four*. The intersections can be sketched as follow. Since the outset of our species, humans are social animals. But they are also unappeasable animals. It leads us to assume that they also relentlessly want to live together, better, and longer and, to this end, they trade, forecast, aggregate, and innovate. I now give more details on these themes, contextually stressing the behavioral and institutional aspects of the matter to emphasize some essential crossings for our tour's aim.

Among the many existing insights on the insatiability of humans, Hobbes sums up the ceaseless voracity of humans as (p. 150) [32] "a perpetual and restless desire of Power after power, that ceaseth only in Death." More recently, B. Russell argued: [33] "man differs from other animals in one very important respect, and that is that he has some desires which are, so to speak, infinite, which can never be fully gratified." This drives me to use the terms *needs* and *wants* interchangeably despite the fact that the latter might evoke less-compelling requirements than the former. The rationale is that by never feeling satisfied, the human being continuously shifts forward his basic necessities, relentlessly chasing new wants and then converting them into needs. So far, there is no clue of any slowdown. Note that, as already observed, insatiability does not imply that more is always preferable to less. By the same token, continuously wishing to live better and longer does not necessarily mean to behave selfishly on any occasion. Humans have a multifaceted behavioral nature that they may tune individually and via economic systems. In our wandering across the *Four*, we shall see many successful cases of intended cooperation.

The next step is to figure out what is the "instrument" used by humans to live together, longer, and better via the *Four*. At this level of generality, this instrument is shared by each of the *Four*. To move forward, I identify this instrument with the *good* as intended by A. Marshall (p. 30): [34] "In the absence of any short term in common use to represent all desirable things, or things that satisfy human wants, we may use the term Goods for that purpose. Desirable things or goods are Material, or Personal and Immaterial."

During our tour, we will be exposed to different kinds of goods. In Chap. 2, we will discuss private goods; in Chap. 4, we will examine public goods and common property resources. In Chap. 5 we will examine the peculiarity of the good "idea." It is worth noticing that discriminating among goods requires far more than a mere matter of classification. Behavioral issues and institutional responses differ according to the nature of the goods. That said, in this break I will focus on other characteristics of goods. These are paramount for our tour's aim, too.

The first distinction refers to economic goods versus free goods and stems from insatiability and scarcity. A good is not scarce, and it is defined as a free good when no matter how much it is desired and demanded, there is never a shortage of it. Scarcity, which makes a good an economic good, is due to two basic factors.

The first is a matter of nature in the sense that the natural insatiability of humans faces the natural exhaustibility of resources, making scarce the (economic) good. There are some subtleties surrounding the notion, however. For example, consider air. As a general matter, in nature air is sufficiently available to be considered a free good. But for scuba divers, air is scarce, and hence, it is not a free good.

The second basic factor for which scarcity makes a good an economic good deals with society in the sense that if we want a good, others may want it as well. This generates another kind of scarcity-related tension besides natural scarcity, namely competition. An example is when in a congested city, there are more cars than parking spaces. In Chap. 2, we shall see how competition is tackled by trading humans via market exchanges.

Other insights may be drawn from the relation between free goods and price—a free good is a good for which supply is not less than demand at a zero price. Therefore, an economic (scarce) good with a zero price—because it is totally subsidized—is not a free good but, rather, a zero-priced economic good. Moreover, and crucially, if a good is offered at a zero price, it will be strongly demanded; hence, it will become increasingly scarce. As a consequence, it will depart more and more from the definition of free good.

Free and economic goods may also be contrasted by talking about opportunity cost and choice. The logic is that, due to scarcity, every choice has an opportunity cost—by emphasizing one objective, it is implied that other objectives are deemphasized.[30] The notion of opportunity cost in particular says that the cost of the chosen alternative is the most valuable option given up. Thus, if our wage rate is $10 an hour, for example, and we choose to consume an extra hour of leisure, it costs us $10 in income—that is, the opportunity cost of the chosen extra hour is $10. Only economic goods have strictly positive opportunity costs. Without scarcity, choosing is easy—there are no opportunities or alternatives that are missed, forgone, or sacrificed. If no good that is valued by anyone is scarce, there is no need to choose among separately valued options; there is no need for social coordination processes that will effectively determine which demanded goods have priority. But this is an idyllic, unreal condition. All we know is that we always encounter economic goods, scarcity, and costly choices. When we execute the *Four*, therefore, we need a way to manage scarcity and mixed behaviors, that is to say, an economic system.

Further considerations regarding goods are the following. If the term good involves *desires*, it does not necessarily equate to *benefit*; a good may be bad. Drinking spirits or smoking are well-known examples, and the related social costs call for the social management of individual choices about goods (cf. Chap. 6). We then buy goods to satisfy our own personal "natural" needs such as food, water, health, and safety, but we also demand goods for "social" reasons. Economists highlight the tendency of humans to "keeping up with the Joneses" (i.e., to value and buy goods by looking at what others have). Elaborating on the fact that humans might want to live better than others, our guides have also posited the presence of *conspicuous consumption,* [35] which pertains to goods bought mainly for their status symbol role (e.g., Ferrari cars). J.M. Keynes [36] claims that some needs are relative in the sense that we feel them only if their satisfaction makes us feel superior to our fellows. Finally, there are *network goods*, or goods valued and bought to be "connected" with other "nodes" of human networks (e.g., cellular phones).

[30] As the traveler will note during the tour, in economics relativity is everywhere.

Institutional settings, behavioral elements, goals, and instruments are not the only commonalities linking the *Four*. Each of these four businesses is essential and immanent in human life, and all are performed by humans in a unique way in the animal kingdom. The *Four* are paramount not in the sense that they are the sole factor allowing humans to pursue their basic desires. As previously remarked these efforts must be framed within suitable economic systems. I have also noticed that human affairs are always surrounded by uncertainty and fortune, which, accordingly, are two other key factors to achieving favorable outcomes. But the point remains: the *Four* are among the essential endeavors put in place by humans to chase their basic wants.

The *Four* are also key because they forge the economic system, hence critically affecting the odds that humans have to fulfil their goals. As we shall see, in one way or another, all of the *Four* impinge on the growth and equilibrium of economic systems. Trading and aggregating continuously shape our systems (Chaps. 2 and 4); forecasting activity is critical for the system to rest in equilibrium (Chap. 3); and innovating efforts unstoppably impinge on both the structure and performance of the system, making capitalism an inherently dynamic entity (Chap. 5).

As for uniqueness, the human being is not the only animal to implement the *Four*, but humans do it in a very special way. For instance, biologists have collected evidence that chimpanzees exchange "services" such as scratching other individual's bodies. However, this social scratch is not comparable to the scale and complexity of the trading activity performed by humans. As a general matter and as easily observable by everyone, no other species is engaged in space explorations, world-wide aggregations, or international trade. Following Russell, this might be due to the unparalleled insatiability in pursuing our basic wishes. Following paleoanthropologists, this might be supported by our special ability in cooperating and communicating. I discuss the uniqueness of each of the *Four* in the next four chapters.

Last but not least, the *Four* are all immanent—these businesses have always been with us and there is still no sign of their going away. History teaches that humans have been unstoppably trading, predicting, aggregating, and innovating for millennia. Looking even farther back in time, the evidence collected by paleoanthropologists sustains the immanence of the *Four*. Importantly here, their works point out that these four endeavors were performed since the inception of our species and, moreover, that the *Four* have tight connections with both the ancestral threefold mantra embodying humans' goals and the two behavioral traits that made us humans.

Paleoanthropologists' findings show that early Sapiens cooperatively lived together in clans with the number of members comprising between 25 and 100. In addition, cooperating and aggregating permitted our ancestors to live longer and better. Symbolic language was surely a key factor in these developments. Thanks to it, then, early Sapiens were able to create new objects (i.e., to innovate). The first tools—such as composite stone tools, long blade knives, and spearheads—required ability for abstract thought to mentally plan a series of steps that could then be executed. Furthermore, the prehistoric toolmakers had the ability to anticipate their needs, since they often carried suitable rocks long distances before making them into tools. Paleoanthropologists have found clues that early hunters likely came right up to their prey before thrusting their spears at them from below. All that requires careful and skillful planning.

Planning is not the same as predicting, but planners are forced to make some assumptions about future scenarios, and that means to predict. There is also more explicit proof of primordial forecasting activities. Our ancestors soon realized the relevance of time measuring and time keeping. Almanacs and calendars based on lunar, solar, and sidereal time reckoning have been recorded since the Paleolithic period [37].

Systematic time patterns might have been used to predict natural phenomena. At some early stage of humankind, humans probably started thinking consciously about seasonality. They might have realized that just as in the previous year, it will be colder and darker out there and that they will find less food and need warmer suits.

What is known is that, once they colonized and cultivated the fertile land of Mesopotamia, humans started to forecast the periodic flooding of rivers by looking at the sky. In the fourth millennium BCE, Sumerians wrote tablets that provide us with the first written evidence of astronomy and astrology in the West. They were able to predict celestial events such as eclipses. Divination seeks to foresee or foretell future events. The earliest evidence for this practice found in China dates back about 6000 years [38].[31] All told, living together, longer, and better implies a more-or-less implicit effort to predict how and where the economic system is going as well as the behavior of others (cf. Chap. 3).

So far, the basic message from paleoanthropology is that early humans were social, innovative, forward-looking beings—that is, they aggregated, predicted, and innovated—to live together and longer. But evidence also shows that our ancestors traded and wanted to live better. Early humans often inhabited caves or rock shelters, when these were available. Soon, natural shelters were enhanced with walls or other simple modifications. One of the earliest known pendants (32,000 years old) is a horse carved in mammoth ivory from Vogelherd, Germany. Body adornments like this are evidence that early humans progressed from merely trying to survive and were then concerned with living better. The unstoppable transformation of needs in wants—or, equivalently, humans' insatiability—virtually started at the sunrise of the human race. Regarding the immanence of trading, scientists excavated ancient artifacts dating back around 300,000 years at the Olorgesailie Basin in southern Kenya. They uncovered weapons made of materials that could not be found there, suggesting our ancestors at the time may have exchanged goods with others [39].

At the end of this first part of the trip, is seems useful to recap what has emerged from the sojourn into the commonalities behind the *Four*. Since the socioeconomic

[31] In passing, this practice can be seen as a systematic method to understand seemingly random events as part of underlying patterns in order to provide insights into a problem at hand. That is, divination tries to tackle risk and uncertainty, in that being an early (obviously non-scientific) attempt to do statistics.

Big Bang, humans started to behave as unique, cooperative, and communicative animals. But individualism is significantly present in many individuals so that humans typically show multifaceted behavior. Behaviorally equipped in this way, humans have been performing four specific activities—trading, forecasting, aggregating, and innovating—which turned out to be as immanent as critical affairs in their life. As social interactions, the *Four* cannot be implemented in a vacuum; they need to be framed within some economic system that, accordingly, constitutes the common background of the *Four*. Behaviors and economic systems have two-way connections, but the latter cannot eliminate the innate coexistence of individualism and collectivism in humans. Taking stock of the elements that have emerged from this behavioral and institutional big picture, we are now in a position to examine trading, forecasting, aggregating, and innovating separately. The *Four* share several common elements, but they are different activities that are derived from specific skills and attitudes and, moreover, they offer unique gains.

References

1. Hayek F A (1956) The Road to Serfdom. Chicago: University of Chicago Press.
2. Edgeworth F Y (1877) New and Old Methods of Ethics. Oxford and London: James Parker. Repr. in Newman (2003).
3. Hodgson G M (2019) Taxonomic definitions in social science, with firms, markets and institutions as case studies. Journal of Institutional Economics 15(2):207–233.
4. Shultz S, Opie C, and Atkinson Q D (2011) Stepwise evolution of stable sociality in primates. Nature 479 (7372): 219-222.
5. Bender R, Tobias P V, and Bender N (2012) Human Evolution Across Disciplines: Through the Looking Glass of History and Epistemology. History and Philosophy of the Life Sciences 34 (1/2):147-184.
6. Boyd R and Richerson P J (2009) Culture and the evolution of human cooperation. Phil. Trans. R. Soc. B. 364(1533): 3281–3288.
7. Locke J (1690) An Essay Concerning Human Understanding. Book II. London: Thomas Basset.
8. Einstein A (1921) Sidelights on relativity. Methuen and co. LTD London.
9. Lacan J (1991) Freud's papers on technique, 1953-1954. W.W. Norton New York.
10. Smith A (1759) The Theory of Moral Sentiments. Cambridge University Press (2002).
11. Smith A (1776) An Inquiry into the Nature and Causes of the Wealth of Nations. University Of Chicago Press (1977).
12. Campbell D T (1983) The Two Distinct Routes beyond Kin Selection to Ultrasociality: implications for the humanities and social sciences. In: The Nature of Prosocial Development, D Bridgeman (ed) Academic Press New York 11-41.
13. Fehr E and Gächter S (2000) Fairness and Retaliation: The Economics of Reciprocity. Journal of Economic Perspectives, 14 (3): 159-181.
14. Jackson M (2011) An Overview of Social Networks and Economic Applications. In Handbook of Social Economics, Ch.12, (eds) Benhabib J, Bisin A, Jackson M O, Elsevier Press.
15. Binmore K (2014) Bargaining and fairness, Proceedings of the National Academy of Sciences, 111 (Suppl. 3) 10785-10788; DOI: https://doi.org/10.1073/pnas.1400819111.
16. Porter R (1983) A Study of Cartel Stability: The Joint Executive Committee, 1880–1886. The Bell Journal of Economics, 14, 2: 301–25
17. Fehr, E. and S. Gächter, (2002), "Altruistic punishment in humans," Nature, 415(10), 137–40.

18. Rapoport A, Seale D A and Colman A M (2015) Is Tit-for-Tat the Answer? On the Conclusions Drawn from Axelrod's Tournaments. PLoS ONE 10(7): e0134128. doi:https://doi.org/10.1371/journal.pone.0134128
19. Smith A (1776) op. cit.
20. Walras L (1926) Elements d'economie politique pure, ou Theorie de la richesse sociale. Paris: Pichon and Durand-Auzias.
21. Arrow K and Debreu G (1954) Existence of an equilibrium for a competitive economy. Econometrica 22 3.
22. Leijonhufvud A (1993) Towards a Not-Too-Rational Macroeconomics. Southern Economic Journal, 60, 1, 1-13, pp. 1-2.
23. Mandeville B (1714) The Fable of the Bees or Private Vices, Publick Benefits. 2 vols. With a Commentary Critical, Historical, and Explanatory by Kaye F B (Indianapolis: Liberty Fund, 1988).
24. Dixit A K (2004) Lawlessness and Economics. Alternative Models of Governance. Princeton University Press
25. North D C (1990) Institutional Change, and Economic Performance. New York: Cambridge University Press.
26. Acemoglu D and Robinson J (2012) Why Nations Fail: The Origins of Power, Prosperity, and Poverty. Crown Business.
27. Machiavelli N (1517) Discourses on Livy. Translated by Mansfield H C and Tarcov N. Chicago: University of Chicago Press (1996).
28. Acemoglu D and Robinson J (2012) op. cit.
29. Hayek F A (1960) The Constitution of Liberty. London: Routledge and Kegan Paul.
30. Williamson O E (2000) The New Institutional Economics: Taking Stock, Looking Ahead. Journal of Economic Literature, 38 (3): 595–613.
31. Trotsky L (1924) Literature and revolution (Keach W ed, Strunsky R translation) Chicago: Haymarket Books 2005
32. Hobbes T (1651) Leviathan. N. Malcolm (ed.), Oxford: Clarendon Press (2012).
33. Russell B (1950) What Desires Are Politically Important? Nobel Lecture, December 11.
34. Marshall A (1890) Principles of Economics. London, Macmillan.
35. Veblen T (1899) The Theory of the Leisure Class: An Economic Study of Institutions. Macmillan.
36. Keynes J M (1930) Economic Possibilities for our Grandchildren. in Essays in Persuasion (New York: Harcourt Brace, 1932), 358-373.
37. Rappenglück M A (2015) Possible Calendrical Inscriptions on Paleolithic Artifacts. In: Ruggles C. (ed) Handbook of Archaeoastronomy and Ethnoastronomy. Springer, New York, NY.
38. Flad R (2008) Divination and power: A multi-regional view of the development of oracle bone divination in early China. Current Anthropology 49 (3): 403-437.
39. Brooks A S et al. (2018) Long-distance stone transport and pigment use in the earliest Middle Stone Age. Science

Trading: Humans Are Heterogeneous Animals

2

2.1 Introduction

In accomplishing the *Four,* most humans have the same ancestral goals and are assisted by common institutional settings. It does not mean, of course, that all humans are identical. It is exactly the presence of differences in human capital, preferences, etc., that stimulates the trade among humans. Were humans all equal in all respects, there would be no gains from trade, and autarchy would be a much more diffuse economic system across the globe. As we shall see, the situation in which there are no incentives to trade is theoretically important: the economic system is in equilibrium (at least as far as the trading activity is concerned). Nonetheless, as seen every day, the no-trade situation never materializes in real-world economic systems. Human beings are always different in some respect; accordingly, there is never a shortage of reasons to exchange.

The solution achieved by humans to tackle the intrinsic heterogeneity of our species (i.e., to trade) is less trivial than it looks. Though it is often taken for granted, the trading activity is not a natural aspect of life in the animal world. Rather, it is a behavior mirroring the peculiarity of humans and of their uniqueness as problem solvers. Humans' trading is unparalleled among animals. As A. Smith put it (p. 29): [1] "Nobody ever saw a dog make a fair and deliberate exchange of one bone for another with another dog." I have already recalled that even if chimpanzees exchange "services," these businesses are not comparable with the scale and complexity of the trading activity performed by humans.

In capitalistic systems, the object of the trading activity is the private property rights of goods, not the good itself. We shall explore property rights at the end of this chapter. Regarding goods, quickly comparing the views of classical economists (such as D. Ricardo and K. Marx) and neoclassical economists (such as L. Walras and A. Marshall) on the value of goods permits us to highlight additional details on the trading activities of humans. Searching for the determinants of value, classical economists focused on the social interactions performed during the productive phase. For classical economists, the value of a good tends to be proportionate to

M. Bovi, *Why and How Humans Trade, Predict, Aggregate, and Innovate*,
Contributions to Economics, https://doi.org/10.1007/978-3-030-93885-7_2

the labor costs incurred in producing them. Marx claimed that the value of a commodity is determined by the quantity of socially necessary labor time required to produce it.

Neoclassical economists instead look at the social interactions between buyers and sellers when they meet in the market. For them, the value of a good is measured in terms of what other things the good could be exchanged for, a quality that economists label value-in-exchange or exchange value. The neoclassical argument goes like this. If all humans were self-sufficient, there would be no problem of economic value. Everyone would produce and consume what he or she values. But as I shall point out below, humans are typically not so skillful, and surely would face big problems satisfying their ever-growing wants by themselves. Specialization and the necessarily subsequent trading activity are therefore ineluctable ways to proceed. Accordingly, it is the value of what one produces in terms of trade that then values one's own ability to fulfill her basic wants.

The change of focus carried through by neoclassical economists had huge effects on how to address economies. It shifted the attention of economists and policymakers away from social classes to individuals, from factories to markets, from objective costs to subjective magnitudes, from production to exchange. Following Malthus and Ricardo, for example, Marx believed that wages were held at the subsistence level by the existence of a large number of unemployed in the system as a whole. Workers just have no choice: work or join the "reserve army." Connections thus flow from the system to individuals. For neoclassical economists, however, the wage on the supply side of labor markets depends on how individuals are willing to exchange consumption (made obtainable by labor and wage) and leisure. Individuals rather than social classes became the basic unit of analysis, and in terms of humans' mixed behavioral nature, the neoclassical economists' main focus was the individualistic side of humans (Walrasians *docent*). Regarding the social interactions within the capitalistic system, then, whereby Marx argued that workers were slaves of the capitalists-producers, neoclassical economists argued that consumers are sovereigns in the sense that their preferences must be carefully considered by capitalists-producers (cf. Chap. 1).

When traveling across trading activities (but this also applies to the other *Four*), another useful preliminary distinction is that of market prices versus fundamental prices.[1] The latter are also referred to as *natural* or *normal* or *long-run equilibrium* prices; the former are also labeled *current* prices. It is self-evident from their names that current prices are what one observes in every moment in the market and that fundamental prices only emerge in the long run, when the system is at "natural" levels. Thus, normal and market prices are typically different and coincide only in equilibrium.

A. Smith remarked that the fundamental price is that "to which the (market) prices of all commodities are continuously gravitating" (p. 73) [1]. Specifically, market demand and supply are the gravitational forces that keep current prices floating

[1] This distinction will also be useful for exploring the forecasting activity (cf. Chap. 3).

around fundamental values. A. Marshall added that the factors affecting natural prices must be regarded as the long run and fundamental supply-side forces that determine the value of produced commodities (such as technology), whereby the forces moving market prices are mainly demand-side and temporary.

All goods, whether reproducible or non-reproducible, have market price. But only reproducible goods have normal prices because the supply of non-reproducible ones cannot be increased in the long run, when the demand for them increases. Therefore, a sculpture by Michelangelo has no fundamental price, only a market price. Somewhat similar is the more recent case of the Bitcoin. Its supply can be increased but only slowly because it, like gold, must be "mined" (via energy-consuming computational means), and it is limited because there are only 21 million Bitcoins that can be mined in total.[2] The rigidity of supply helps to explain the huge volatility of its market price because if the supply does not react, then any movement in the demand is fully reflected in prices.

Another key concept for the trading activity is the gain from trade, which has been left somewhat implicit so far. It is often insufficiently considered by many traders, possibly because of the high frequency and impulsiveness of the act of exchange. Typically, people appreciate these gains only when they are not enough. Robinson Crusoe's story, which is often told by economists, puts forward the idea of the gains from trade. After being cast away, Robinson could have just what he was able to do, which forced him to live a poorer life than before. His life in the Island of Despair (a suggestive name, indeed) was very different from that in England.

There are two other real, aggregate-level, examples. Tasmania was discovered in 1650, and, due to their insulated and insufficiently populated economic system, Aboriginal Tasmanians at that time still lived in a relatively primitive way with respect to the Dutch explorers who first met them. At the other extreme, in the thirteenth century, Venice (a small city, after all) became an economic superpower, exploiting its commercial connections that made up the *Silk Road* network.

International trade also benefits firms by letting a small country's industries attain an efficient scale and by imposing them to compete seriously on an international level. An indirect clue about the importance of trade can be drawn from the fact that these days, small economies (i.e., with limited domestic markets) are typically more open to international trade than larger ones. In 2020, for example, Italy, Spain, France, the UK, and other advanced but relatively small systems have seen a ratio of the country's total trade (the sum of exports plus imports) to the country's gross domestic product more than double compared to that of the USA (about 60% vs 27%).

Trading also has ulterior welfare-enhancing aspects. In his 1748 book *The Spirit of the Laws*, Montesquieu advanced the idea that international trade leads to peace

[2] Mining cryptocurrencies is costly and slow. According to a study by the European Union, in 2018 the estimated annual electricity consumption of Bitcoin was equivalent to the annual electricity consumed in the Czech Republic. Regarding the speed of withdrawal, despite miners' efforts, from January to December 2020 the number of Bitcoin in circulation worldwide has increased from 18.19 to 18.61 (in millions).

among nations. Instances of the strategic dividend associated with the trading activities are diffuse in human history. Even among humans who, very likely, were not aware of Montesquieu's hint. In 1922, B. Malinowski [2] published a book where he meticulously wrote about Trobriand people living on the Kiriwina island chain (nearby the island of New Guinea). These people sailed across the other islands to exchange shell ornaments and other products, making a clear distinction between trade and gift and used both to build up partnerships. More recently, specifically in the aftermath of WWII, the early stages of the European Union were based on trading activities because, inter alia, trading is better than bombing. The current renewed interest in the Silk Road (the so-called Belt and Road Initiative) suggests that the search for this kind of trade-related benefits is still alive and kicking.[3]

Another way to appreciate the advantages of the exchange is to explore situations where trading activities are artificially reduced. Before the two world wars, international trade was hampered by a wave of protectionist policies that may have exasperated nationalism, favoring the emergence of Nazism.[4] In those years, the USA also raised its tariff rates so that the subsequent contraction of trade may have magnified the severity of the Great Depression. More recently, the sanctions banning US and other countries' companies from trading with Iran or North Korea have badly affected the economy of the latter two. It sounds somewhat ironic to observe that politicians impose trading limitations to other nations and contextually encourage their citizens to "buy national." In both cases, many consumers lose their gains from trade.[5] Protectionism can also spur costly trade wars. In 2018, the Trump administration introduced billions of dollars in new tariffs on Chinese imports and threatened tariffs on other countries. Following a tit-for-tat strategy, China retaliated by announcing tariffs on US imported goods. A recent Moody's Analytics study reports that in just one year, the trade war with China costed Americans at least 300,000 jobs. Even the experience of the Brexit is suggestive of how insulating may be costly. According to the Office for Budget Responsibility (an independent public body funded by the UK Treasury), data show that the long-run effects of leaving the European Union will reduce the UK's GDP by around 4%. An impact even bigger than that of the current pandemic.

Besides offering the outlined gains, trading enhances both cooperation and communication. On the one hand, it may shift individual behavioral attitudes toward pro-sociality, improving the social capital permeating the system. On the other hand, trading also leads humans to improve their communication. Under the British, for example, the use of the English language spread throughout the world from the

---

[3] It is perhaps worth noticing that the Silk Road has a long history: Greeks and Romans benefited from the commerce created by the route along it.

[4] In fact, the Nazi Party official name included the term National: "National Socialist German Workers' Party."

[5] A rationale is that "buy national" campaigns sustain well-organized groups while consumers are typically much less organized. An element that, understandably, politicians need to consider with due attention.

sixteenth through the nineteenth centuries. In market systems, then, the role of trading activities goes beyond the simple exchange of goods. By linking supply and demand, the market price encapsulates a lot of information—the buyer's willingness to pay and the seller's cost (more on that soon).

Though trading improves human life, it, of course, cannot prevent all problems and may create others. In human affairs, alas, one-size-fits-all solutions do not exist. In this stopover, for instance, it must be observed that free trade is not always the best solution. A. Smith stresses that the exchange must be "fair and deliberate," a hint that applies to both individuals and human aggregations. Regarding nations, for example, barriers, quotas, and tariffs are a good thing if they aim to restore fairness. The contrast of social dumping is a case in point. As a general matter, international trade needs fair competition, but countries have very different economic, social, and political histories and models. Likewise, trading affairs among individuals are socially desirable only under some conditions. Among them, trade must be voluntary and enforceable (see also the Chap. 6). The point is that for this activity to be functional and inclusive (i.e., to improve the whole system and not only parts of it), the exchanges must be performed according to certain rules. For example, as we shall see at the end of this chapter, well-defined and well-protected property rights may turn socially and environmentally unsustainable interactions into peaceful and efficient ones.

The needed institutional setting operating in the background of humans' trading depends on the socioeconomic environment that, in turn, affects the adaptive behavior of humans. It is relatively easy to perform frequent exchanges within a village where tight social connections can lead to the accumulation of sufficient amounts of social capital. Economists refer to these as personal market exchanges, which may be based on reciprocity-trading gifts, favors, and assistance across time because trust and reciprocity are high and transaction costs are low in this context. Whereas trade involves larger groups and longer distances, social interactions are usually one-shot experiences. Also, trade is also often performed among individuals who do not know each other. These so-called impersonal market exchanges impinge on humans' multifaceted behavior and call for the evolution of the institutional setting. Impersonal trade magnifies the possibilities for conflict over the exchange. Studying merchant courts at the Champagne fairs of the twelfth and thirteenth centuries, our guides[6] have argued that these can be seen as institutions supporting impersonal exchange relations over time. This institution indeed provided proper incentives for gathering information, honoring agreements, reporting disputes, and adhering to judgments. By centralizing certain record-keeping functions and effectively permitting only merchants in good standing to remain at the fairs, this institution also enhanced social capital and reduced transaction costs.

D. North argues that negotiation and enforcement in regions far away typically entails the development of standardized weights and measures, notaries, consuls,

[6]Milgrom P et al. (1990) The Role of Institutions in the Revival of Trade: The Medieval Law Merchant, Private Judges, and the Champagne Fairs, Economics and Politics, 1:1-23.

merchant law courts, and other similar formal institutions. Moreover, pirates and bandits are a threat to "out-of-the-wall" commerce, calling for inclusive institutions even at the supranational level. All considered, then, markets, impersonal exchanges, opportunistic behaviors, and transaction costs all have sizes that tend to expand hand in hand and that call for institutional responses. Against these developments, insatiable humans neither stop their trading efforts nor change their mixed behavior but, rather, manage the emerging issues taking advantage of their innate cooperative skill. In light of our journey, it is worth stressing that similar dynamics are shared by all of the *Four*—they are never applied in an institutional vacuum and are always subjected to humans' multifaceted behavior.

The sojourn continues with the exploration of the discrepancies that lead humans to implement their trading activities. In the next sections, specifically, I will discuss differences in human capital, information, and preferences. In these brief excursions, insights on why and how humans trade mainly stem from neoclassical economists. They will assist us in exploring the individual-level behavior behind exchanges in simplified Walrasian-like economic systems. In the last section, I will return to the institutional setting and, in particular, to property rights.

2.2 Different Preferences

Preferences are a wide-ranging concept in economics because mankind has a spectrum of preferences that is dramatically vast—tastes and habits (in eating, dressing, etc.), emotions (shame, fear, anger, etc.), *modus operandi* (in decision making, etc.), and psychological attitudes (aggressiveness, extraversion, propensity toward risk, etc.). This massive gamut makes the human race a highly heterogeneous entity.

Economists do not posit that some preferences are more rational than others. As D. Hume remarked, there would be nothing irrational about his preferring the destruction of the entire universe to scratching his finger. Preferences, then, may be given and stable in the sense that they permanently escort us over the entire course of our life. But there are exceptions. It is not unusual that a new friend changes our preferences about music, food, sport, fashion, etc., or that our propensity for risk varies as we age and/or after we have certain experiences. As far as preferences go, humans are the result of a mixture of DNA and social interactions. In short, preferences consist of humans' disparate attitudes pushing individuals to act in a specific way. Figuratively thinking of trading, one may look at the incentive of gains from trade as being the fuel and preferences as the wheels to direct the trading activity toward the satisfaction of the basic human wants.

It is easy to see why different preferences lead to trade. I have something that I do not want but you want; you have something that I want and that you do not want—the exchange naturally materializes (especially among humans, as observed). Imagine two early humans, Sapiens A and Sapiens B, who meet. Each has one different good,[7] and their preferences are such that they are eager to exchange their goods. These two Sapiens could exchange the goods in disparate ways. Their trade might be based on theft, gambling, gift exchange, or ultimatum offers such as take-it-or-leave-it. Assume that they learn to manage their interaction by implementing the exchanges under some more evolved behavioral rule than the jungle law. In particular, conjecture that the Sapiens eventually perform their trading activity according to "market exchanges," which means that the trade is bilateral and deliberate. Say then that the two goods are private. This clearly implies private property rights, but this stop on our tour concentrates on the behavioral aspect of the trading effort, thus, I postpone the discussion on rights (cf. Sect. 2.4).

There is a last consideration, however. Because changing one or more assumptions may direct the social interaction toward dramatically different solutions, the traveler must remember that we are currently visiting a Walrasian system in which two Walrasians trade via market exchange two private goods; this is just one model among many. We are now in a position to scout three key elements of trading: the market mechanism, the price, and the money.

Whereas the unsatisfactory initial allocation of goods is the starting point of the trade among the two Walrasians, the exchanges end when all the gains from trade have been exhausted. That is, the trading activity stops when at least one of the two Walrasians cannot improve her welfare via exchange (which, by definition, is a Pareto efficient solution). Comparing the situation before and after the trading activity shows that, besides being efficient, the market exchange is a positive-sum game. The two partners deliberately trade because they both gain from that. Accordingly, the new allocation achieved via the market exchange is such that both individually and collectively, they are better off. Observe, then, that the gain is eminently psychological or immaterial. Even though both Walrasians gain from trade, by definition, there is no new material production in the pure-exchange system we are traveling in. Thus, the mere redistribution of given physical endowments increases both the individual and collective psychological well-being. Considering how many market exchanges are executed, virtually every moment in modern capitalistic systems is suggestive of the size of the gains from trade at the aggregate level.

So far, there is neither any clue on what the role of the price is nor is there any indication about who sets prices. But someone must do the job in order to determine market prices that, as observed, are determined by demand and offer. The market price indeed accomplishes a key coordinating, informative role among the trading partners who follow the so-called Walrasian pricing rule: when at the current price, the demand for a good exceeds the available quantity, the price indicates that that good is excessively demanded and the rule says that the change in price has the same sign as the excess demand. When the current price signals that there is no excess demand, then the two Walrasians exchange and that price is said equilibrium or market clearing price.

[7] The two goods are "initial endowments" obtained as, for example, manna from heaven. Otherwise stated, the economic system that we are currently visiting is of "pure exchange"—there is no production.

It remains to be said who sets prices. Walras hypothesizes that another Sapiens enters the system and starts acting as auctioneer. This new, hypothetical actor randomly chooses the price, while the two agents decide the desired quantity at those prices. The Walrasian pricing rule goes on with no exchanges until the prices are such that the total amount that each agent wants to buy of each good is equal to the total amount available. In the competitive (or market or Walrasian) equilibrium eventually achieved, all the gains from trade have been exploited, and the prices are such that each Walrasian is choosing her most-preferred affordable basket of goods. Otherwise stated, the market price is the objective measure of what an agent is subjectively willing to give up (of her endowment) in order to secure a desired satisfaction (exchange value).

But its role goes beyond that. Being rapacious and self-regarding by definition, the two trading Walrasians need some working way to manage their behavior. In competitive capitalistic markets, directions come from the market price—even these days. The logic is that when two Walrasians exchange, two opposite "worlds" are connecting and collapsing: one subjective and the other objective. There is the subjective push to trade according to one's own preference in order to obtain what each Walrasian *wants* to get. Instead, the price objectively indicates the finite resources of the Walrasians, or what each *can* get.

Trivially,[8] consider a city where drinkable water is scarce and, hence, it is an economic good. As observed in the Prologue, policymakers may decide to supply it for free (e.g., subsidizing it). To the extent that the citizens are not sufficiently able to manage their behavior in this situation, then the demand will be high, the resource might be wasted, and eventually even exhausted. Instead, a price that increases with demand reduces the demand and also the waste because the price makes it costly to do that. Although under peculiar conditions (Walrasian system, private goods), the described mechanism teaches humans that they cannot have all that they want, hampers waste of valuable goods, and guides the trading activity toward a solution that is efficient. Sustainable, and enhances the well-being of all the participants.

As most people typically take for granted that trading is a very human and clever solution to the intrinsic heterogeneity of our species, just as many take the above outlined mechanism for granted. Yet its functioning is very astonishing. Walras figured out a hypothetical auctioneer; A. Smith talked about an invisible hand. One of our guides, V. Smith, was unhappy with these abstractions and skeptical about the mechanism. In the 1950s, he ran laboratory experiments using students to see the market mechanism at work [3]. In a two-person exchange experiment, V. Smith addressed how a single buyer and seller of a good reached, or failed to reach, mutually agreeable terms for trade of that good. Subjects were found to produce single-price market equilibria even though none of them desired this outcome. When

[8]To be sure, the example is deliberately trivial, it does not consider many elements, and it is only aimed to make clear the situation we are currently traveling across. During the tour, hopefully, the traveler will learn more about these topics.

they repeated the exercise, prices tended to converge around the competitive equilibrium. The number of units being transacted was also Pareto efficient, exhausting the gains from trade without anyone being in charge of the market. In short, V. Smith was the first human to explicitly and mindfully observe the astonishing invisible hand at work.

The social interaction among trading Walrasians can be made more realistic—never forget that we are tracking simple models of an immensely complex system. As is well known, traded goods are typically measured in terms of their dollar (euro, yuan, etc.) value: the largest dollar amount a person would be willing to pay for a good is a measure of its personal worth to that person (value-in-exchange).

The reference to the dollar steers toward another institutional arrangement that humans smartly invented to sustain their trading endeavors—money. The story may be told as follows. It is possible that the Walrasians A and B bartered. But when the trade starts involving more and more goods, services, and individuals, then the difficulty of the barter shows up. As mentioned, the size of the trade and the need of institutions go hand in hand. The point is that barter trade needs, in economists' parlance [4], the double coincidence of wants: a trader with meat but preferring vegetables must find someone who precisely owns the right quantity of vegetables and wants the right quantity of meat.

It is easy to figure out that the probability of the exact matching quickly collapses to zero as the trading activity involves more and more goods. It comes not as a surprise, then, that according to archeologists, metal objects were introduced as money since around 5000 B.C. (the Mesopotamian shekel). Our official guides add further details. They stress that money is an institution aimed to reduce transaction costs per exchange so that the potential gains from trade become easier to realize. Specifically, economists emphasize that money has three main functions. It is a medium of exchange, and it provides a unit of accountability in easing trading activities. Also, money functions as a storage of value because humans want to be able to delay their consumption until they are ready to make a purchase.

Reflecting on the insatiability of humans, which continuously boosts the evolution of their trading activities, money is ever evolving as well—from the Mesopotamian shekel to mobile and digital currencies via commodity money and fiat money.[9] Though it is easy to see why monetary economies are more evolved than systems based on barter, some details are less evident, yet important, for our tour. Somehow, the trading partners must agree on what will be acceptable tender for making payments and settling debts among themselves. General agreement to the convention, not the particular media agreed upon, is what makes money such a valuable institution in economic systems. This positive feedback pushing humans to converge toward a common medium makes money similar to language, network goods, and social norms—the more we use them, the better they work. Money also spurs institutions such as central banks because modern market systems are better off

[9] Fiat money is a government-issued currency (e.g., US dollar) that is not backed by a commodity such as gold.

when there is a non-market entity with the power to create and manage this key institution. We will come back to money in Chap. 3.

2.3 Different Human Capital, Information, and Propensity to Risk

In the previous section, I endowed the trading Walrasians with different goods without specifying how they obtained their goods (or money). I talked of manna from heaven. But more realistically (and more generally), before trading, humans have different availability of goods for disparate reasons such as legacy, skills, transfers, and gifts. In the first part of this tour stop, I shall focus on human capital, that is, the acquired knowledge and skills that an individual brings to an activity.

Regarding our two trading early humans, A and B, for example, you might think that they have different abilities in hunting and/or gathering. All we know is that humans feature very heterogeneous levels of human capital. The vast majority of us would like to be the new Einstein, an acclaimed sport champion, or the like. But the hard truth is that very few humans are so gifted, which justifies why they are so special, famous, and rich (scarcity boosts prices). All the other humans show a wide range of talents and skills, which further magnifies the heterogeneity of the human race. Willingness, efforts, study, training, and the like surely help to increase our human capital, and this is why we devote a lot of effort and time to these activities, both individually and as a society. In fact, humans try to improve their knowledge and abilities differently, longer, and more intensively than any other animal. Not only is human childhood the longest in the animal world, but humans have also been establishing and improving complex educational institutions to accompany young humans in their passage from family of origin to their own position in the economic system in their adulthood. This notwithstanding, the basic point remains. In spite of all our individual and collective efforts, heterogeneity in human capital is a persistent trait of individuals and economic systems. Both individuals and systems should accept the presence of this kind of inexorable inequality and find efficient and peaceful ways to cohabit with it.

Luckily, trading activities enter the scene, acting as a sort of Paretian Robin Hood. Trading improves the human condition and raises the well-being of all humans, both the more and the less gifted. This is the positive message of D. Ricardo's law of comparative advantage.[10] Consider another two Sapiens, C and D. In one hour, C can produce €180 by hunting and €30 by gathering; D can produce €1 by hunting and €20 by gathering. Using economic lingo, C has an absolute advantage: she is more productive in both productions. The intriguing point is that despite the absolute advantage, both individuals—and, hence, the economic system as a whole—will

[10] In fact, this D. Ricardo' law originally dealt with international trade, but the logic also holds in other contexts. More importantly, this law does not consider institutional and historical factors which may make the free-trade solution a bad one.

benefit from specializing and exchanging. It is easily seen. To produce €30 by gathering, C should lose €180 by hunting. Thus, C is better off by hunting for one hour, producing €180, and then hiring D as a gatherer. C may hire D, paying her up to €150 (180–30), and remain better off. More (stuff) is obtained with less (overall work).

The richness of the social interactions among humans is really huge, and economists have examined several cases deriving from the trading activities related to disparate human capital. Among them, one finds its rationale in the practical impossibility that two workers have exactly the same characteristics. It implies that the market for each particular bundle of labor services can be quite thin and, clearly, the situation becomes even worse when more skilled humans are involved. These markets, such as entry-level legal, business school, and medical labor markets, are labeled matching markets. This name derives from the fact that the participants must be appropriately matched in order to trade with each other. Each individual cannot simply choose what she wants (even if she can afford it), but she has to be chosen. In matching markets, price adjustments alone do not solve the social interaction; they need application procedures, selection criteria, or other rules of the game.

A. Roth has studied these matching markets, showing yet another case whereby human trade and behavior spur institutions. Inter alia, Roth examined the evolution of US market for new doctors and suggested a solution [5]. Students who graduate from medical schools in the USA are typically employed as residents (interns) at hospitals. Until the 1950s, the market for new doctors was largely decentralized, but market forces created problems of unraveling and congestion. The former emerged because competition for medical students forced hospitals to offer residencies (internships) earlier and earlier to students. This caused matches to be made before students could produce evidence of their human capital and, perhaps, even before they formed their preferences regarding the specialization they wanted to practice. Congestion results when a marketplace does not give participants enough time to evaluate as many of the transactions as they would like or compare different potential positions. In the market examined by Roth, indeed, competition led hospitals to impose tight deadlines on accepting offers and led medical students to make quick decisions.

Because of unraveling and congestion, offers are not made in time to ensure mutually beneficial trades, so markets do not clear. In these cases where heterogeneous services are traded, offers must be made to specific individuals rather than to the market. How these thin markets allocate resources, then, depends on the institutions that govern transactions. The decentralized market for new doctors was substituted by an institution which is now called the National Resident Matching Program (NRMP). Its web page states that NRMP uses a computerized mathematical algorithm, based on Ruth's suggestions, to align the preferences of applicants with the preferences of program directors in order to produce the best possible outcome for filling training positions available at US teaching hospitals. NRMP is successful, annually meeting the needs of more than 50,000 medical students and graduates who compete for more than 40,000 residency and fellowship positions. Roth argued that the success of the NRMP was due to the fact that its algorithm produced stable matchings.[11] Since the match is Smithian (fair and deliberate), the argument goes, if the algorithm produces unstable matchings, then doctors and hospitals would have an incentive to bypass the algorithm by forming other, more preferred, matches (such as direct contacts between doctors and hospitals). To reiterate, when dealing with the *Four,* efficient outcomes depend on behaviors and rules.

Information is yet another essential element in economic systems, one which must be appropriately considered to learn about interactions among humans. Trading activity is one of these interactions. It may well happen that otherwise identical individuals acquire different quality and quantity of information at some point. This kind of heterogeneity, coupled with the related incentive to gain from trade, has unsurprisingly led humans to implement new kinds of exchanges and institutions. Consider the case with different information on future stances[12] as formalised, for example, in forward contracts (in which subscribers agree today on the details of a transaction at a specified future date). Until 1865, both grain and cotton traders operating in Chicago used to speculate in futures. In that year, they agreed to establish formal futures markets to formalize their local tradition [6]. The positive distinctive features of a futures market[13] are that contracts are standardized, transactions costs are minimized, and liquidity is high so that contracts can be, and typically are, bought and sold many times during their lifetime. In doing so, futures markets help to motivate the collection and dissemination of relevant information as well as permit to spread—hence to reduce—risks (more on that below). Regarding any other institutional development functionally sustaining the *Four*, futures markets spread rapidly across capitalist countries involving more and more types of assets.

Operating in futures markets are speculators who, thanks to their unique skill and information set, attempt to profit from future price changes. For example, "long speculators" expect the price to rise above the current level; hence, they purchase futures contracts to buy in future periods at current prices.

Despite being different from other markets, even in a futures market, the price is a measure of the exchange value. Specifically, if this kind of market exchange is performed in well-functioning markets and it is based exclusively on different information (and not, for example, on different risk-attitude or other kinds of heterogeneity), then the market price quantifies exactly the difference in the price expectations of the traders. It can be observed that in this sort of social interaction, only the most successful traders can survive in the market over time. Even though there are losers, the selection process is nonetheless a good thing for the system as a whole. In fact, it implies that the prices set in futures markets are a reliable source of information about what might happen in the economic system, a source which is publicly available for everyone in need. Futures markets offer a measurement of risk

---

[11] In the cooperative game theory jargon, the solution of an interaction is stable when no coalition can deviate and make its members better off.

[12] In Chap. 4, I shall talk about the difference in information between the principal (e.g., the employer) and the agent (the employee). In Chap. 3, I shall dig deeper on how economists think humans form their expectations.

[13] In futures markets, participants trade specific quantities of a commodity or financial instrument at a specified price for delivery on a specified future date.

(i.e., the possibility to associate probabilities[14]) in that reducing uncertainty (more on that below and in Chap. 3).

Examining Walrasian capital markets, E. Fama argues that markets are strongly efficient when market prices embody all available information [7]. In this case, market prices enable resources to be allocated to their highest-valued uses. Worth stressing during this current excursion is that this efficient market hypothesis (EMH) is realized by trading activities induced by disparate information. If the price of the asset does not already reflect all available information, Walrasians would trade on it thereby quasi instantaneously moving the price until the information is no longer useful for making money via trading. Since all information is always correctly reflected in prices, it is impossible to "beat the market." As usual, homogeneity, in this case in the information set, kills trade. However, this conclusion holds under very tight assumptions on the functioning of markets and ability of operators. Among others, for example, P. Samuelson [8] observed that the stock market is "micro efficient" but "macro inefficient." The EMH, he argued, is suited for individual stocks "for the reason that the minority who spot aberrations from micro efficiency can make money from those occurrences and, in doing so, they tend to wipe out any persistent inefficiencies." The EMH, instead, is much less suited for the aggregate stock market in the sense that long waves in the time series of aggregate indices of security prices exist above and below the various definitions of fundamental values (the Shiller's CAPE ratio *docet*).[15] In view of our journey, a useful takeaway is that no-trade periods scarcely can materialize in real-world economic systems.

There are other cases where disparate information sets at the individual level may impinge on both behaviors and the trading activity performed in capitalistic systems. Although synthetized, the following examples offer a glimpse of how heterogeneous information among humans may have contrasting effects on their trading endeavors.

Excessive trade (with respect to ideal situations such as those studied by Fama) may emerge when differences in information (and in human capital) induce herd behavior. In real-world financial markets, for example, untrained traders typically follow the experts' hints. Going along with well-informed, skilled operators may be understandable from the standpoint of the single amateur investor. After all, if many professionals are trying to figure out reasonable prices, why waste one's time to do the same job? But considering many of them, the strategy induces herd behavior, which may generate excessive demand and trade (we shall return to this topic in the Chap. 6).

There are then situations in which dissimilar information sets may lead the trading activity to contract (the opposite of the previous case). A classic example is the presence of asymmetric information. As explained by G. Akerlof in his analysis of the *market for lemons* [9], asymmetric information shrinks the market for good-quality cars despite the presence of humans who are willing to trade used cars. The

[14] As said in the Prologue, risk is measurable uncertainty and uncertainty is unmeasurable risk.

[15] Available at http://www.econ.yale.edu/~shiller/data.htm

trading humans studied by Akerlof are Walrasians even if the customer is not fully informed.[16] This latter is searching for a used car but lacks information about the quality of the cars in the seller's shop. Facing uncertainty, this otherwise Walrasian customer imagines that half of the cars are good and half less good. Accordingly, she attributes to all the cars the average price. In doing so, cars with above-average quality are undervalued and others (the lemons) overvalued. The fully fledged Walrasian seller knows that the Walrasian customer values all the cars at the average price, and, accordingly, he puts on the market only the overvalued lemons. In turn, the customer knows this and lowers the average price at which she values the cars in the shop. Again, the seller knows this and puts on the market cars with even worse quality. Clearly, this adverse selection spiral continues in the mind of the two Walrasians until only really bad cars are actually marketed. The moral of the story is that asymmetric information hampers exchange that would improve the welfare of all the participants. This is why the state offers consumer protection laws and establishes authorities, such as US Federal Trade Commission, aimed at supporting customers. Recall, then, that opportunism may be costly and reputation beneficial in market systems. In fact, humans have also reacted to asymmetric information, enriching this kind of market with free after-sell services and guarantees, user-based valuations, and the like. This is yet another case supporting that efficiency depends on behaviors and rules. It also recalls the importance of social capital in executing the *Four* in capitalistic systems.

According to our guides [10, 11], another example of the difference in information leading to a reduction in trading activities may happen in labor markets. Occasionally, humans may rationally choose to remain unemployed even if they could work, which amounts to fewer exchanges ("labor vs money"). In looking for an answer, economists have elaborated on the so-called search models. These models aim to explain the circumstances under which humans find it in their interest to not sign an employment contract while searching for work. These humans are assumed to be fully informed Walrasians, but it is also assumed that they must pay for information. Basically, the rationale is that in labor markets characterized by uncertainty and in which information can be costly, to close a contract, both employers and employees must search. The exact location of the better matches is unknown and discovering them is costly in terms of time, effort, and money. In the case of the market for new doctors, for example, we saw that without a working algorithm, such as the NRMP, doctors should search hospitals by themselves, and this makes information an economic good. The idea is then to approach the labor market as a matching market (between firms and workers) and the job search as a costly information-gathering activity.

Walrasians must then compare the costs of search and benefits of matching. If it is not advantageous to extend too much time on the search, the worker may well have preferences leading her to not accept offers below a minimum level of matching. The rationale for smaller-than-Walrasian trading activity in labor markets with costly

[16] If not otherwise stated, Walrasians are fully informed humans (cf. Chap. 1).

search is not smaller-than-Walrasian rationality in decision making but, rather, the imperfect information over the location of one's best job opportunity. In passing, note that this conclusion sounds similar to what was said about the market for lemons—in both cases the trading efforts of otherwise Walrasians are affected by lack of information, not by irrational behavior. To increase the efficiency of labor markets, humans have addressed search problems with state initiatives such as the UK government's "Jobseeker's Allowance"—which is an unemployment benefit for people looking for work—as well as exploiting the Internet. The latter is rapidly changing the way workers search for jobs and employers recruit workers. Sites such as Monster.com and HotJobs.com are examples of how humans have eased this sort of hunting-gathering activity in the modern savannah.

A final possibility that I want to discuss in this tour stop on information and trade is that more complete information may shrink socially useful exchanges. After reading what has been said so far, one may well wonder—How can more complete information be bad for exchanges? Never forget the immense complexity of behavior, systems, and the ways they can interface. Consider health markets. If private health insurance companies can discriminate between individuals—for example, on the basis of genetic data or the person's current state of health—someone with genes indicating potential health problems could not obtain medical insurance at an affordable price. Thus, in many countries, the law prohibits conditioning medical insurance fees to information regarding the individual concerned.

Humans are insatiable, forward-looking, heterogeneous, clever animals who dislike uncertainty. This has led them to invent contingent markets, that is, markets where exchanges involving different states of nature are performed.[17] Before proceeding, it is worth recalling that in our tour, a risky event is measurable in the sense that it is possible to measure or estimate a probability as, for example, in the case of roulette wheel result or events that have occurred often enough to build a basis of prediction. Uncertainty (or ambiguity), instead, is unmeasurable risk (cf. Chap. 1). Needless to say, since the socioeconomic Big Bang, in implementing the *Four,* humans face both ambiguous and risky situations. If a world without uncertainty is still really far away (if it can exist), history teaches that some ambiguity has been downgrading to risk, which enlarges the opportunities to gain from trade. As observed, for example, futures markets help to measure risk in that reducing ambiguity. I thus devote the next discussion to inspect how humans and, specifically, Walrasians approach trading activities under risk.

Walrasians are supposed to be fully informed and able to measure risks but may have different attitudes toward risk. As a consequence, there would be gains from trade even if all this sort of humans were identical in all the other respects (e.g., endowment and information). Suppose a Walrasian wants to participate in a fair lottery (i.e., a bet whose expected payoff is zero). If she is risk neutral, all that she values is the expected payoff. As a consequence, she is indifferent about whether to

[17] In contingent markets, contracts are made to exchange funds contingent upon an event or combination of events or contingencies thereof.

gamble or not to gamble because, on average, gains and losses offset one another. From a behavioral standpoint, the cases of risk aversion and risk-loving are more interesting because these risk-sensitive Walrasians also look at the risk related to the bet. Specifically, risk-averse agents prefer not to participate in a fair lottery, whereby risk-loving individuals prefer to gamble. Otherwise stated, whereby the former ponder the risk and the latter ponder the thrill.

It is worth stressing that risk aversion is not an aversion to put in place risky exchanges. We are visiting Walrasians, and risk-averse Walrasians have no problem gambling if the odds are favorable; they are risk-averse, coherent humans. Needless to say, the presence of risk and disparate propensities toward risk led humans to enrich economic systems with other types of trading activities, markets, and institutions. Risk loving agents populate speculative markets; risk-averse humans are ideal customers of insurance companies. In any case, in Walrasian markets, the price (indirectly) quantifies psychological attitudes. For example, the difference in price between two assets which are identical except for their different risk quantifies the different risk of these assets as perceived by agents. The perceived risk explains why amid turbulent periods, low-risk financial assets, such as German treasury bonds, are so much in demand that their yield goes below zero.[18] Despite the fact that money is not a free good, in the last few decades, the situation has become such that some individuals are willing to lend their own money for free for up to 10 years (which, these days, is a sort of watershed separating negative and positive yields for the German Bund). By the same token, the insurance premium measures the risk aversion of the insured—how much she is willing to pay to reduce risk to an acceptable level. But it needs functioning insurance markets, and this calls for the state to intervene by establishing ad hoc watchdogs (e.g., Japan's Financial Services Agency).[19]

2.4 Property Rights and Trading

The institutional setting is crucial for peaceful, sustainable, and successful social interactions among humans. In the Prologue, for example, we saw that Acemoglu and Robinson argue that inclusive political institutions are a must-have for nations to prosper. Perhaps theirs is too extreme a view, but in our journey, it is hard to deny the importance of formal institutions as outlined in the Prologue. In the previous sections, then, the trek was mainly devoted to the heterogeneities behind the exchange, only glimpsing some institutional issues and responses while procrastinating others. In the story of the comparative advantage, for example, one should ask why Sapiens C is more productive—because of higher human capital or

[18] The higher a bond's price, the lower its yield. If each year the bond pays 5% of its face value (say 100) as interest, the yield is lower if the bond's price is above its face value.

[19] I shall talk about other institutional devices emerged in insurance and financial markets in the Epilogue.

just because he can exclude Sapiens D from the most fertile areas by claiming property rights over these areas? Is it possible that other rules of the game would improve their system? This tour stop touches upon these issues and, specifically, on property rights, which are among the most important rules of the game in helping humans execute the *Four*. I have already grazed the importance of property rights, inserting them into the inclusive institutions set and stressing their role for a socially sustainable resolution of human interactions. Hence, I devote this stopover to scout property rights with the goal of outlining their importance for the *Four* in general and trading efforts in particular. The standpoint still remains, by and large, within the realm of neoclassical economics.[20]

According to our guides, property rights are the exclusive authority to determine how a resource is used. Economists stress that individuals do not own something but, rather, own socially structured rights to use something in certain ways [12]. If we are the owner of land, their argument goes, we own the right to till it, mine it, and sell these rights, but not the right to throw the soil at people or to force someone to buy it. Property rights are crucial for the *Four* because they determine what the system lets individuals do. As mentioned in the Prologue, institutions such as property rights are the rules of the game, and not knowing who has what rights, it is not possible to understand human behavior within an economic system. Finally, these rights are essential rules because they solve potentially dangerous social interactions and reduce the waste of socially useful resources.

One way to proceed is to explore the intersections of capitalism, private property rights, and the *Four*. Property rights held by individuals, i.e., private property rights, are a key ingredient of market systems. This is so because capitalism strictly necessitates the general rules of property and contracts to frame not only exchanges but also production, human and physical capital formation, and, more generally, each of the *Four*. Private property rights furnish incentives to work and to maintain wealth and durable goods; they establish time horizons for investment, production, and exchange. They are among the most important institutional devices invented by humans to manage the endeavors we are traveling across. It is sometimes overlooked that private property rights provide the incentives for individuals to economize on resource use because the user bears the costs of their actions. For example, the market value of our car or house depends on how we take care of it. Working as a sort of built-in penalty, private property rights teach humans to behave responsibly because it is costly not to do so. Incentivizing individuals to produce, invest, etc., as well to preserve socially valuable private goods, private property rights often improve the system more than what top-down arrangements or anarchy can do. The state, of course, must be able to enforce private property rights avoiding

[20] As repeatedly mentioned, the tour can only briefly stop in some site leaving unexplored many others. Regarding private property, for example, an alternative view can be found in the Marxist literature. In a nutshell, according to Marx private property allows the appropriation of the means of production and is an institutional obstacle in the achievement of a better system. Hence, he suggested to abolish it which, according to the description of capitalism in our tour, would lead to another kind of economic system.

unjustified accumulation of wealth. In fact, economic inequality is not a problem of property rights but, rather, of the state, which must not throw the baby with the bath water.

Changing perspective, when property rights are absent or difficult to assign or enforce, problems arise as in the case of public goods and common resources (fish stocks, wood, pastures, etc.). Think about how often humans overconsume public goods such as the atmosphere, the ocean, and the like (cf. Chap. 6) or situations like the "tragedy of commons" that we shall explore when we will visit communities and their common pool resources (Chap. 4). Additional insights can be drawn by comparing situations where property rights are well-established to those where they are not so well-established. Acemoglu and Robinson claim that a significant part of the different performance of economies such as, on the one hand, Congo and, on the other side, the USA or Australia is due to the fact that European colonizers put greater emphasis on private property in the latter. These days, most land in sub-Saharan Africa still has no formal documentation of who owns it or has rights to use it. Various initiatives are underway to address this with the belief that land registration and titling can promote investment, reduce poverty, and encourage better natural-resource management. According to the World Bank, if poor countries improve the opaque procedures surrounding land ownership alone, there will be a significant increase in food production. H. de Soto [13] has then stressed that in rich Western countries, it is usual to use buildings and land both for immediate physical purposes and as collateral. In developing countries, this double life of capital is much less diffused, which badly affects their economic system. For de Soto, specifically, the lack of capitalizable property rights (i.e., property rights that can be used as collateral for loans) is a major reason why the poor stay poor in developing countries.

Another example comes from China. Starting in the late 1970s, this country moved a long way toward a greater role of private property in its economic system. Our guides [14] have collected evidence of this process, showing that between 1978 and 2015, private wealth increased from 115% to 487% of national income. During this period, China has enjoyed a very rapid rate of economic growth. The essential contribution of private property in this development is emphasized even by Chinese policymakers. In 2004, they declared private property of citizens "inviolable" by an amendment of the Chinese constitution. On the behavioral side of the matter, one may argue that even Chinese policymakers agree (or must admit) that humans have an ineluctable individualistic side and that is better to manage it rather than try to change it.

For property rights to be so incentivizing, however, they must be enforceable. Several economic problems arise when property rights to goods are either not possible, not protected, or not easily implemented. F. Hayek [15], a staunch advocate of free markets, claimed that "Law, Liberty and Property are an inseparable Trinity." To reiterate, an efficient state is key for capitalism to be a functional system. Economists also conjecture that if the state is unwilling or unable to protect private property, then private institutions emerge to fill the gap uncovered by the state. These could take the form of neighborhood patrols,[21] but they can also be dangerous paramilitary or mafia-like organizations [16]. In this respect, property rights are key for humans' endeavors because they produce social order and social coordination.

So far, I have briefly delineated the general validity of property rights in human affairs, and in the next chapters, I will offer further details as we explore common property goods (Chap. 4) and intellectual property rights (Chap. 5). But there are also more specific links with the main target of the current sojourn, trading. To start with, recall the questions about property rights raised by the comparative advantage story, and that even the trading endeavor of early Sapiens A and B needed some working rule of engagement. To use the economists' jargon, individual property rights in that sort of pre-state stage of human history might have been a common-interest (e.g., I do not steal you, you do not steal me) social interaction.[22] Early trade, then, spurred the introduction of money in the economic system. But, again, money is related to private property because it is a symbol of what others in the system owe you; it is a symbol of your claim on the system's resources.

What is perhaps more important to stress in this stop, however, is that what is bought and sold is the private property rights, not the good itself. This is easy to see considering what is traded in real estate markets—in these markets the goods may be located someplace else and immovable, such as land and buildings. This clarification allows us to refine the notion of market in capitalism—it is an arrangement and process for comparing people's demands and offerings and for conducting exchanges of private property rights. An essential feature of private property rights, indeed, is transferability (or alienability), i.e., the right to sell your rights. In principle, property rights should be freely transferable in order to allow resources to move to their most highly valued uses. But, as usual, the complexity of both human beings and economic systems makes things less easily manageable than desired. There are exceptions that, limiting the alienability of property, hamper humans in their willingness to trade.

On some occasions, constraining the impetus of humans to trade is good, and at other times, it is not. A case where limiting trade is positive refers to the *rule against perpetuities* (or rule against remoteness of vesting). It requires that future trust interests—that is, interests that do not take effect immediately—must be certain to vest within a defined period of time known as the perpetuity period. An explanation for this rule is to reduce the Dead Hand control, i.e., the attempt to control property after the death. The problem consists in a trade-off. One the one hand, one should have the complete freedom to tie up property in perpetuity. On the other hand, private property rights should be controlled by the living and not the dead because the dead cannot respond to changes in circumstances as they arise—the Dead Hand can impair the alienability and productivity of property. In particular, the rationale to

[21] According to the *New York Times* (Mar. 23, 1973), in the early 1970s there were about 7000 citizen self-help groups in New York City.

[22] D. Hume argued that the history of property is the history of conflict and theft, but he also saw property rights arising as a solution to that conflict: a social convention arises spontaneously to establish peace by recognizing existing holdings as if they were property.

limit the control of property by those no longer alive is that it discourages potential buyers by preventing them from developing the property as they see fit and may prevent the property from being developed to economic advantage.

Recall that trading, or alienability, aims to transfer goods to those that most value them. Imagine that a landlord wants to convey land to his son with restrictions on alienability to prevent the land from being sold outside the family. Hypothesize, then, that his son is incapable of maintaining the estate—that will deteriorate the property to the point of becoming unproductive (e.g., unusable for farming). Since there is the need to balance between the living and the dead, it is a matter of Dead Hand vs Invisible Hand.

Several other legal restrictions to the alienability of property are definitively justifiable and easier to see than the Dead Hand issue. Points in case are legal restrictions aimed to stop trading children, women voting, endangered animal species, etc. Likewise, it is surely wise to stop *ex lege* the possibility that young humans ("minors") buy or sell specified rights referring to alcohol, guns, specific movies, or marriage licenses. It is also defensible to limit agreements to work for, say, over ten hours a day.

In contrast, there are cases whereby restrictions on trading cannot be easily defended. Among them, there are limitations that make agreements to sell at a price above some politically selected limit illegal. The crux is that this kind of constraint reduces the strength of private property and market exchange both as coordinating tools of behaviors and as a means of resolving conflictual social interactions. To the extent that property rights can be voluntarily exchanged, an economic system with more complete private property rights makes market exchange values more influential. Consider rent controls, i.e., policies that aim to cap house price increases. On the positive, possibly more visible side, they are intended to keep housing affordable at least for the most vulnerable parts of a population. However, the policy has its drawbacks. In Sweden, for example, rent controls effectively toppled the government. In Germany, the matter was subject to a year-long legal battle. Meanwhile, lawmakers in the Netherlands, the UK, and Ireland have all had similar discussions about their property markets.

To see the difficulty of rent controls, we now explore the case when the presence of more complete property rights makes discrimination more costly. Suppose a woman wants to rent an apartment from a landlord who does not like her for reasons linked to her race or sexual inclinations or religion or the like. The more the landlord has the right to set the rent at whatever level he wants (i.e., there are no legal price ceilings), the more the woman can offset her "diversity" by offering a higher rent. Note what this higher rent means for the landlord: it makes it more costly for him not to accept the deal. The landlord has thus an incentive to start a market exchange with the woman. If they cannot close the contract, it means that there is no equilibrium price at which both are freely willing to trade. But if they eventually close the contract, it means that both are gaining from trade. Accordingly, this kind of unconstrained trading activity may offer an exit strategy for unpleasant social interactions.

Of course, the market solution is not perfect because the woman must pay a higher rent, but the management of this behavior with different institutional tools may lead to even worse solutions. Compare a situation whereby, as before, the market price can solve the social interaction (i.e., the parts reach a deal) with that where there is the inability to exchange at market clearing prices due, for example, to price fixing law. This reduction in the trading of property rights may lead to social interactions based on less impersonal and more discriminating allocative methods (by gender, marital status, pet ownership, eating and drinking habits, and so forth) with respect to the market price. The woman would have no chance to rent even if she were willing to pay a higher rent. In other words, with price controls, non-pecuniary discriminating features necessarily receive greater weight and the exchange shifts from price competition to a nonprice competition that can even stop exchanges that would have increased the well-being of the trading partners.

But there are other more indirect costs that are derived from price caps. These may hinder other landlords from renting their apartments which shrinks market opportunities (hence the gains from trade) for potential tenants. In the long term, these caps may also reduce the market for rent because fewer new houses can be built. Finally, applying antidiscrimination laws has drawbacks because proving discrimination is difficult and contested decisions involve long-lasting, complex, and subjective judgments. These transaction costs are far from being trivial and should be considered. This is a general point when addressing the *Four* and is worth emphasizing. Perfect solutions are very rare, if they exist at all. Only imperfect ones abound. While perfection could be considered an ultimate goal or a situation toward which to strive, comparisons must involve only feasible—typically imperfect—solutions, taking into account both direct and indirect potential costs and benefits.

Further insights on the links between property rights and trading may be drawn from our guides' research on the fact that, other things being equal, property rights tend to be made more precise as resource values rise. This standpoint permits us to address a basic question—how do property rights emerge in economic systems? The answer found by H. Demsetz provides another example of the ability of humans to find functioning ways to carry out their businesses and, in particular, of how private property rights may develop among trading individuals. Demsetz advanced a cost-benefit analysis suggesting that property rights are expected to materialize in human societies when their advantages become relatively greater than their disadvantages [17]. Elaborating on a research by the anthropologist E. Leacock, he examined the emergence of property rights in land among Indians and explained that it was a way of preventing overly intensive hunting of valuable animals. Following a consolidated tradition, the story goes, the Indians used to hunt beavers and then sell their furs within a social arrangement that allowed free hunting. The fluidity of this trading system was challenged when white traders arrived and increased the demand for beaver's furs. In line with the trading instinct and behavior of humans as well as with the Walrasian pricing rule, the growth in demand quickly inflated the price, and the monetary incentive led Indians to capture more beavers. Soon, the Indians realized that they could have been left with an insufficient population of beavers (Malthus *docet*). Hence, they changed the rules of the game in order to achieve a happy ending to their trading efforts.

The Indians' institutional move was to substitute the free access arrangements with private rights in land. By owning the right to exclude others from their land, Indian families were provided with an incentive to inventory their animals. Under a free access arrangement, such inventories would have been depleted by other hunters. Crucially, the institutional transition toward private property took place only after the benefits of doing that were greater than the costs.

A countercheck found by Demsetz allows us to appreciate the cost-benefit analysis performed by Indians. He examined other Indians living in another, more southernly, territory. Unlike the northern land, the morphology of this territory was such that the animals could run around in wide spaces so that the cost of establishing who could hunt which animal—i.e., the cost of instituting a private property system—was high. This large cost also had to be compared with the little commercial value of the hunted animals. According to Demsetz's view, it was then unsurprising that southern Indians did not introduce property rights.

For our tour's purposes, two things are worth noting in this story. First, the Indians' institutional move was deliberate; it did not emerge spontaneously. Second, and even more important, the story of the Indians emphasizes that the social function of private property rights lies in aligning individual behavior with collective interest in the sense of allowing and supporting transactions between the owner and other contributors. This important idea deserves to be conveyed directly through our guides' words (p. 24): [18] "private rights can be socially useful precisely because they encourage persons to take account of social costs. The identification of private rights with anti-social behavior is a doctrine as mischievous as it is popular."

References

1. Smith A (1776) op. cit.
2. Malinowski B (1922) Argonauts of the Western Pacific: An Account of Native Enterprise and Adventure in the Archipelagoes of Melanesian New Guinea. Routledge and Kegan P. LTD, London.
3. Smith V L (1962) An experimental study of competitive market behavior. Journal of Political Economy 70 (2): 111-37.
4. Jevons W S (1875) Money and the Mechanism of Exchange. London: Macmillan.
5. Roth A E (1984) The evolution of the labor market for medical interns and residents: A case study in game theory. Journal of Political Economy 92: 991-1016.
6. Williams J C (1982) The Origin of Futures Markets. Agricultural History, 56, (1): 306-316.
7. Fama E (1970). Efficient Capital Markets: A Review of Theory and Empirical Work. The Journal of Finance, *25*(2): 383-417.
8. Samuelson P A (1998) Summing Up on Business Cycles: Opening Address. In Fuhrer J C and Schuh S (ed), Beyond Shocks: What Causes Business Cycles. Boston: Federal Reserve Bank of Boston.
9. Akerlof G (1970) The Market for Lemons: Quality Uncertainty and the Market Mechanism. The Quarterly Journal of Economics, 84 (3): 488-500.
10. Stigler G J (1962) Information in the labor market. Journal of Political Economy 70: 94–105.

11. Rogerson R, Shimer R, and Wright R (2005) Search theoretic models of the labor market: A survey. Journal of Economic Literature 43: 959–988
12. Alchian A and Demsetz H (1973) The Property Right Paradigm. The Journal of Economic History 33(1): 16-27.
13. De Soto H (2000) The Mystery of Capital: Why Capitalism Triumphs in the West and Fails Everywhere Else. New York: Basic Books and London: Bantam Press/Random House.
14. Piketty T, Yang L, and Zucman G (2019) Capital Accumulation, Private Property, and Rising Inequality in China, 1978–2015. American Economic Review, 109(7): 2469-96.
15. Hayek F A (1973) Law, Legislation and Liberty. Vol. I: Rules and Order. Chicago: The University of Chicago Press.
16. Gambetta D (1993) The Sicilian Mafia: The business of private protection. Cambridge, MA: Harvard University Press.
17. Demsetz H (1967) Toward a Theory of Property Rights. American Economic Review, 57(2): 347-59.
18. Alchian A A and Demsetz H (1973) op. cit.

Forecasting: Humans Are Prone-to-Predicting Animals

3

3.1 Introduction

Since the socioeconomic Big Bang, the human being plans and forms expectations. Incessantly. We are not the only animal to predict. Marmots, bears, bats, and bumblebees spend the months they are awake reproducing and preparing for the next hibernation. The behavior of some animals may affect the forecasting of weather emergencies or earthquakes, and biologists posit that many animals anticipate the arrival of summer because they sense that the days are getting longer. All this activity seems to derive from animals' senses, which are superior to ours: scientists claim that animals can sense the environment and its changing states (humidity, air pressure, etc.) much better than humans.

Possibly because of their inferior senses, humans predict more cerebrally. Of course, the greater use of brain implies neither that other animals are not smart, nor that humans' forecasting exercises are just a matter of rational thinking or, as economists typically state, coherence. As we sometimes hear, humans swing from being thinking creatures that feel to being emotional creatures that think. It is yet another way of saying that humans are complex, adaptive behavioral entities with the addition that the human brain is a multiplex organ where, sometimes chaotically, rationality and irrationality coexist.

In his lifelong research on cognitive psychology, D. Kahneman [1] has posited that human thinking can be imagined, although for pedagogical purposes only, as stemming from two separable systems. One is intuitive and emotionally inflected, which makes it a fast and generally effective "machine for jumping to conclusions." The second is slow and rational; its scope is to check the responses made by the first system and to understand the world more rigorously than intuition allows.

M. Bovi, *Why and How Humans Trade, Predict, Aggregate, and Innovate*,
Contributions to Economics, https://doi.org/10.1007/978-3-030-93885-7_3

This seems to be a widespread attitude—humans accomplish all of the *Four* by blending emotions and rationality.[1] In trading, we make rational choices, but departures from coherence are far from being rare (cf. Chap. 6). We aggregate for emotional motives, but we also base this decision on some logical reasoning (cf. Chap. 4). Inventions and innovations, then, are the results of rational choice and innate imagination (cf. Chap. 5).

The fact that, for necessity or virtue, humans rely more on their brain than on their inferior senses with respect to other animals offers a first clue as to why the expectation formation mechanism of humans is unique. Then, evidently, the idiosyncratic symbolic language of humans plays a crucial role in making special the way in which humans stitch together present and future circumstances. The mix of emotions and rationality, as well as the special skill of humans in making abstractions makes humans complex forecasting entities who predict for disparate and unique reasons. An excursion across some of these drives pinpoints the degree of diversification, suggests that humans have an innate predisposition to look forward, and highlights the gains from forecasting.

Humans forecast for a sense of control. It is a basic need. Just as early Sapiens and Sumerian farmers did, if we can mindfully prognosticate what will happen, we have higher chances of controlling events. To the extent that we do not know what will happen next, we cannot relax and must constantly be on the lookout for danger. H. Simon [2] stressed that one of the most powerful influences on fear is uncertainty. The less we know, the more threatened we feel. Humans predict to prevent, and they are continuously at work in order to "downgrade" ambiguity to measurable risk as well as to reduce the latter. Short-term weather forecasts and the prediction of smoking-related diseases are points in case. We hope that as soon as possible, scientists will be able to insert all conceivable natural disaster (as well as any other possible uncertainty) in humans' risky-event set. Besides natural events, forecasting to control is also targeted to others' behavior. Since human beings first communicated with each other, we have told lies. As O.J. Williamson put it (p. 51) [3], humans use a "full set of ex ante and ex post efforts to lie, cheat, steal, mislead, disguise, obfuscate, feign, distort and confuse." All that implies that we need to forecast others' behavior.

Despite all our efforts (and, as we shall see, partly because of them), everyone knows that today's economic systems are still very risky and uncertain. In trading, innovating, and aggregating, we are constantly looking forward, trying to decide the best course of action to achieve our goals and to avoid potential discomforts. Lack of knowledge means we do not know what we need to know to protect ourselves, which equates to a lack control over health and safety, i.e., over living longer and better. As we are learning in this tour, even the market system can be thought of as a mechanical device to address an uncertain environment given our inadequate senses

[1] The view that emotions and rationality are perpetually in battle for domination is sustained by neuroscientists (for instance, Sapolsky R M (2017) Behave: The Biology of Humans at Our Best and Worst, Penguin Press).

to figure out the future (recall the excursion in future and contingent markets. See also Sect. 3.3).

On several other occasions, however, the scope of our forecasting efforts is less decisive. We perform predictions just to have fun, or for the sake of excitement and thrill to get rich. Many humans forecast to bet on the royal baby's name, the next world champion, the next political leader, and so forth. Perhaps because of their purpose, these types of forecasts seem to have a significant emotional content. As a sort of permanent worldwide experiment, national lotteries are examples of that. Most players are aware that these bets are unfair from their perspective—the payout to the successful punters is always less than what they should have received if the odds had reflected the true chances. Buyers are well-informed of that because it is explicitly written on lottery tickets, or it is readily available on the lottery website and at retail outlets. On the other hand, it is easy to learn that the seller has a systematic advantage—in several countries a nontrivial part of government revenues derives from national lotteries or the like. This notwithstanding, many gamblers do believe that numbers have memory so that there is room to perform reliable predictions and to implement systematically winning strategies. Despite statistics on past numbers simply cannot help to predict future drawings, some stackers put more chances on *hot* numbers, while others, magnifying the irrationality of this kind of prediction, select *cold* numbers. Since 1662 economists have been stressing that the lottery is a fool's tax [4], which, from the mere statistical standpoint, is definitively right.

Unlike numbers, however, humans have memories and emotions. Putting aside compulsive gamblers, even normal people who are aware that the mathematical expectation of the lottery is negative may still rationally buy lottery tickets. They can do that for emotional motives. They may participate for the pleasure to dream about what they could do with all that money. In this sense, buying a scratch-off ticket is not so different from buying a movie ticket. As professional advertisers highlight, after all, both offer a brief emotional escape from everyday life and, as our guides teach, the market price quantifies how much we are willing to pay for that.

Finally, the forecasting tendency of humans sometimes takes the appearance of pure curiosity. It is so when we look forward to having an idea of what to expect in the afterlife or when we speculate about future economic systems, imagining how technology could improve the world.

If predicting afterlife is impossible, all forecasting exercises are far from being easy. As the great physicist N. Bohr nicely warned, "it is difficult to predict, especially the future." When guessing about future technological scenarios, for example, humans only occasionally get it right, and even brilliant, well-informed humans make big errors. In 1889, T.A. Edison foreshadowed that "Fooling around with alternating current (AC) is just a waste of time. Nobody will use it, ever." In 1943, IBM Chairman and CEO T.J. Watson suggested that there was "a world market for maybe five computers." In 2005, P. Tetlock [5] reported a study of 284 political and economic "experts" and their predictions. He found that these skilled humans performed worse than they would have if they had simply assigned equal probabilities to each of the potential outcomes. But mistakes and difficulties have never stopped our inclination to predict. Quite the contrary. For good or ill, when tackling human affairs, humans never give up.

To recap, humans carry out forecasting efforts in disparate ways, for disparate reasons, and with only occasional success. It is a matter integral to their behavioral nature, but it also deals with the fact that humans operate in complex uncertain systems. Modern economic systems are tightly interconnected, amplifying the need to forecast. If the need to forecast others' behavior because of opportunism is timeless, in modern economic systems the quality and quantity of events that we have to forecast as well as the frequency of the prediction efforts that we must face is much larger than those of our predecessors. At a personal level, we need to predict the traffic jam, to perform family planning, to forecast the possibility/duration/participation of a strike, to trace the evolution of financial and real estate markets, to decide whether to continue to study and what to study, to borrow at a fixed vs variable rate, to choose the best retirement plan among many alternatives, and so on. The presence of network goods such as smartphones or services such as Facebook implies then that we have to figure out whether our fellows decide to systematically use them. The effects of social complexity on forecasting materialize even in the birth of new forecasting tools and new kind of professional forecasters. Because of the continual evolution of economic systems, tools have been evolving from the observation of omens to machine learning; forecasters have been developing from oracles to data scientists.

This preamble indicates a way to dig deeper into forecasting exercises. Specifically, I shall frame the exploration by separating two kinds of predictions, stressing their feed-backs with individual behaviors and economic systems. The first deals with economic subjects, that is, the prediction of others' behavior in social interactions. The second deals with economic objects, that is, the prediction of variables such as prices and GDP growth, labor market and public finance evolutions, etc. Though different and discussed distinctly, these two forecasting exercises are not separate businesses. A hint about their intersection comes from the *beauty contest* concept elaborated by Keynes (p. 156): [6] "It is not a case of choosing those which, to the best of one's judgment, are really the prettiest, [. . .] we devote our intelligences to anticipating what average opinion expects the average opinion to be." In predicting economic objects such as stock prices, i.e., Keynes suggested that one should predict not the objective value of the stock but, rather, what others think about that value. These days, a somewhat similar insight can be drawn from W. Buffett's hints. The Oracle of Omaha (Buffett's nickname) has often written about how "Mr. Market" can swing from euphoria to despondency, bidding up or driving down a company's stock price based on manic-depressive emotions rather than any big changes in the fundamental business and outlook. Rather than inspecting fundamentals, he therefore claims that a successful strategy consists in selling when others are euphoric and buying when their sentiment is depressed. Finally, it has been argued that individuals can have different information, hence different expectations, on economic objects so that forecasting the forecasts of others could be a central element of their decisions. This is the case even when others have no real economic connections with them [7].

3.2 Forecasting Economic Subjects

Forecasting economic subjects—i.e., others—is perhaps the most important and high-frequency predictive emprise in a human's life. It is innate and inescapable in view of our alacrity to live together, longer, and better. Since the socioeconomic Big Bang, humans face situations whereby they must predict what decisions others will make and how others will behave. There are strong incentives and large gains in these kinds of forecasts. It is essential to the social interactions that make up our personal and professional lives because we strategically tune our behavior according to what we expect others will do. We are aware that the outcome of our choices will depend on the actions and beliefs of others. Though this kind of forecasting involves predominantly few individuals, the economic system as a whole has an impact on it. As observed, for example, the more the network in which humans operate is interconnected, the more important and frequent this endeavor becomes. This positive correlation between forecasting activity and system sophistication parallels the fact that the size of trading efforts goes hand in hand with the complexity of the economic system.

How do humans perform this sort of exercise? Differently from other animals. When one ant touches another with its antennae, it assesses whether the other ant is a nestmate and, sometimes, what task the other ant has been performing. The ant uses its recent experience with chemical interactions to decide what to do next. Dogs' superior sense of smell help them to collect a lot of information about other dogs. Though humans form their expectations of others by extracting information from chemical interactions [8, 9][2] and body language, informal institutions (as defined in the Prologue) and beliefs turn out to be more critical factors, making unique the way in which humans predict their fellows' behavior.[3]

We use our beliefs about what we think others should do to predict their behavior. Everyone has a set of beliefs about how others will act in different social situations. Believing that someone is a (un)trusty seller, for example, will lead us to expect from him a (bad)good behavior and to behave accordingly. We are willing to pay more for an employee that we believe to be serious and committed to her obligations. In Sect. 4.2, we shall learn that in the belief that workers' productivity depends on the wage paid employers may pay higher (efficiency) wages. That may be good for the economic system because it enlarges the social capital by both deterring lack of integrity and rewarding reliability.

---

[2]Evidence shows that when people are exposed to disgusting odors, dirty surroundings, or repellent videos (e.g., showing a man eating a large mouthful of writhing worms), then they are led to self-identify as conservative or to show more negative attitudes toward an entire social group. Cf. [8, 9]

[3]It is perhaps instructive to see beliefs, preferences, and institutions in action all together. Consider the case of driving that we will occasionally meet in the tour. Driving on the right-hand side of the road is an informal institution, a convention, which is supported by laws (formal institutions). People do not prefer driving on the right but prefer avoiding crashes and fines. The belief that others will drive on the right sustains the institution of driving on the right, which in turn sustains the belief.

Just like the other activities included in the *Four*, forecasting must be wisely implemented for the successful achievement of human goals. As usual in humans' life, potentially useful devices occasionally perform poorly, and unfortunately, more often than desired, beliefs perform poorly. Since the time of the ancient Greeks, "the apparel oft proclaims the man," as Shakespeare much later put it, but "oft" is less than always, and, at least occasionally, the apparel turns out to be a poor leading indicator.

Beliefs may be either outmoded and offensive or false because they are elaborated upon by our brain so that they are formed by a mix of rationality and emotions. Some beliefs may be inferred by first impression and, as such, may incorrectly attribute a bad character to good people or vice versa. Per a familiar phrase, first impressions are long lasting, and that makes forecasting errors persistent. Some beliefs lack reasonable factual foundations not only due to ignorance, but occasionally as an apparently conscious rejection of those values and facts behind the problem. In cases whereby shared beliefs mislead forecasts and behaviors, those beliefs spread uncertainty and inefficiency, and they reduce cooperation throughout the system.

Though via different tools with respect to those used in ancient times, even these days a good person may be ostracized or pilloried. From Spanish inquisition to the fake news diffused by modern mass media, humans may form distorted beliefs, impinging dramatically and unjustly on individuals or groups. For example, in the 1800s in the USA, racist sentiment led to the publication of false stories about African Americans' supposed deficiencies and crimes. These days, data show a decline over the last 40 years in the number of homicides carried out by people identified as suffering from mental health problems, but inappropriate representations increase stigma, ostracism, harassment, and victimization of these individuals by the public. Socioeconomic boundaries may be sustained by the belief that the behavior—and the poor performances—of a group of people is almost exclusively determined by their disposition with structural and situational factors having little, if any, influence. This leads to say, for example, that the poor as a group deserves what it gets.

Such beliefs may stem from the so-called *attribution effect*, according to which we believe that the behavior of others is explained by their intrinsic qualities in a given situation without considering the influence of the situational factors [10]. Clearly, this psychological bias operates not only on clusters based on income, but also on human aggregations based on, for example, religion, race, etc. Symbolic language is an instrument and, as such, it may be used for good or bad. Stereotypes produce similar distortions in humans' forecasting the behavior of others—Asians are good at math, Republicans are rich, male drivers are aggressive, etc. Our guides offer scientific evidence on that. Describing a man as (pp. 6–7) [11] "very shy and withdrawn, invariably helpful but with little interest in people or in the world of reality, [. . .] with a need for order and structure, and a passion for detail," most people deduce that he is more likely to be a librarian than a farmer. This is just because the description fits better the cultural stereotype of a librarian. Beliefs then integrate and differentiate economic systems as well as maintain the status quo. In any case, beliefs are an important ingredient when humans put in place their efforts to predict economic subjects.

Regarding informal institutions such as norms, I have already mentioned that acting as a coordination tool, they drive behaviors and reduce uncertainty in humans' interactions (cf. Chap. 1). If you are an absolute beginner, you probably wait for others before applauding during an opera so that the audience's clapping is typically synchronized. The fear of being sanctioned, the will to signal membership in the group, or simply following the lead of others are among the coordinating forces. This tour stop affords the possibility to say more about that, of course, with special attention to the activity we are currently visiting.

Acting as a behavioral guide, informal institutions help to forecast human behavior because they suggest the behavior expected from an individual toward others and from others toward himself. Humans expect each other to behave according to particular customs. Dress codes and norms of etiquette such as wearing a hat to dinner, showing up late to a meeting, and interrupting someone as she speaks are leading indicators that a person does not care. Informal institutions have strong forecasting power because they are long-lasting or fade away slowly. For example, until 2002, diplomatic immunity protected UN diplomats from parking enforcement actions, so diplomats' actions were constrained by cultural norms alone. As easily predictable—and this is the point—data show that diplomats from high-corruption countries (as ranked by survey-based indices) accumulated significantly more unpaid parking violations than other diplomats [12].

Expectations and informal institutions are tightly intertwined. As has been said, informal institutions have strong forecasting power because they are persistent, but this persistency depends on expectations as well. Once a particular way of doing things becomes established as a rule, it continues in force because we conform to the rule given the expectation that others are going to conform. This is so because failing to coordinate via norms is inherently costly, and fulfilling others' expectations is one way to not incur costs. For instance, we speak using words with the "expected" meaning to avoid misunderstandings. In some cases, there is also an external formal check, for example, driving on the "commonly expected" (right or left) side to avoid crashes and traffic fines.

Even the way in which humans learn what norms are is informative on the wide intersections of informal institutions and expectations. If a behavior does not provoke reactions and/or it is expected, then we think of it as a norm. Norm, indeed, is short for normal (behavior). Human beings dislike abnormal behaviors and like expected behaviors because that reduces uncertainty, keeping their life manageable and ordered. All that facilitates predictions, coordination, and, hence, the execution of all the affairs we are traveling across. In sum, informal institutions are useful forecasting tools, and expectations help to sustain them.

Informal institutions constitute valid devices for humans, and just as beliefs, they must be used wisely when predicting economic subjects. This is a timeless issue. Many of Plato's dialogues, indeed, dramatize the habits and processes that lead humans to false conclusions. Several centuries later, D. Hume [13] posited that irrational prejudices can be formed by overgeneralizing from experience; the imagination is unduly influenced by any "superfluous circumstances" that have frequently been observed to accompany the circumstances that actually matter. And paradoxically, he went on, the only way to correct the pernicious influence of general rules is to follow other general rules, formed by reflecting on the circumstances of the case and our cognitive limitations. In addition, norms within a given community tend to be uniform because people make less diverse choices than they otherwise would. It is both economically and socially costly not to conform. Different communities, however, might center around different norms because the evolutionary process producing norms is inherently random. Norms, thus, may contextually integrate and differentiate so that, consequently, forecasting others' behavior on the basis of our own informal institutions may be misleading. What is normal for us may not be so for other people. The digression on the definitory *caveat* made in the Prologue is illustrative of how conventions may help convergence or induce divergence even among scientists.

Game theory can be fruitfully exploited to add details about the interplay between informal institutions and expectations. A short introduction to the notion of Nash equilibrium (NE) turns out to be particularly useful in the current tour stop because, on the one hand, it helps to predict economic subjects and, on the other hand, it needs informal institutions. The NE is an equilibrium because it stems from strategies that are mutually best responses to one another. Even when the other person's choice is revealed, no rational individual wants to change his behavior.[4]

The utility of the NE in the present tour stop is that it allows us to avoid the infinite regression problem typically affecting the interactions among humans. When humans interact, the reasoning is often of the kind "I think that you think that I think. . . .." Thanks to the NE one can avoid considering all the intermediate moves and safely predict that, eventually, the rational players will behave according to the Nash equilibrium.[5] In a sense, it is like when a master of chess after a couple of moves tells a (rational) rookie how their game will end—there is no need of intermediate moves.

Even with rational players, the NE cannot solve all forecasting problems. Due to the richness and complexity of human interactions, there is no one-notion-fits-all, and several social interactions have multiple Nash equilibria. For instance, people can queue for service, or they can push; when greeting someone, they can shake hands or use other forms of greeting (as in these pandemic days where I imagine many of us have witnessed nice coordination failures). Widows can wear black or white (as in Eastern Asia), drivers can coordinate to drive on the right or left (as in England), and so forth.

[4]In Table 1, the double coincidence of the best replies can be seen in the cell "Confess; Confess" (cf. Chap. 1).

[5]To be sure, the Nash equilibrium concept does not necessarily predict how people will behave in the real world. It offers indications about how purely rational humans might behave, what one might expect to happen in a world where no one does anything wrong.

In some circumstances, there is no purely rational reason for selecting one equilibrium rather than another—is it more rational for widows to wear black or white? But, of course, real-life social interactions always find a unique solution. Humans never remain locked in a sort of limbus whereby their social interactions remain "hanging." They always converge toward one of the available equilibria. Here is when norms and conventions enter the scene as fruitful predictive instruments. Acting as behavioral guides and uncertainty-reducing tools, they coordinate people's expectations in situations with multiple equilibria and can thus be seen as humanly devised equilibrium selectors. For example, the commonly accepted convention to drive on the right (in left-hand drive vehicles) solves the Driving Game. In view of our tour, it is worth stressing the intersections of rationality, informal institutions, and equilibrium. British are not irrational because, unlike many other humans, they solve their Driving Game by choosing to drive on the opposite side. As observed, what allows informal institutions to survive in the long run is not their rational content but, rather, the fact that they coordinate behavior toward an equilibrium. This, in turn, is related to the forecasting efforts under scrutiny because the equilibrium nature of norms lies in the fact that humans follow a behavioral rule because they expect that others will do the same. In our guides' parlance, representing equilibria of games of strategy, informal institutions are supported by a cluster of self-fulfilling expectations [14].

Further insights can be drawn from T. Schelling's works on focal points [15]. He showed how beliefs, informal institutions, and proneness to predict may help humans to coordinate their actions toward a solution with insufficient information and without explicit communication. Just as with norms, specifically, the focal point acts as an equilibrium selector; it is the solution based on shared expectations. Following Schelling, consider the case of two individuals who have fixed a day to meet in New York City but have said nothing about either the time or location. The abstract representation of the game provides no way to distinguish different times and locations, and hence no hope that the two will actually meet. Schelling instead reported that in informal surveys, nearly every respondent indicated that they would attempt to meet at noon, and a majority chose Grand Central Station (perhaps an informal conventional meeting point at that time) as a location.

Focal points and forecasting also operate at a macro level in the sense that the game may involve much more participants. A point in case is the decimal number system, whereby the natural predisposition of humans to forecast may have led many of them to expect that the number ten was a focal point. The reasoning might have run like this. Humans have ten fingers, and virtually all of us started counting by using our fingers. Everyone tends to expect that all others implement the same learning process. Accordingly, individual expectations and behaviors converged and very many human networks ended up using the decimal numeral system. Expressing it in the terms of our trip, focal points are forecasting tools permitting us to attain cooperation when humans can just rely on symbolic thinking.

If the complexity and uncertainty of social environments occasionally lead to multiple equilibria, they also push humans to exert strategically their innate instinct to forecast. When humans cannot predict and do not know what to do, they look to others, and it may be strategic to give them clues on how to behave. Due to social complexity, sometimes logic suggests being predictable; sometimes it suggests doing the contrary. Unpredictability can put another party off-balance. It can confuse others, cloud their thinking, cause them to waste time and effort, and trick them into making a mistake. Consider the penalty kick in professional soccer games. The shooter must decide where to shoot the ball and the goalkeeper where to dive. Since videos on the past behavior of professional players are easily available, both players should behave in order to be as less predictable as they can.

In other—possibly more numerous—contexts, being predictable can expand the trust others have in us and may assist us in social interactions. Recall that social capital is important when dealing with the *Four*. Economists have been arguing that particular economic agents, such as a central bank, should behave predictably. The rationale goes as follows. Central banks are institutions created to keep inflation low and financial markets ordered; thus, people's expectations on inflation and their trust in central banks are key. If the central bank makes it clear that, for example, it will raise policy interest rates[6] when inflation is above its published target and then systematically acts as announced, then it gains reputation among agents. The confidence of the general public in the low and stable inflation rates announced by the central bank strengthens over time. In turn, it means that the inflation expectations of agents used as a basis for wage and price determination tend to converge to the target of inflation set by the central bank. Our guides say that this kind of behavior by the central bank provides the economy with a solid nominal anchor. This anchoring is important not only for controlling the wage-price spiral but also for easing the burden when the system is hit by a shock. In a situation whereby the economy is exposed to an inflationary shock, the time/costs of bringing inflation back to pre-shock levels is/are shorter/lower if agents' expectations are anchored to those of the central bank.

Transparency, reputation, credibility, and accountability are thus considered crucial ingredients for effective central banking. The modern central bank provides households, firms, and markets with all relevant information on its strategy, assessments, and policy decisions as well as its procedures in an open, clear, and timely manner. The European Central Bank began using forward guidance in July 2013, which means that it is providing information about its future monetary policy intentions based on its assessment of the outlook for price stability. Likewise, in the USA, the Federal Open Market Committee (FOMC) publishes a statement immediately following each of its eight annual FOMC meetings that describes the Committee's views regarding the economic outlook and provides a rationale for its policy decision. This notwithstanding, central banks always keep some margin of unpredictability. FED chief J. Powell acknowledged this at the Jackson Hole

[6] In the USA, for example, the Federal Reserve manages the fed funds rate. The latter is the interest rate banks pay for overnight borrowing in the federal funds market and influences other interest rates, such as credit cards, mortgages, and bank loans. A higher fed funds rate, hence, tends to reduce consumptions and investments and, eventually, inflation.

conference in August 2020: "We are not tying ourselves to a particular mathematical formula that defines the average." Even these special economic agents must wisely mix cooperative behavior and opportunistic behavior in their social interactions. The reference to expected inflation leads us to visit the second forecasting activity that this tour wants to touch upon.

3.3 Forecasting Economic Objects

While forecasting others is an ancestral affair for a social animal such as the human being, the prediction of economic objects such as prices, interest rates, labor markets developments, and the like has been becoming increasingly fundamental in modern economic systems. There is no need to be a professional forecaster to be involved in forecasting economic objects these days. For every individual or group of humans forecasting economic objects is a high-stakes game to play virtually every single day. In order to save their purchasing power and to perform adequate intertemporal decisions, modern Sapiens must predict the consumer price index, interest rates, real and financial assets price dynamics, etc. Human aggregations such as modern firms must develop and manage human resources plans, production policies, selling strategies, and so on. Today, policymakers must imagine scenarios and predict the costs and benefits of their moves from several viewpoints. Just as with the other human activities which we are traveling across, all this forecasting activity has large gains, and close relations with both behaviors and economic systems.

Economists have been arguing that expectations on economic objects drive behavior. If someone figures out that she has no chance of finding a job (economists talk about *discouraged workers*), then she will not adequately prepare herself for the job market and/or will put insufficient attention to her job search. The big issue of this forecast-induced behavior is that it may magnify the likelihood that grim expectations will materialize. Alongside discouraged workers, poor people may as well get trapped in a permanent state of poverty because their own gloomy expectations to improve steer them to be insufficiently proactive.[7] In the usual mixture of emotions and rationality, dark individual expectations may be based on both bleak objective macroeconomic stances and psychological attitudes. Whatever the source, acting side by side with attribution effects these self-isolating behavioral attitudes may reinforce socioeconomic differentiations within economic systems.

Luckily, most humans typically display a more reactive behavior. Our guides have argued that this greater activism in forecasting activities may be spurred by monetary incentives, as when humans face a rising cost of poor predictions. If employees/lenders earn fixed wages/interests, for example, underestimating price developments in high-inflation environments would lead them to lose significant purchasing power. In inflationary environments, therefore, humans typically institute some price indexation mechanism. As perhaps the traveler imagines at this stage

[7] Cf., for instance, Banerjee A V and Duflo E (2011) Poor Economics: A Radical Rethinking of the Way to Fight Global Poverty, Public Affairs.

of the tour, the most proactive humans are the Walrasians. As I mentioned, they are supposed to be optimizing fully informed people. But obviously this does not mean that they know the future. By and large, their forecasting skills can be expressed, borrowing from A. Lincoln: "You can fool all the people some of the time and some of the people all the time, but you cannot fool all the people all the time."[8] More precisely, Walrasians promptly and efficiently exploit all available information, especially about future dynamics, in such a way that their forecast errors are entirely random. In other words, Walrasians' forecasting errors are unpredictable; thus, their errors have neither systematic bias nor memory (i.e., no significant correlations with past errors). This is the sense of rational[9] expectations (RE) which, in line with the Lincoln's quote, implies that Walrasians cannot be surprised systematically as time passes. We shall return on RE later on to recall here that inside modern economic systems, human life is complex. Due to the cost of gathering and elaborating on information, in fact, our guides have allowed the possibility that Walrasians can rationally choose to be inattentive to news, updating sporadically information and expectations [16].

All in all, forecasting, behavior, and economic systems are all closely related, and in this stopover, I will concentrate on some of the feedback between expectations and systems at the aggregate level. We will also explore how the forecasting activism of humans makes money a veil in the system and how it impinges on the macroeconomic equilibrium. To this end, I select the guides mainly from macroeconomics, which, by definition, is more focused on the whole system than on individuals.

According to J.M. Keynes [6], the founding father of macroeconomics, expectations and uncertainty (which implies that risks are unmeasurable) play a key role in capitalistic systems. He argued that once expectations and uncertainty (real or simply perceived by agents) are taken into account, one can clarify a number of puzzling departures of real systems from the ideal systems studied by economists such as Walras. Writing during the worldwide Great Depression of the 1930s, Keynes advocated that uncertainty explains why a state of depressed expectations can persist and can lead to a protracted recession or even to a depression. He approached the economic system very differently from the neoclassical view prevalent at his time. On the one hand, he was mainly interested in the behavior of the system as a whole rather than on the micro behavior of the individuals living therein. On the other hand, Keynes focused on short-term[10] issues whereas Walras dealt with the equilibrium of the system and, hence, on its long-term conditions.

[8]As recalled in the Prologue most standard economic, even microeconomic, models are interested in the aggregate behavior of many individuals, not in the behavior of a single individual. In these models, the Walrasian is the representative agent.

[9]A better term would be model-consistent expectations. In the main text, I talk about RE equilibrium as the consistency condition that each agent's choice is a best response to the choices by others. Sometimes it seems that economists do not bother to confuse laypeople using misleading terms. In turn, laypeople seem occasionally to criticize economics without bothering to learn sufficiently what economists really intend. Definitions matter.

[10]Keynes finely distinguishes between long-run, long-term, and long-period. Due to my bird's-eye perspective, I brutally use them interchangeably.

Keynes' attention on the short term was due to the ambiguity of capitalistic systems, which, according to him, shapes the expectations of individuals (henceforth, I refer to these humans as "Keynesians"). Because of uncertainty, Keynesians form expectations, attaching great weight to facts about which they feel somewhat confident. Crucially, the argument goes, these facts must refer to the near future because Keynesians just cannot be confident on faraway scenarios. Specifically, Keynes put forward the idea that in forming expectations, Keynesians tune to the cited weight in such a way that confidence is more crucial than relevance. Regardless of how relevant they are to the decision that will be made, elements about which Keynesians' knowledge is vague are given less weight than facts about which humans are more confident. Remarking on the importance of confidence in the expectation formation mechanism, Keynes went on to say that the state of confidence of Keynesians is constantly in flux. When it is high, the system thrives; when it is depressed, the economy contracts. Because of these naturally alternating states of optimistic and pessimistic expectations, the economic system as a whole inexorably suffers from reiterated fluctuations, which explains his focus on business cycles.[11]

Despite his interest for the short term, Keynes also had a view about the long run. Still in contrast with the prevailing view at his time, Keynes believed that many equilibria were possible and that the Walrasian full employment equilibrium was only a limiting case (which explains the term *general* in the title of his masterpiece). Again, forecasting is the main character of the scene. Keynes distinguished investors, who operate in financial markets with a short-run view, from entrepreneurs, who must necessarily form long-term expectations in light of their industrial perspective. Because of the impossibility of achieving reliable estimates of risk in an uncertain system, these long-term expectations are for Keynes essentially based on exogenous *animal spirits*, i.e., on the emotional side of the human brain. As he put it in his 1936 General Theory, animal spirits are "a spontaneous urge to action rather than inaction, and not as the outcome of a weighted average of quantitative benefits multiplied by quantitative probabilities." Against this backdrop, in this layover, it is instructive to compare the situation faced by two types of humans, namely Walrasians and Keynesians.

Walrasians are supposed to operate in a simple but complete economic system populated by well-selected, hence efficient, speculators who continuously seek information, act on it and in the process incorporate the information into the price. Walrasians, thus have at their disposal all the necessary futures and contingent markets—today they can afford to know (probabilistically) all the price implications of, respectively, any future event and every state of the nature. Two considerations lead to believe that in Walrasian systems there is a tendency for the predicted prices to be correct. First, a sort of Darwinian selection eliminates less skilled forecasters

[11] From the normative standpoint Keynes' followers suggested to fine-tune the economy to reduce or eliminate the business cycle. Even in the best case of benevolent policymakers, however, this raises a question: if the system is as uncertain as Keynes feared, how then can the government obtain the necessary information in due time?

from the market. In financial markets, for example, rational arbitrageurs profitably trade to eliminate the effects of belief distortions of irrational "noise traders" on security prices.[12] Second, the correctness of predicted prices is sustained by the number of speculators. The rationale goes like this. Few predictions may well be wrong, but the more the speculators, the higher the probability that the average forecasts converge on the prices that actually will prevail in future. F. Galton referred to it as *vox populi* and J. Surowiecki as *wisdom of crowds* [17, 18]. In 1906, F. Galton was visiting a country fair whereby about 800 people were trying to guess the weight of an ox. In a celebrated experiment, he discovered that, despite none of the participants getting the right answer and several individuals' errors being large, the average guess was extremely close to the actual weight of the ox.[13] For Walrasians, therefore, the future is probabilistically priced in; uncertainty is "contractually covered." As a matter of fact, for Walrasians ambiguity is not an issue as they are supposed to live in a risky environment (this should be suggestive of the benefits for the system stemming from the speculators' job).

Keynesians, instead, are supposed to operate in a world which is more uncertain than risky. This has significant consequences for firms' investment because entrepreneurs' long-term expectations behind those investments turn out to be based on animal spirits rather than objectively addressed fundamentals. Again using Keynes' words (p. 162–163) [6], "Human decisions affecting the future, whether personal or political or economic, cannot depend on strict mathematical expectation, since the basis for making such calculations does not exist; and that it is our innate urge to activity which makes the wheels go round, our rational selves choosing between the alternatives as best we are able, calculating where we can, but often falling back for our motive on whim or sentiment or chance."

Inserting this view in a game theory setting, investment decisions may then be seen as a game that may converge toward good or bad equilibria, i.e., toward solutions with more or less investment spending. Just as norms push toward one of the multiple possible equilibria, the emotional-driven long-term expectations of Keynesians-businessmen determine the solution of their game. If the solution turns out to be the bad equilibrium, such as in the Great Depression, the government must intervene because the price mechanism cannot push the system away from it. The bad equilibrium is in fact due to the insufficient demand caused by low investment and employment that, in turn, depends on grim expectations. Reducing prices (*latu senso*: interest rates, wages, etc.) would not stimulate supply but just shrink the aggregate demand even more.

---

[12] However, economists have found robust evidence that, due to capital constraints that limit arbitrage and risk aversion of arbitrageurs, typically there remain inefficiencies in market prices. See also Sect. 3.3.

[13] The *vox populi* effect is also captured by the television game show known with the name of "Who Wants to Be a Millionaire." In this game, the contestants face several questions and can "Ask the Audience" for help. Though some of the audience members may be wrong, the answer given by the audience as a whole typically turns out to be correct.

To be sure, Keynes did not conceptualize an erratic economic system totally at the mercy of expectations deriving from capricious animal spirits. In the above reported citation, he says, "calculating where we can." He thought that long-term expectations could also be steady and even when they suffer changes, there were other factors that could exert compensating effects. Moreover, Keynes offered exceptions to the uncertainty "dictatorship." For instance, he conceded that the ambiguity of investing in buildings could be shared between investor and occupier, or even completely transferred from investor to occupier, by means of long-term contracts.

It is now time to turn our attention to how humans' forecasting activity on economic objects makes the money a veil or, equivalently, a neutral presence in the system which means that it changes nominal values but does not affect quantities. To this end, a bit of history of macroeconomics turns out to be functional to see the connections of forecasting, economic systems, and the institution "money." The story, where forecasting is key, may be told with the help of the Phillips curve. In 1958, W. Phillips uncovered an empirical regularity in macroeconomic data that since then has been referred to as the Phillips curve (PC) [19]. The PC shows an inverse relation between the unemployment rate and the rate of wage inflation.

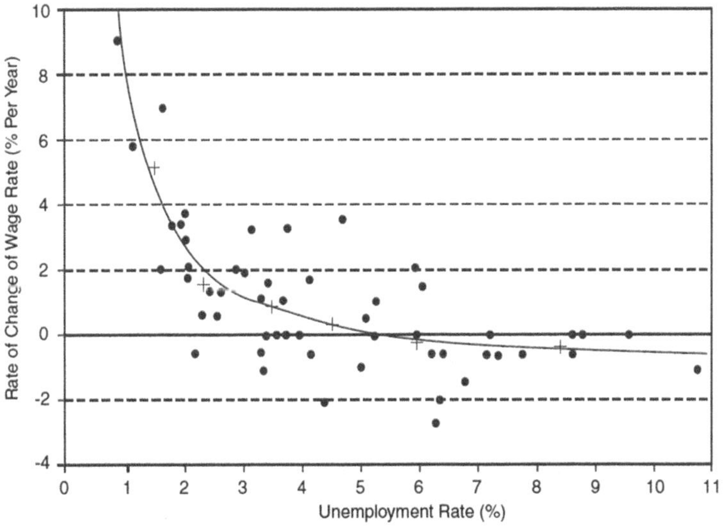

Inflation-Unemployment Relationship in the UK, 1861–1913. Source: Phillips (1958)

Despite stating a mere correlation between prices (*latu senso*) and quantities in labor markets, the PC turned out to be a key discovery in economics. The PC was in line with the Keynesian idea that the long-run level of unemployment could be successfully addressed by policymakers and offered a number of stable pairs of unemployment rate and inflation rate from which policymakers could select the preferred one. According to the PC, governments facing high unemployment could "buy" more employment, paying for it with little inflation—virtually *à la carte*.

But the economic system is a complex, uncertain entity hit by shocks of disparate nature. If the Great Depression of the 1930s led Keynes to concentrate upon the demand side of the economic system, 40 years later a supply-side (oil) shock led other economists to challenge Keynes's arguments. In all that expectations are paramount and, crucially, this was something that the PC did not take into account. In a few years, in fact, an inflationary shock coupled with the frenetic forecasting activity of humans challenged both empirically and theoretically the relation detected by Phillips.

On the empirical side, the problem was that in many countries the 1973 oil shock produced higher prices while it kept quantities (output and employment) virtually untouched—a phenomenon that economists since then refer to as stagflation.[14] The nice menu embodied in the PC was thus suddenly subtracted from the policymakers' options.

From a theoretical standpoint, in the late 1960s (hence before the first oil shock) M. Friedman and E. Phelps correctly claimed that the proneness of humans to forecast implies that the PC has no trade-off in the long run. Specifically, they argued that the long-run PC is vertical at the level of what they labeled the *natural* rate of unemployment.[15] This natural rate is determined by real factors such as the structure and the rate of growth of the economy but—and this is the point—it is something which is independent of the rate of inflation. The rationale may be sketched as follows. Employers and workers typically behave according to real (relative) prices/wages, not to nominal (absolute) prices. That is, humans are only interested in the purchasing power of money, what money can buy. In economists' parlance, humans do not suffer from monetary illusion. This said, suppose that unemployment is at the natural rate. The real wage is constant: workers who expect a given rate of price inflation insist that their wages increase at the same rate to maintain their purchasing power. Conjecture then that policymakers, without any advice, implement an expansive monetary and/or fiscal policy in an attempt to lower unemployment below its natural rate. This positive policy shock raises demand, leading firms to raise their prices faster than workers had anticipated. With higher revenues, firms are willing to employ more workers at the old wage rates and even to raise those rates somewhat. At the beginning, seeing that their nominal wages have risen, workers wrongly think that what is augmenting are real wages and, as said, they behave according to this. Thus, they supply more labor and the unemployment rate falls. Surprised workers do not realize right away that their purchasing power has fallen because prices have risen more rapidly than they expected.

As Lincoln argued, yet humans cannot be fooled for long, and their illusion disappears sooner rather than later. As workers come to anticipate higher rates of

[14] Stagflation is the contraction of the words stagnant (flat GDP growth) and inflation.

[15] Recall that in economics the term natural is used as a synonym of long-run equilibrium (cf. Chap. 2).

price inflation, they revise their behaviors, insisting on increases in wages that keep up with inflation. Eventually, real wages and unemployment return at their pre-shock natural levels. However, the price inflation and wage inflation brought on by expansionary policies continue at the new, higher rates. That is, once workers' expectations of price inflation have had time to adjust, the natural rate of unemployment is compatible with any rate of inflation—in the long run, the PC curve is vertical. The importance of forecasting is also reflected in the refinement of the name of PC—now it is known as price-expectation augmented PC (PEAPC).

As telegraphic as it is, this account of the PC-PEAPC is nonetheless useful in our trip to reach the intersection of forecasts, behaviors, and market system. Humans are forward-looking animals; hence, they behave in anticipation of scenarios they expect will occur. Their forecasts, in turn, affect the economic system—only when expectations are confirmed the system lies in its steady (natural, long-run) state. This two-way feedback is suggestive of how expectations are strictly related to the notion of equilibrium in market systems, which I further discuss below.

In 1958, P. Samuelson, a prominent neoclassical economist, analyzed the following environment [20]. He devised a simple (Walrasian-like) social interaction between two groups of Walrasians—young and old—with one private good that, crucially, is perishable. In this system only the young can work and produce the good, but, not astonishingly, all Walrasians are eager to consume it. Since the good cannot be stored, the Walrasians must then devise some mechanism to transfer part of the production in every period to those who are old. Samuelson, of course, hypothesized that humans were eventually able to find a solution to their interaction. He supposed that the Walrasians, officially through the state or informally through custom or the like, made a grand consensus on the use of *greenbacks* (i.e., money) to permit the cited intertemporal transfer. Unlike the good, greenbacks can be stored. Though the greenbacks cannot be consumed, each generation of young Walrasians want to exchange part of what they produce for greenbacks because they expect that future generations will do the same. In this economic system, thus, the institution "money" is based on a very human intergenerational social contract.[16]

Clearly, what is important to highlight in the current stopover is the forecasting activity rather than the trading one. In the present framework, specifically, the problem for the young is that they need to forecast the value of money when they are old. But this value depends upon the decisions of the next generation and therefore upon the forecasts that will be made by the next generation. The Walrasians therefore live in a system that, despite being very simple,[17] requires forecasting the forecasts on economic objects of others. In this two-cohorts economic network, the equilibrium requires an evolved use of humans' forecasting instinct. Specifically, and crucially, it needs the expectations of future prices to be the same as the prices

[16] In Chap. 2, money emerged as a tool to improve "contextual" barter trade.

[17] Recall that all models must be a simplified version of real world. What is important is that they, once the working hypotheses are cleared, achieve useful results in a scientific way. The general validity of these results is necessarily limited—no model fits all in economics.

that actually prevail, i.e., it requires that expectations be correct. In other words, an equilibrium is a price in each period and a choice by young people in each period of how much to sell to the market, given the price when they are young and the price when they are old, such that the amount of money brought into the market by old people is the same as the amount of money young people want to carry into the future. We have already met this requirement and we have referred to it as market clearing. But in this stop time—hence the forecasting activity—it is crucial for equilibrium.

Recall that Walras theorized equilibrium as a rest point of the system established in terms of quantities and prices. Modern neoclassical macroeconomists, instead, view equilibrium as consistent situations where people's expectations, choices, and behaviors validate and reinforce each other. As noticed, they have elaborated the notion of rational expectations [21]. Intuitively, these RE take into account the fact that in many economic situations, the outcome depends partly on what people expect to happen. The price of an agricultural commodity, for example, depends on how many acres farmers plant, which in turn depends on the price farmers expect to realize when they harvest and sell their crops. Outcomes, in turn, impinge on expectations because RE-Walrasians cannot commit systematic forecasting errors and adjust their rational expectations accordingly. The two-way feedback of expectations and outcomes, therefore, suggests that the former must be formed rationally such as to be consistent with actual economic environments.

Further insights on the connections of humans' forecasts and capitalism pop up contrasting Keynes and RE macroeconomics. Stressing the role of uncertainty and animal spirits, Keynes argued that Keynesians' expectations are an exogenous, destabilizing, subjective element of the market economy. RE macroeconomists, instead, maintain the ultimate stability of market processes whereby rational expectations cannot affect the system in the long run because RE-Walrasians conform their prediction to the stable path of the system.

Whatever the case, the message from this stopover is that the predictive activities of humans are crucial ingredients of economic systems. The gain from correctly forecasting objects emerges in maintaining stability in the system. Expectations should not (if Keynesians) or cannot (if Walrasians) diverge too much and/or for too long from fundamentals. This holds both at the individual level—e.g., the price of a stock must reflect the fundamental value of the firm—and at the aggregate level—e.g., intertemporal decisions must be such that aggregate demand is not systematically larger than the system-wide fundamental, or natural, capacity of production. Otherwise, the system dangerously overdrives. When prices in financial markets are significantly decoupled from fundamental values, for instance, economists suggestively warn about the presence of *bubbles* (cf. Chap. 6). In the next section, we will visit other ways in which, according to our guides, humans may tackle their forecasting exercises. Before doing that, however, let me briefly detour into the relationship between professional economists and forecasts on economic objects. After all, economists belong to the human race; thus, what follows affords the opportunity to examine other angles of humans' forecasting activity.

Unlike what many laypeople think of economics, and in spite of the fact that a nontrivial number of economists are often involved in predicting economic objects, forecasting is not the main scope of the economic science. I hope this book, despite being far from exhaustive, is sufficiently convincing regarding that. It is possible that the large mass media coverage of forecasts about inflation, GDP, public finance, labor and stock markets, etc. has been diffusing this biased view. In late 2008, for example, the news quickly became viral that during a briefing by academics at the London School of Economics on the turmoil in the international markets, Britain's Queen Elizabeth asked: "Why did no one see it coming?" For many laymen, and even for scientists of other fields, this was recorded as just another failure of economists and their supposed science.[18] In defense of the economists' forecasting efforts, I observe the following.

First, sensationalism leads to magnifying bad news, such as economists' failures in the current case, which clearly spreads a biased view about economists. But economics do have predictive ability. The problem might be that this skill is taken for granted; thus, it lacks the sensationalism needed to be in the spotlight (in passing, note that this paradoxically implies that the norm is to think of economists as good forecasters). Economics correctly predicts that when supply is lower than demand, then prices tend to rise. The current interruption of international supply chain is a point in case. They also forecast that an increase in prices stimulates lower demand and higher supply. If structural, then, economists argue that higher prices lead to rise in the investments in the research and development of alternative goods as, for example, happened in the aftermath of large and sustained oil shocks, which led to new energy saving products. As mentioned in Sect. 2.2, then, economists satisfactorily predict that the higher (real or perceived) the risk surrounding the asset of a firm or country, the lower the asset price. Of course, these are all conditional (ceteris paribus) predictions. To take a more specific example of the forecasting skill of economists, as early as 1974, W. Nordhaus predicted that the amount of carbon in the atmosphere will have reached 487 ppm by 2030, surprisingly in line with current estimates (420 ppm) and dynamics (about 2.5 ppm/year).[19]

Second, focusing mainly on forecasting hinders the fact that economics is able to offer reliable explanations on several issues as well as suggest valid solutions to fix them. Moreover, the fact that economists cannot predict crashes does not mean that they do not understand them. Considering again the 2008 financial crisis, what is really important is that economists provide a coherent analysis of the reasons for a possible impending crisis. Regarding normative hints, it is worth noting that the vast majority of policymakers around the world have responded to the COVID-19 pandemic by implementing expansive macroeconomic policies that surely have attenuated the socioeconomic effects of the negative shock (at least in the short-

[18] In fact, the crisis surprised many but not all economists. In the Epilogue, for instance, we will have a look at H. Minsky's job that, as early as the 1970s, offered an explanation of the perverse dynamics likely behind the 2008 financial crisis.

[19] https://en.wikipedia.org/wiki/Carbon_dioxide_in_Earth%27s_atmosphere

term, because the current generosity of policymakers will likely affect future scenarios). This is so because most economists recommend proceeding in this way.

Third, critics should take into account that predictions heavily depend on the quality and quantity of datasets used for elaborating them. Nonprofessional economists often do not figure that typically, economists have at their disposal less reliable and more lagged data than other scientists can afford. To have an idea of the difficulties of producing reliable data in economics, just note that the most watched, cited, and forecasted macroeconomic variable, the real GDP, is itself an estimate attempting to synthetize in one digit the quantity of the millions of goods and services produced in a system. Since its construction is subjected to never-ending revisions, then, economists must even choose whether to forecast the time series of "provisional" or "semi-definitive" or "definitive" values.

Fourth, what about the forecasting record of the other sciences? Referring to the current COVID-19 pandemic, for example, why did no one (including the Queen Elizabeth) ask, "Why did no one see it coming?" to physicians? And what about geologists and earthquakes?

Finally, unlike weather forecasters or other scientists, economists cannot afford the "luxury of exogeneity"—they are inside the system; they are part of a complex game in which they are active players, not just exogenous spectators. In 1929, I. Fisher, one of the most known economists at that time, was attacked for his prediction that the stock market had reached a permanently high plateau. Given his stature, yet, if in the 1920s he had instead warned of a crash before the crash actually happened, the collapse probably would have happened earlier, and he would be blamed for having started it, for having been the bird of ill omen.

This is neither to say that economists should not attempt to predict nor that they are free from faults when they perform forecasting exercises. I agree with the view that economists should be more explicit and forceful in stressing that economic forecasts must be taken as prudently as they deserve. Moreover, the further one predicts, the less one can be confident. It is not a weakness to provide interval forecasts or to use fan charts. In defense of economists engaged in forecasting, admittedly, the fact is that policymakers typically—and reasonably enough—want very precise indications. US President L. B. Johnson once said to an economist, "Ranges are for cattle. Give me a number" [22].

To sum up, two basic considerations emerge. First, we need more economics, not less. Second, if humans' life is hard, economists' life is even harder.

3.4 Psychological Forecasting

Forecasting involves the future; hence, certainty is excluded from the forecaster's dictionary. If economic systems were "just" risky and humans were fully-fledged Walrasians, then they would know the probability distribution of all the possible configurations of the system generating the alternative states of nature.[20] But real-world humans often have only limited time, information, and computational capacities with which to make inferences about what is happening, let alone make predictions about what will happen. Not to mention that in economic systems, several situations are uncertain, which makes risks unmeasurable. Even professional forecasters' expectations embody some subjectivity. They typically base their predictions on objective procedures (such as time series analyses) and then adjust the outcomes using subjective judgments to allow for the influence of factors or information not included in the objective algorithm. It seems to be a winning strategy. Economists have shown that central banks that include judgments when constructing optimal policy projections of the target variables and the instrument rate perform substantially better [23].

The predictive attempts of ordinary humans are much more delicate. Regardless of whether they are forecasting economic subjects or objects, this business is a very hard task for them. Experience may help, but it teaches bad habits along with good ones. The complexity of modern economic systems may then lead them astray. On one hand, it may make conditions so volatile that one must search for the signal amid a lot of noise. On the other hand, it may make situations so heterogeneous that each time is virtually the first time—past errors bring no information in systems with so little memory. In addition, previous predictions may not give the right hint—a good forecast does not necessarily end up with a good result, just as a bad prediction does not necessarily lead to a bad result. For example, a bad shooter unaware of how to use a gun with a bend scope may hit the target, although for the wrong reason. Even more information may be harmful. Our guides claim that "a wealth of information creates a poverty of attention" [24] and offer evidence that forecasts of stock earnings decrease in accuracy as new information is added [25].

All that may lead ordinary humans to forecast differently from Walrasians. A number of insights can be drawn by Hume's discussion of probability, which finishes with a section on common cognitive biases [26]. Among other considerations, he argued that the more recent the observations we draw on, the stronger our belief in the conclusion.

D. Kahneman and A. Tversky (KT), the guides I have chosen for the excursion on these themes, somewhat follow Hume's arguments. Their prescriptive standpoint offers several hints on how humans actually measure risk, address probability, and deal with forecasting. Among other things, KT lifelong research helps to understand whether humans actually behave as Walrasians. The short answer that can be drawn by the results of their laboratory experiments is that humans often behave differently from Walrasians [11, 27, 28]. Let us then refer to this kind of humans as the "Kahnemanians." This sort of human typically searches for information by direct observation, recollection of memory, first-hand experience, or rumors. In predicting,

[20] As a matter of fact, neoclassical economists observe that what is necessary is only that Walrasians behave "as if" these calculations were performed. Their argument may be sketched as follows. The calculations necessary when driving a car and determining whether it is safe to pass someone ahead are incredibly complex. Yet there is no need to be a genius to drive a car.

Kahnemanians act like intuitive scientists who base their decisions on simplified, abstract models. Facing risky, if not uncertain, environments and little time to ponder, Kahnemanians tend not to optimize but, rather, to use bounded rationality, to search clues around them, to implement heuristics (i.e., quick and dirt inference mechanisms that guide their predictions). Heuristics do not involve much computation and do not lead to compute probabilities, as an emotionally detached statistician would make. In this sense, heuristics are devices not dissimilar from informal institutions—when humans face problems in implementing the *Four*, they typically proceed excogitating some instrument to solve their issues. All in all, the KT's job offers several clues on how humans execute their forecasting activity and points out that the laws of logic and probability play a small role, one which is surely smaller than that assumed to be behind the Walrasians' way of reasoning. A brief description of some of these psychological biases should clear the matter and add details on the human endeavor currently under scrutiny.

Kahnemanians suffer from the *availability bias*. It is the tendency to judge an event by the ease with which examples of the event can be retrieved from memory or constructed anew. Thus, our forecasts may depend on what we remember which, in turn, is potentially influenced by the frequency of exposure to an issue due to social or mass media influences. For the sake of example, a few days of cold weather may induce one to believe that the predictions about the effects of global warming are not so accurate. Mr. Trump once tweeted, "It is freezing in New York—where the hell is global warming?" In so doing, he may have disparate goals as well be aware of climate change issues, but his message suggests that (at least part of) the general public is thought of as believing in the *law of small numbers*. Still, although the road you use to drive across might be no more dangerous than it has ever been, seeing an accident causes you to overreact. The probability you assign to the prediction of having an accident increases, and you become an extra cautious driver for the next week or so. Likewise, the participants in the stock market often predictably overreact to new information, creating a larger-than-appropriate effect on stocks' prices (W. Buffet *docet*).

Kahnemanians display *illusion of control*. As mentioned, humans forecast for a sense of control. Most of us, however, do that under the illusion of being able to control random events. This illusion of control leads Kahnemanians to predict that the risk of dying in a car accident is lower than that of dying in a plane accident. Evidence shows that this tends to hold even if one is informed that the objective probability of dying in a plane accident is significantly lower. The "logic" is that when you are the driver, you can think you can control the events. When gambling, likewise, one can see people trying to control the outcome of a slot machine or that of a die by the way they press the handle or they roll the dice. If the devices are fair this behavior cannot have an impact on the results; it is just an illusion. Nonetheless, a nontrivial number of humans insist and persist in forming biased predictions.

The *confirmation bias* involves seeking and/or concentrating on information that sustains preexisting beliefs. It impacts on how we gather, interpret, and recall information. For example, Kahnemanians who support or oppose a particular issue will not only seek information to support it, they will also interpret news stories in a way that upholds their existing ideas. Unlike what can happen in the Walrasian world, this kind of bias naturally magnifies the persistence of forecasting errors.

The *hindsight bias* refers to the tendency of Kahnemanians to view events as more predictable than they really are. Even in the case whereby one is able to form a probability statement about the outcome of a risky event, ex ante none cannot know for sure what is going to happen. After an event, Kahnemanians are instead often sure that they knew the outcome of the event before it actually happened. There is strong evidence and instances are easily found about that, but I imagine that the traveler is well aware of the fact that when something has gone differently from what one predicted, humans tend to say, "I was sure" or "I knew it all along." Again, it may affect the persistence of forecasting errors.

Kahnemanians suffer from *overconfidence*, i.e., they have more confidence than they should objectively have. Specifically, Kahnemanians tend to exaggerate the precision of their predictions as well as the degree of certainty that their prediction is correct. The first type is a sort of attempt to reduce the real risk as in the case of an investor assuming that yearly gains or losses are bounded in a range of, say, $\pm$ 10% even though history and experience shows a much wider range. The second type of overconfidence bias is certainty overconfidence, a typical example of which is shown by students (and well known by teachers). Students might be 90% certain each answer is right, while test scores average a good deal below 90%.

Kahnemanians employ *anchoring-and-adjustment*. When they face ambiguous situations, they are influenced by whatever available anchor is at hand. When forecasting the value of a variable from explicit information about previous values of that same variable, for example, Kahnemanians typically form expectations using the starting information, or anchor, and then adjust away from that anchor to take account of the major features of the series. At the end of the procedure, however, they tend to leave final estimates too close to the original anchor.

These heuristics are closely intertwined and may reinforce each other. For instance, evidence showing that 93% of American drivers rate themselves as better than the median may be the result of certainty overconfidence and illusion of control. Confirmation bias may then make this belief long-lasting. This applies even to forecasting economic objects. Economists [29] have found multi-year continental-wide evidence showing that when asked about the current economic situation and future outlooks, the average European relentlessly repeats the following mantra: "As usual, it has gotten worse than I expected. Especially for others. Nevertheless, I still think that it will get better. Especially for me." Note that this means that the average citizen judges, and expects, that his/her particular situation has got, and will get, systematically better than that of "himself/herself." In financial markets, illusion of control may explain the tendency to improperly neglect objective risks while the law of small number may lead to irrational exuberance (cf. Chap. 6). On the other hand, many heuristics are tied to the biology of memory, which accounts for mechanisms of selective recall. This implies an overreaction to news that leads to biased forecasts just as heuristics and the rule of thumb may lead to commit errors. This happens even in a systematic way and with slow, if any, tendency to correct. As noticed there is evidence that in financial markets, rational speculators persistently operate side by side with irrational "noise traders." These psychological distortions may also interact with stereotypes and beliefs for the worse [30]. Evidence from labs points out that gender stereotypes influence posterior beliefs, beyond what a Bayesian model would predict [31].

This said, these forecasting shortcuts have some advantage. For instance, overconfidence may be good if it sustains self-esteem, and there is some evidence that realism and depression go hand in hand [32]. Our guides then argue that heuristics may be effective in cases whereby it may be more important to predict quickly rather than focus on accuracy [33]. On the other hand, finally, a small optimistic bias is compatible with—and may be induced by—objective computations [34].

All considered, there are reasons to believe that psychological forecasting is worse than optimal forecasting but not always. In real life systems thus Walrasians, Keynesians and Kahnemians coexist, hence, objective and subjective forecasts coexist as well occasionally, significant differences between market prices and fundamentals materialize.

References

1. Kahneman D (2011) Thinking, Fast and Slow. Macmillan.
2. Simon H A (1957) Models of man: Social and rational. New York: Wiley.
3. Williamson O E (1985) The Economic Institutions of Capitalism. New York: The Free Press
4. Petty W (1662) A Treatise of Taxes & Contributions. History of Economic Thought Books, McMaster University Archive for the History of Economic Thought.
5. Tetlock P (2005) Expert Political Judgment: How Good is It? How Can We Know? Princeton University Press.
6. Keynes J M (1936) The General Theory of Employment, Interest and Money. New York: Harcourt Brace and Co.
7. Townsend R (1983) Forecasting the Forecasts of Others. Journal of Political Economy, 91(4): 546–588.
8. Bloom P et al (2011) Disgusting Smells Cause Decreased Liking of Gay Men. Emotion 12(1): 23-7.
9. Smith K B et al (2011) Disgust Sensitivity and the Neurophysiology of Left-Right Political Orientations. PLoS ONE 6(10).
10. Ross L (1977) The intuitive psychologist and his shortcomings: Distortions in the attribution process. In Berkowitz L (ed), Advances in experimental social psychology New York: Academic Press. pp. 173–220.
11. Kahneman D (2011) op. cit.
12. Fisman R and Miguel E (2007) Corruption, Norms, and Legal Enforcement: Evidence from Diplomatic Parking Tickets. Journal of Political Economy 115(6): 1020-1048.
13. Hume D (1739) A Treatise on Human Nature. Selby-Bigge L A (ed), Oxford: Clarendon Press (1896).
14. Bicchieri C. and Muldoon R (2010) Social Norms. The Stanford Encyclopedia of Philosophy.
15. Schelling T C (1960) The Strategy of Conflict. Harvard University Press.
16. Reis R (2006) Inattentive Producers. The Review of Economic Studies 73(3):793–821.
17. Galton F (1907) Vox Populi. Nature 75:450–451.
18. Surowiecki J (2005) The Wisdom of Crowds. Anchor Books.
19. Phillips A W (1958) The Relation between Unemployment and the Rate of Change of Money Wage Rates in the United Kingdom 1861–1957. Economica November: 283-299. The PC is also frequently depicted in the space "GDP growth; Inflation."

20. Samuelson P A (1958) An Exact Consumption-Loan Model of Interest with or without the Social Contrivance of Money. The Journal of Political Economy 66(6): 467-482.
21. Muth J A (1961) Rational Expectations and the Theory of Price Movements. Econometrica 29(6): 315–335.
22. Mansky C (2007) Identification for Prediction and Decision. Cambridge, MA: Harvard University Press.
23. Svensson L E O (2005) Monetary Policy with Judgment: Forecast Targeting. International Journal of Central Banking, 1(1).
24. Simon H (1971) Designing Organizations for an Information-Rich World. In Greenberger M (ed) Computers, Communications, and the Public Interest. Baltimore, MD: The Johns Hopkins Press.
25. Davis F D, Lohse G L, and Kottemann J E (1994) Harmful effects of seemingly helpful information on forecasts of stock earnings. *Journal of Economic Psychology (15):* 253-267.
26. Hume, D. (1739) op. cit.
27. Kahneman D, Slovic P, and Tversky A (1982) Judgment under uncertainty: Heuristics and biases. Cambridge, UK: Cambridge University Press.
28. Kahneman D (2003) Maps of bounded rationality: Psychology for behavioral economics. American Economic Review, 93(5):1449-1475.
29. Bovi M (2009) Economic versus psychological forecasting. Evidence from consumer confidence surveys. Journal of Economic Psychology 30 (4):563-574.
30. Bordalo P et al (2016) Stereotypes. Quarterly Journal of Economics 131(4): 1753–1794.
31. Coffman K B, Collis M, and Kulkarni L (2019) Stereotypes and Belief Updating. Harvard Business School Working Paper, N. 19-068.
32. Bovi M (2009) op. cit.
33. Gigerenzer, G. and S. Mousavi (2014) "Risk, uncertainty, and heuristics" Journal of Business Research 67(8):1671–1678
34. Brunnermeier, M.K, and J.A, Parker (2005) "Optimal Expectations" American Economic Review (95):1092-1118.

Aggregating: Humans Are Social Animals 4

4.1 Introduction

Physically, Homo Sapiens is not the most powerful species in the animal world. Living together is then a natural strategy to live longer and better. Since the socioeconomic Big Bang, humans have been well aware that unity is strength and that there are gains from aggregating. In this trek, we shall learn that living together leads to the accumulation of various kinds of capital. Sapiens stand united as other species do, but differently. Only human beings gather together in countless numbers with no other link than common abstract ideas such as state, people, firm, liberty, rights, and justice. Think of the famous French motto: "*Liberté, Égalité, Fraternité*" ("liberty," "equality," "fraternity"). Throughout history, our unique behavioral traits have helped us form special, increasingly inclusive aggregations—from families to clans, from villages to cities, from nations to the United Nations.

So far, I have only touched upon the concept of social capital, but as many travelers might fairly argue, it is a paramount element in our tour. This stopover in aggregating activities is the right place to expand on the notion a bit more. For the purposes of our tour, as said, it is a mixture of trust, trustworthiness, willingness to respect the rules of the game, and civic engagement that emerges as humans participate in groups, and its power derives precisely from its ability to promote cooperation among the participants and to reduce transaction costs. In a nutshell, social capital is an important private input to producing social output. When individuals learn to trust one another so that they are able to make credible commitments and rely on norms of reciprocity, they are able to achieve far more than when these forms of social capital are lacking. United we stand is good, and inclusive institutions are necessary. But trusting each other helps widen and reinforce social interactions and steers them toward a happy outcome. Since ancient times, indeed, among the most dangerous sins were considered those that deny the trust on which social relations among humans are based—fraud and treachery

M. Bovi, *Why and How Humans Trade, Predict, Aggregate, and Innovate*, Contributions to Economics, https://doi.org/10.1007/978-3-030-93885-7_4

(Dante's Inferno *docet*[1]). The modern sharing economy is premised on leaps of faith in perfect strangers: we rely on reviews on Amazon, climb into a stranger's car through carpooling or Uber, stay at someone else's house via Airbnb, and look for love on several dating apps. The *fiat* money that we use these days is a type of money that is not backed by any physical commodity such as gold or silver and derives its value solely from the trust of people. J. Stiglitz observed that it is trust, more than money, that makes the world go round. K. Arrow extolled trust as a lubricant of a social system, an "extremely efficient" mechanism for easing transactions and promoting prosperity. In sum, social capital is an essential ingredient in all human aggregations because it supports the other ingredients of the economic system in managing the innate behavioral multiplicity of humans. Unfortunately, social capital is not a commodity that can be bought easily. It is not a panacea, it is hard to increase via policies, and it suffers from various drawbacks and vagueness [1].

In light of our tour is worth observing that the need of this sort of capital is relative, i.e., it depends on the peculiar nature of the good about which coordination is needed. As we shall see, some goods are hardly excludable, and this makes them more subject to opportunism than private goods.[2] Accordingly, one would expect that successfully human groups dedicated to the provision of hardly excludable goods are more likely to produce greater social capital than those dedicated to the provision of private goods. Recall that humans are adaptive animals.

Social capital has tight links with economic systems and with formal institutions that go beyond the nature of the good. As said in the Prologue, an economic system rich in social capital does not need to rely on diffuse formal institutions and, in so doing, individuals learn how to manage their interactions by themselves. A system typically resorting to the state and formal institutions, instead, shrinks the possibility of individuals to form trust which, in turn, calls for even more formal institutions because this is what individuals expect. On the other hand, the state can foster social capital, easing the connections between public agencies, firms, and other social aggregations, and facilitating the alignment of the interests of the various economic agents. Evidently, this boosting materializes only if the state an honest and efficient mediator, otherwise the state reduces the social capital. Trusting citizens ease the efforts of policymakers, while an virtuous efficient state promotes trust in the population. As per social relations in capitalistic markets, they may stimulate the search for reputation and the enlargement of social capital because suppliers in competitive markets must take care of customers.

Social capital intersects with nature and culture in the birth and development of human clusters. Our guides have argued that when human groups are based on blood relationships, then the social capital operating in their clusters is higher with respect to when inner connections are social. In particular, economists have contrasted the

[1] Dante put the circle of fraud closer to the pit of hell than murder. Possibly for someone this is too extreme a view, but it wants to stress how large and widespread the social damage emerging from opportunistic fraudulent behaviors can be.

[2] In Chap. 5, we shall see that similar issues affect the outcomes of innovating.

Chinese clan with the European corporation that emerged in pre-modern times [2]. The European corporation (such as the independent city, communes, and business associations) is a voluntary association between unrelated individuals established to pursue common interests. The Chinese clan, instead, is a kin-based organization consisting of patrilineal households that trace their origin to a common male ancestor. Results show that in Chinese clans, kinship enhances stronger moral commitment and loyalty, reduces enforcement cost, and, hence, implies a comparative advantage in pursuing collective actions. This suggests that kinship impinges on the functioning of human clusters, yet our guides also observe that the reasons leading to form clans rather than corporations are eminently cultural and institutional. As we shall see in Sect. 4.3, in fact, sociopolitical historical developments may play a role in the formation of social capital.

In human aggregations, of course, the degree of individualism and collectivism is an important element. There are cases whereby nature is the first driver of these traits in human aggregations. In East Asia, for example, rice is the main source of food. Rice farming requires a massive amount of communal work—terracing mountains, building irrigation systems, and harvesting crops. In Western countries, however, wheat and meat are typical sources of food. Both wheat farming and herding are individual tasks—farmers and herders often spend days alone, causing individualism to be more widespread in the West. In 1987, M. Thatcher (UK's prime minister at the time) stated, "There is no such thing as society, only individuals and families." It is not a matter of East vs West. In some parts of northern China, it is easier to grow wheat than rice and evidence shows that rice-growing southern China is more interdependent and holistic-thinking than the wheat-growing north.[3]

If natural, cultural, and institutional factors may steer the average human who populates certain social aggregations toward (more or less) individualism and to produce (more or less) social capital, it, as observed in the Prologue, does not mean that humans lose their innate mixed behavioral nature. As for the interaction we are currently visiting, if individuals prefer to conform to the prevalent behavior, they may have more incentive to behave opportunistically if others are other-regarding. Manifestations of self-regarding behaviors at the cost of the collectivity, such as tax evasion, corruption, and free riding (obtaining a benefit at another's expense or without the usual cost or effort), are, although to varying degrees, a significant presence in all human clusters. When asked if they prefer to live in a corrupt society, for instance, most humans predictably say no. When asked how many people would pay a public official a small sum of money in exchange for higher priority in treatment, the same humans typically say they believe most people, including themselves, would do it.

Given the opportunity, Asian businessmen act not dissimilarly to the Smithian butcher. Think about Chinese immigrants in Western countries. A handful of studies show that the descendants of East Asian immigrants to America typically tend to

[3]Talhelm T et al (2014) Large-Scale Psychological Differences Within China Explained by Rice Versus Wheat Agriculture. Science 344: 603-608.

become as individualist as European Americans in one or two generations.[4] Humans adapt their innate multifaceted behavior, but the latter always tends to materialize. There is evidence that starting from the late 1980s, Chinese have become more individualistic or, better, less collectivist. The existing literature stresses this rise of individualism in mainland China, identifying industrialization, economic growth, urbanization, and population mobility as leading socioeconomic factors behind it. But it may also be that innate individualism is the driver of these socioeconomic developments. A public opinion poll conducted in countries from around the world (2005 World Public Opinion Survey) has found that the individual-based free market system is "the best system on which to base the future of the world" for 74% of Chinese. In the United States, the percentage is 71, while in France is only 36%. Mixed behavior is widespread. Data highlight that while Hong Kong Chinese recognize the imported individualistic culture's superiority in status attributes (e.g., competence, achievement), at the same time, they maintain positive evaluations of Chinese culture on solidarity attributes (traditional moral values).[5] Western Europe's transition to a modern economy and its successful post-WWII reconstruction, on the other hand, benefited from its social welfare systems rooted in generalized morality. Regarding behavior, thus, before being Asian, American, European or whatever aggregation one belongs, we are all complex human beings (Plato *docet*).

Living together may be nice and fruitful, but it is hardly easy.[6] The same symbolic language that drives humans to aggregate also creates dramatic conflicts. History is rich with stories of wars within and between families, clans, tribes, cities, and nations. Likewise, the multifaceted behavior of humans sustains the structural tendency of humans to integrate and disintegrate at the same time. Aristotle had a clear view about the tensions that arise when humans aggregate. He claimed that if unity is strength, it must nonetheless preserve diversity. In his words (Politics, Book II), "Is it not obvious that a state may at length attain such a degree of unity as to be no longer a state? Since the nature of a state is to be a plurality and intending to greater unity, from being a state, it becomes a family, and from being a family, an individual; for the family may be said to be more than the state, and the individual than the family. So that we ought not to attain this greatest unity even if we could, for it would be the destruction of the state. Again, a state is not made up only of so many men, but of different kinds of men; for similars do not constitute a state." These days, our guides have found indications that strong family ties are negatively correlated with the level of social capital enjoyed by an economy and that these tight entanglements imply more household production and less participation in the labor

[4]Mesoudi A et al (2016) "How Do People Become W.E.I.R.D.? Migration Reveals the Cultural Transmission Mechanisms Underlying Variation in Psychological Processes," PLoS ONE 11: e0147162.

[5]Ho-Ying Fu J and Chiu C Y (2007) Local culture's responses to globalization: Exemplary persons and their attendant values. Journal of Cross-Cultural Psychology 38(5): 636–653.

[6]Recall that in social interactions among humans the solution always shows some drawbacks.

market by women, young adults, and the elderly [3]. As a general matter, facts point out that when dealing with human aggregations, the stronger the intralinks, the weaker the interlinks.

In sum, there are complex junctures within and between human aggregations. Individuals, groups, and systems all affect, and are affected by, each other. All that makes the aggregating efforts of humans very interesting to examine. In this chapter, I will briefly explore some peculiar social aggregations that have arisen over time, sketching out the reasons why they are persistent elements in capitalistic systems, how the life inside them goes on, and what the behavioral and institutional aspects of the matter are. As the traveler will note, humans aggregate in different ways, for several reasons, and with disparate success but, in any case, when they aggregate they accumulate various kinds of capital.

4.2 The Family

The family is one of the oldest human aggregations. Historians claim that the family was the basic unit of society in ancient Mesopotamia. Looking at the scope and administration of the family, Aristotle posited that the family is the natural aggregation for the supply of men's everyday wants and that it must be organized hierarchically with the man acting as the ruler.[7]

In this stopover, I will mainly pay attention to the concepts of family and household as regarded in the Western world. Following the OECD glossary, I define households as the arrangements made by persons, individually or in groups, for providing themselves with food or other essentials for living. The family within the household is then made up by those members of the household who are related through blood, adoption, or marriage. In our tour, I will occasionally use the terms "family" and "household" interchangeably with the hope that the context helps the traveler recognize the concept I am talking about. Despite being affected by the usual definitory *caveat*, the mentioned definitions nonetheless highlight various important aspects of this human way of aggregating. In stating that the household deals with the arrangements aimed to provide humans with food or other essentials for living, the definition highlights that the family is an economic system unto itself. In stressing that the connections of family members are also institutional, the definition highlights that the family is a very human aggregation; institutional bonds are based on the very human symbolic language.

The founding father of family economics, G. Becker, offers a rationale for limiting this tour stop to families living in modern Western economic systems. In 1991, he wrote (p. 1) [4],: "the family in the Western world has been radically altered—some claim almost destroyed—by the events of the last three decades." In ancient times (although still today in some places), the marriage establishing the

[7] In fact, this is a case of social regress because the role of women in ancient Egypt was practically equivalent to that of men.

family was an informal arrangement signed by handshakes between men, with women merely playing the role of the object of the contract. This approach mirrored the role of the family as well as the aim of the marriage, which in those economic systems often belonged more to trading than aggregating instincts. The familiar link was, in fact, a way of raising physical capital, constructing political alliances, organizing the division of labor by age and gender, etc. Until the 1950s, even in developed Western countries, Aristotelian social norms said that men were supposed to finish school, get a job, marry, and have children. That was less important for women, for whom the crucial steps were marriage, childbearing, and childrearing. But, as Becker noted, in the last few decades, many Western countries experienced huge sociopolitical-cultural-technological winds of change that dramatically altered the framework whereby humans aggregate in family. Among them are the possibility of same-sex marriage, the ability to divorce, the decline in fertility rate and in the number of religious weddings, the rise of the proportion of children living in single-parent families, an increase in women's participation in labor force, and a rise in women's median age at first marriage.

These preliminary indications are evocative of the reasons why the family is a key social cluster for both individuals and the system. Trying to offer an answer to the question of why humans form families and to the issues they face in doing that, our guides have emphasized that what is behind the establishment of a family in modern economies is a sequence of complex decision-making problems.

The first step is the decision to live together. Of course, love is a strong incentive for that. However, although economists have considered the role of love [5][8] as a determining factor in a couple's decision to live together, they typically consider other elements that highlight the gains from this sort of aggregating effort. Among them, the family unit benefits from the presence of public goods such as children and home. The fact of being non-rivalrous and non-excludable makes clear why children and home can be considered public goods—both partners can equally enjoy the public goods "produced and owned" by the family.

As an economic unit, then, the family can take advantage of increasing returns to scale. In other words, the needs of a household grow with each additional member but not in a proportional way. Needs for housing space, heating, electricity, etc., will not be three times as high for a household with three members than for a single person. More specifically, the OECD [6] compares income inequality and poverty using a scale that divides household income by the square root of the household size. Thus, a household of four persons is thought to have needs twice as large as one composed of a single person. In addition, the family may exploit comparative advantages to divide labor among its participants. It also gains from risk pooling or, if unmeasurable, from reductions in uncertainty. Individuals who face idiosyncratic income risk have an obvious incentive to provide mutual insurance so that the

[8] G. Hess, for example, questioned whether love is more important to a lasting marriage than economic compatibility [5].

family can reduce the uncertainty and risk ineluctably permeating economic systems. For example, one partner could work when the other is sick or unemployed.

A case in point is what our guides refer to as the *added worker effect*, i.e., an increase in the labor supply of married women when their husbands become unemployed [7]. Although different from precautionary saving, this is yet another way to achieve the desired level of income smoothing induced by the aversion to risk featuring the typical human being. Economists [8] have found that couples with a higher correlation of income are more likely to divorce, which, changing the perspective, supports the role of mutual insurance among married people with low or negatively correlated incomes.

Our guides [9] have then considered the risk of living without the insurance offered by the annuity market.[9] They have estimated that the gains that a single person can expect on marriage are equivalent to 10 to 20% of their wealth. Finally, the family can enhance credit and coordination of investment activities. For example, one partner works when the other is in school, i.e., when he/she is investing in his/her human capital.

Data confirm that living together and longer go hand in hand. Empirical analyses for the USA show that the death rate for unmarried people is significantly higher than for married individuals living with their spouses [10]. Although this effect is significant for all categories of unmarried, it is strongest for those who had never married. Regarding living better, the logic is similar to the gain from trade: to the extent that the union is fair and deliberate and there are no barriers to exit (i.e., to divorce), living together implies that both parties are better off. Data for the USA affirm the presence of Paretian improvements[10]: men seem to obtain a "marriage premium," women bear no marriage penalty in their individual incomes, and both men and women enjoy higher family incomes compared to unmarried individuals.

Once the family is formed, economists continue, other decisions must be made. Since these choices deal with the life inside the family, preferences and behaviors of participants may be even more crucial than during the first step. The family is a complex decision unit in which the partners may well have different objectives regarding the amount of money necessary for consumption/saving, work/leisure activities, and decisions on fertility and childcare. Our guides [11] argue that cooperation leads to Pareto-efficient outcomes (there is no alternative decision that would have been preferred by all members). From a game-theoretic perspective, indeed, marriage is a typical example of repeated interactions between the same players, and cooperation is easier to support in such contexts.

[9] Annuities are long-term insurance contracts where people invest their money. In return for their investment or premium, individuals get income in the form of regular payments that may help them when they retire. There are also annuities aimed to spousal protection.

[10] Lerman R I and Wilcox W B (2014) For Richer, for Poorer: How Family Structures Economic Success in America. Report, American Enterprise Institute (AEI) and Institute for Family Studies, October. Paretian improvement is a condition whereby goods can be reallocated to make at least one person better off without making any other individual worse off. Pareto efficiency is achieved when no more Paretian improvements are possible.

But as everybody knows well, life inside the family unit may be tumultuous. The multifaceted behavioral nature of humans is put to the test within the family. Family members constantly negotiate over food, parental attention, access to external benefits such as school, and allocation of work within the household. This bargaining may end up with inefficient allocations when individuals put their own interests ahead of those of the family. The contextual presence and the contrast between self-regarding and other-regarding behaviors are typical inside humans, and this is reflected in all human networks.

Even special aggregations such as families—whereby in principle, pro-sociality should be an obvious trait—are not an exception. For example, parties may hide information to increase their personal share of resources. According to a recent survey, indeed, 27% of Americans have kept a financial secret from their partner [12]. Since bargaining can involve bluffing and posturing, there is no certainty that an agreement will be reached, and the game may have many equilibria. As already noticed, humans always find their way to solve multiple equilibria, but the solution may be good or bad.

As shown by A. Rubinstein in his influential model of bargaining, however, at least in theory, a fairly reasonable dynamic specification of bargaining can yield a unique (subgame perfect) equilibrium [13]. Let me report just the practical insights from his model that are most interesting for our trip—when bargaining, the more impatient and risk averse you are, the less you will get. This sounds like bad news for women who, typically, are thought of as being more risk averse and more patient than men. However, there is still no conclusive evidence on which gender, if any, is more risk averse and more patient [14].

Another hint revealed by our guides' work is that, as far as consumption and work choices go, family behavior typically differs from that of a single decision maker even in the case of cooperative and efficient behavior [15]. This shows once again the complexity of the human being and, possibly because of that, its aggregations—humans do not merely add up as numbers do.

So far, we have inspected the family, keeping a sort of introspective view that magnifies the behavioral side of the matter. But the decision to live together or live alone is never taken in an institutional vacuum. The family is a society, and as Latins reminds us, *ubi societas, ibi ius* (where there is a society there must be the law). As usual in our journey, well-established rules of the game may help solve tricky behavioral issues and improve the efficiency of the system. Facing the decision to marry, for example, one should be aware of who owns what or whether property and income would become community property. The presence of the institution of "divorce," then, has led some individuals to constrain behaviors via formal prenuptial agreements. For sure, negotiating a prenuptial agreement before marriage is rather unromantic, yet it can prevent nasty, excessively expensive court battles (recall that in human affairs there are no costless solutions). Because everything is already spelled out in the agreement, everyone knows exactly who gets what, and there is no room for argument.

In the last few decades, the interaction of culture, institutional settings, and technological progress has drastically changed the relationships between the members of the family. These developments have also impinged on the role of the family in the economic system; thus, ties are mutual. Though I briefly describe below some of the bidirectional feedback separating one-way directions, it should be clear that I do that merely for expository reasons; in our journey simultaneity is the rule, not the exception.

From family to economic system—what happens within the family influences the economic system. Data for the USA gathered by our guides [16] quantify the macroeconomic effects of the reduced amount of time that women invest in housework and childcare. Incorporating the value of nonmarket household production (such as housework, cooking, odd jobs, gardening, shopping, and childcare) has raised the level of nominal GDP 39% in 1965 and 26% in 2010.[11] This decline reflects the steadily decreasing number of hours households spent on home production because the drop in women's home production was not compensated for by an increase in men's hours. Updated works confirm that the situation in 2017 is not different [17]; habits die hard, even as old as Aristotelian ones are still with us.

The family-level decision to have fewer children, then, mechanically affects the size and age structure of the population living in the system. In turn, this impinges on the sustainability of partially funded pension systems (which use contributions from current workers to pay benefits to current retirees) and, hence, public finance. Since firms and governments are structurally net debtors in the system, family savings are crucial, especially in view of the increasing trend of public debt in several countries (started well before, but exacerbated by, the COVID-19 crisis): The US Congressional Budget Office has recently forecasted that in 2050, the debt will be twice the GDP. Intra-family choices regarding education also affect the accumulation of human capital and labor productivity in the system. Finally, the phenomenon called assortative matching may increase the economic inequality recorded in the system. In fact, it is the tendency to marry like with like in certain dimensions, such as education or income, and, clearly, this peculiar sort of homophily or homogamy acts as a multiplier of economic inequality [18].[12]

From economic system to family—how policies affect family decisions. Consider, again, the institution of divorce. It may negatively impinge on the decision to marry because it may reduce the marriage capital accumulation in the form of children, shared experiences, and personal information [19]. In addition, economists have argued that a child living in a blended family [20][13] may end up with poorer outcomes [21]. Various factors explain such findings, including parental stress, family conflict after separation and remarriage, inferior maternal time allocation within blended families, and economic hardship leading to family disruption. This

[11] According to the System of National Accounts, the output from these nonmarket, unpaid domestic and personal services does not add to GDP. One of our guides, P. Samuelson, joked that if a man marries his maid, GDP falls.

[12] Matching by education increases income inequality because household income is strongly correlated with the partners' level of formal education

[13] The blended family is characterized by stepchildren (born from an earlier marital union) living together with their half-siblings who are the joint children from an ongoing union.

notwithstanding, calling off a divorce does not imply eliminating the problems between the spouses (following the typical increasing formalization of human affairs, the institution of divorce simply formalized de facto situations where problematic couple lived separated at home). The possibility of divorce may then have a positive effect on the individual decision to marry because it allows couples to replace bad marriages with better ones. The positive consequences, whereby a higher aggregate divorce rate facilitates remarriage, may thus be better for both individuals who divorce and those who remarry.

A more specific example of policy affecting decisions dealing with family is what economists call the "power of the pill [22]." In the USA in the late 1960s, the birth control pill was made legally available to young unmarried women. This lowered the costs of long term professional education for women and raised the age of first marriage. By the same token, in the 1970s, poor American black women responded to poor marriage markets by choosing to raise children on their own. This choice may not have been feasible without the expansion of welfare programs [23]. Finally, as previously noted, economists have determined that poor macroeconomic conditions may impact the labor supply of married women, giving rise to the added worker effect.

It seems instructive to offer an example of the simultaneity in—and the complexity of—the interlinks between behavior and economic systems when one examines the family. Consider technological progress and social progress in the form of higher female participation in labor markets. Time-saving devices (e.g., washing machines and microwaves) have reduced the time required for home production (e.g., childcare, preparing food, and cleaning), freeing up time for work. Needless to say, women are beneficiaries of this. Higher female participation in labor markets has then been accompanied by greater possibilities to work for women. In modern economic systems, the "Service Revolution"—the huge increase in the share of the service sector in GDP—accounts for at least half of the long-term variation in female working hours [24].

But the increased share of female participation implies a reduced amount of time that women invest in housework and childcare, which is typically not balanced by a parallel increase in these activities by men. Fast technological progress and slow-changing customs have thus triggered a flourishing market for baby-sitters and housemaids that, in turn, has prompted a strong increase in female immigration from East Europe to West Europe and from South America to North America. Immigration has strong and hard-to-manage effects on the system, possibly making technological change easier and faster than social progress.

The increasing share of female participation, on the other hand, may undermine those long-term relationships that cement the family together and reduce the fertility rate, again impinging on the economic system. Smaller populations may bring benefits in reducing the consumption of natural resources and system's impact on the environment. However, as noticed, a system with fewer young workers and a larger proportion of older people poses problems for economic growth and the maintenance of social welfare systems such as pensions and healthcare. To encourage women to have more children without entering too heavily in their personal decisions, many capitalistic countries with insufficient replacement fertility rates[14] have then implemented family-oriented policies (financial transfers and tax breaks for parents with children, child-related leave and provision of childcare, as well a variety of measures that help with gender equality, reconciliation of work and family life, etc.). At least as measured by standard macroeconomic indicators, the connection of economic system performance and lower fertility rate shows a positive balance. Data from United Nations[15] indicate that in 2019 fertility was 1.7 births per woman in Europe and Northern America, 2.9 in Northern Africa and Western Asia, and 4.6 in sub-Saharan Africa. Part of the explanation lies in the increased number of women participating in paid labor which, as observed, statistically expands the GDP. But a more fundamental question naturally arises, one which again emphasizes the simultaneous connections of the life inside households and inside systems—does higher income per capita cause lower fertility or vice versa? The difficulty of establishing the causation may be inferred by looking at recent policy interventions. The Malthusian standpoint[16] recommends family planning in order to increase income per capita, a view shared by the World Bank and, until recently, by China (the only-one-baby-girl policy).[17] G. Becker, instead, suggested that the opposite causation is more likely: higher income per capita causes lower fertility. The rationale for women to choose more income than more children in rich countries is the following. On the one hand, in advanced countries, women have more chances to have careers and earn money; thus, they face greater opportunity costs to produce and to look after children. On the other hand, in advanced countries, children cost more—in terms of money and time—due to the higher education (and lifestyle) level needed to live in rich economic systems. Considering the healthcare system, it is also possible that higher income per capita causes lower fertility because of higher opportunities for pregnancy prevention as well declining infant and child mortality rates. Considering the lack of social safety net, likewise, in poor countries, children are needed to provide care for their parents in old age. Not to mention that, of course, poor and rich countries may have different culture.

There are another two points worth stressing when exploring the conjunction of human aggregations such as the family and economic systems. The first refers to the persistent presence of the family in capitalism and the second to cultural transmission.

As long as the economic system is relatively underdeveloped, the ties among different households are simple and infrequent. Most of the *Four* are implemented

---

[14]Replacement level fertility is the level of fertility at which a population exactly replaces itself from one generation to the next. In developed countries, replacement level fertility can be taken as requiring an average of 2.1 children per woman.

[15]United Nations (2020) World Fertility and Family Planning 2020 Highlights.

[16]According to this view, population growth unavoidably outpaces output growth; thus, it must be taken under control (cf. Section 5.1).

[17]The recent grim demographic performances recorded in China have led Chinese policymakers to a major policy shift. China has announced that it will allow couples to have more children and has implemented baby bonuses.

within the family. But increasing social complexity calls for more evolved ways to combine efficiently the participants who, by definition of complexity, inflate exponentially. As social coordination tools, market systems have accompanied households when a complex society was to be coordinated. But if capitalism and the family are both economic systems, then they are competitors, and as capitalistic systems become more developed, competition among them becomes stronger. As observed, for example, the family offers some insurance to the participants. But if markets and/or the state do the same job (e.g., insurance markets, unemployment benefits, and public pensions), then humans do not need to rely on the family. Similarly, in developed systems household chores and care responsibilities can be increasingly outsourced by couples as a strategy for better combining work and family life.

Now, if the system offers what the family does, why do humans continue to aggregate in families in developed capitalistic countries? Besides obvious emotional and biological considerations as well the importance of cultural transmission (see below), the rationale is the following. The social safety net provided by the state may be inefficient and, however, in capitalistic systems the state typically prefers not to impinge excessively on individual decisions; thus, the support provided by the state needs to be complemented. As per the market solution, due to the peculiarity of the social interactions at play finding valid alternatives may be hard as well as morally and culturally unacceptable. A significant share of households, e.g., just want to take care of loved ones personally. It has been also suggested that exchanges within the family are easier because of the intrinsic advantages in monitoring (due to proximity), in enforcement (due to access to nonmonetary punishments and rewards), and in knowing each other [25]. In addition, belonging to a network helps participants to enhance trust and to coordinate strategies with each other. The social capital and moral support linking participants in the market are smaller with respect to what can emerge within the family. Our connection with ancestors, and our concern for progeny, forms a story in which the sense of belonging and common fate is paramount. Possibly, this is why in some countries (e.g., Italy and France) written norms explicitly state that in impersonal economic affairs individuals must behave as a "good family man." That is to say, the state tries to export to the market the informal norms and rules of behavior operating inside the family to coordinate individuals toward better collective outcomes. In sum, it is unsurprising that the family is still a key institution in mature capitalism and that risk pooling and social safety nets in these systems are still provided by markets, state, and households. Blended solutions are typical in human endeavors.

Looking at the family as a social safety net paves the way for cultural transmission: the better and more secure our familiar safety net, the more we feel comfortable trying, falling, and therefore learning and growing. An excursion on the persistence of family within capitalistic systems and on the links between them, indeed, cannot refrain from casting an eye on cultural transmission. In this part of the stay, specifically, the aim of the visit is twofold. First, I highlight that cultural transmission is key to linking young humans to the economic system. Second, I stress that cultural transmission contextually differentiates and integrates the system.

The first question to address is—what is it that cultural transmission transmits? The short, trivial answer is "culture," but it calls for defining the concept of culture that, admittedly, so far has remained too vague. When I speak of culture during this journey, I refer to the subjective aspect of culture rather than to its functionality.[18] Specifically, culture here is made up by the values, beliefs, preferences, and norms prevalent among members of a particular human aggregation[19] [26]. In light of our journey, two things must be emphasized. First, knowing this definition of culture, we can say that in our trip, cultural transmission in families concerns the transfer of preferences, beliefs, and norms of behavior as a result of social interactions across and within generations. Second, this interpretation makes self-evident how intertwined individuals and society are. In fact, one may wonder whether culture can exist only as an interpersonal or social entity.

Be that as it may, since culture refers here to the accumulation over time of beliefs, norms, and other institutions essential to the functioning of economic systems, then cultural transmission turns out to be critical in human behavior, economic systems, and, accordingly, in humans' way of executing the *Four*. As per aggregating, Aristotle believed that the family was instrumental in the existence and preservation of wider human clusters (specifically city-state such as Athens, in his book *Politics*). This is for two main reasons, both dealing with cultural transmission. First, the family is where humans learn to live together so that then they can aggregate in larger social groups. Second, the abstract concept of "public" cannot develop until individuals have understood the private domain. Aristotle's view thus stressed that the family works as a sort of training camp in relation to the development of wider social clusters. Cultural transmission within families is thus fundamental for linking children to wider social aggregations.

Young humans learn the rules of the game via cultural transmission, and social interactions within the family is paramount in such learning. Modern psychology argues that what learned during our childhood will shape our future behavior. The values transmitted to a child about abortion, sex-related issues, gender equality, stereotypes, religion, etc. in a traditional family are different than those the same child would learn in a modern family. This evidently impinges on how children will mix their multipart behavioral nature in social relations during their adult life. By the same token, cultural traits at systemwide, family and individual levels tend to reinforce each other via cultural transmission. A collectivistic culture—such as that prevailing in, for example, an Asian country—magnifies conformity, harmony, and interdependence, whereas individualistic cultures put more weight on autonomy, self-interest, uniqueness, and personal achievements. Accordingly, a good child in collectivistic culture is one who quietly and attentively listen to parents and teachers; a good child in individualistic culture is instead one who proactively looks for her

[18] An alternative definition of culture emerges by taking a more functional orientation. Culture denotes certain activities undertaken by people, and the products of those activities, which have to do with the intellectual, moral, and artistic aspects of human life.

[19] This is the most adopted definition in the papers collected in [26]

way, use as much as energy to emerge and to form personal opinions. It can be added that in the learning process aimed to progressively insert individuals into the economic system via the family, nurture seems to be more important than nature. The latter, in fact, gives humans less than the system requires of them. Nature only gives us the physical ability to speak. Nurture, instead, gives us the social ability to communicate. We acquire a language interacting with other speakers, not from parental genes. Though it takes time, moreover, cultural transmission is much faster than natural selection in forming behavioral patterns. Economists have studied indepth the decomposition of the cultural (or environmental) and genetic effects on cognitive and psychological traits. B. Sacerdote has surveyed that part of the large "nature vs. nurture" literature examining how the intergenerational transmission of educational attainment, income, and health vary when a child is being raised by adoptive rather than biological parents. His conclusions point out that both the biological and the nurturing parents contribute a great deal to the transmission of income and education to their children [27].

Behaviors and attitudes are affected not only by what is transmitted but also by how parents raise their children. Child psychologists[20] argue that childhood influences core aspects of adult behaviors and attitudes and have found a close relationship between the type of parenting style and children's behavior. Specifically, they categorize four key parenting styles. Authoritative—parents encourage kids to be responsible, to think for themselves, and to consider the reasons for rules; Authoritarian—parents expect their orders to be obeyed without question, children's behavior is mostly shaped by punishment and children's emotional needs are low priorities; Permissive—parents are responsive and warm, but also reluctant to enforce rules; Neglectful—parents offer their children little emotional support and fail to enforce standards of conduct. Accordingly, for instance, the children of authoritative parents are more independent, more active, develop greater self-esteem, and better social skills than children raised with different parenting styles.[21] In line with the heterogeneity of human behavior, data show a diversified picture. In the United States, roughly 46% of parents use authoritative parenting style, 26% authoritarian parenting style, 18% permissive parenting style, and 10% neglectful parenting style. Another expected result is that authoritative parenting is diffuse among European-American parents, while Asian-American parents have a more authoritarian style.[22] In sum, nature and nurture enter the scene, and parents are able to shape

[20] Maccoby E E and Martin J A 1983 Socialization in the Context of the Family: Parent-Child Interaction. In: Handbook of Child Psychology. Socialization, Personality, and Social Development. New York: Wiley.

[21] Replacing the words "parents" with "state" (as intended here) and "kids" with "citizens" the taxonomy seems somewhat apply to economic systems—authoritative brings to mind capitalism (as intended here), authoritarian brings to mind planned-economies, and permissive brings to mind anarchy.

[22] Shen J J, Cheah C S L and Yu J (2018). Asian American and European American emerging adults' perceived parenting styles and self-regulation ability. Asian American Journal of Psychology, 9(2), 140–148.

the behavior of their children only partially. As all parents know, for good or ill children and adolescents also learn from mixed-behavior peers and maintain a significant part of their natural mixed behavior.

Let us now turn our attention to how cultural transmission within families may contextually differentiate and integrate the system. To this end, one remarkable element in modern societies is the lack of that sort of "within-cluster" homogeneity known as *melting pot*. Basically, this materializes when a dominant group succeeds in assimilating minorities into its hegemonic culture. The empirical evidence instead confirms the presence of persistent heterogeneity in the cultural traits of many economic systems (as we all know, for instance, immigrants all over the world generally strive to maintain various traits of the culture of the country of origin). In searching for explanations, economists have specifically studied the resilience of ethnic and religious traits across generations. Instances abound—orthodox Jewish communities in the USA, Basques and Catalans in Spain, Corsicans in France, and the Irish Catholics. According to empirical analyses [28, 29], in the USA, during the period from 1972 to 1996, intermarriage and socialization rates were consistent among Protestants, Catholics, and Jews, with a strong preference for raising children who identify with their own religious beliefs. Only 1% of whites in the USA, then, marry blacks even though blacks make up more than 10% of the population.

Our guides justify these statistics based on the different efforts parents use to transmit their culture to the children which, in turn, depends on the relative position of the family within the society [30]. The logic goes as follows. Families that belong to a cultural majority do not need to devote many resources to socialize their children. With high probability, children will spontaneously adopt or imitate the predominant cultural trait in society at large, which is exactly what their parents desire for them. Conversely, families belonging to a cultural minority need to socialize children more intensely because there is higher probability of horizontal (peer-to-peer) and oblique (e.g., from teacher to children) transmission of undesired cultural traits. For minorities, vertical (from parents to offspring) cultural transmission is more important. Since they are relatively more attentive to avoid non-vertical cultural contamination, they are not culturally absorbed by the majority—individual behavior triggered by cultural heterogeneity shows up as a resilient element of the system as a whole. Homophily, intergenerational rigidity (i.e., the similarity in socioeconomic status between parents and offspring), and assortative matching may then enter the scene, exacerbating the level of socioeconomic segmentation in the system. To be sure, all these factors widen the economic inequality within the system. Bad equilibria are not so infrequent in human societies—for too many humans, vertical transmission of cultural traits, homophily, homogamy, and other forms of social rigidity can make the American Dream just a dream.

4.3 The Productive Firm

In this stopover, I shall deal with the peculiar social cluster called the firm and, in particular, the productive firm. The focus will be on why and how humans aggregate to produce as well as on what gains and issues they meet in doing that. In this respect, commercial firms may be seen more as pertaining to the trading endeavors discussed in Chap. 2. Under the definitory *caveat*, the kind of firm I am chiefly interested in is broadly close to the concept of enterprise as defined by the System of National Account: "An enterprise is an institutional unit in its capacity as a producer of goods and services." Henceforth, I will use the terms "firm" and "enterprise" to mean "productive firm." In addition, I will concentrate on the typical firm operating in market systems. In our brief trip, I must leave unexplored other kinds of productive aggregations, such as cooperatives, employee-managed firms, state-owned enterprises, and the like. As economics teach, scarcity implies costly choices.

As observed, the household is an economic system; as such, it was organized to produce for its own use whatever was wanted. In pre-capitalistic economic systems, consequently, households had few interconnections. But as shown by the *Four*, humans have eagerness and skills unique in the animal kingdom. When households became more productive—because of improved human capital and/or new tools—they started producing for sales rather than for household use only. A. Smith suggested that human societies develop in stages according to the dominant forms of production—hunting, pastoralism, agriculture, and commerce. But humans want more and more. Once family and trading became insufficient for humans' insatiability, another kind of aggregation was needed in the economic system, one more specialized in productive activities. And humans concocted the enterprise which, in human history, emerged later than the household because it responds to higher levels of human wants. By the same token, the productive firm is more recent than the family because it needs to be inserted into sufficiently developed economic systems populated by sufficiently evolved human beings. Capitalism helped shift the coordination from within the family to the market via the productive firm. There is today no developed market system whereby the household is the sole or the chief productive unit. Enlarging the perspective to have a more inclusive view one may say that humans living in modern capitalistic economies can afford to coordinate their efforts via three major visible operators—the household, the firm, and the state—and one invisible mechanism—the market. Social capital, of course, is intimately intertwined with both all operators and the mechanism.

As usual in human affairs, a new form of social aggregation does not solve all problems, and it raises new ones. Since the outset of our species, humans know that working together is helpful. Since then, however, they have been also learning that several difficulties arise because of the less prosocial side of the humans' behavioral nature. Production, furthermore, involves not only the physical transformation of inputs into outputs but also the transfer of property rights between the owners of resources, commodities, and labor services. In this effort to exchange rights, organizational and institutional constraints arise. Contrast firms, markets, and households on these themes. In the market, the invisible hand coordinates decentralized decisions; in hierarchical human aggregations such as the firm, coordination may be tougher to achieve. In both households and firms, then decision making may pertain to single individuals as well as to a group of humans, but the social capital inside enterprises is likely smaller. Phrases such as "in this firm, we are like a family" are true only occasionally, and the larger the enterprise the lower the probability that this is true. These are the institutional and behavioral issues that we will touch upon during our stay in this type of aggregation that only humans can conceive.

Since the firm is a complex social organism, it has been addressed in several ways by our guides, and a telegraphic account of that turns out to be a good starting point in this tour stop.

Paralleling the view about consumers' behavior, in standard neoclassical theory, the firm is seen as a cost-minimizing, profit-maximizing entity. Just as consumption choices derive from constrained maximizations (cf. Chap. 2), the neoclassical firm maximizes its profits by economizing inputs under exogenous technological constraints. It is a black box that merely transforms inputs into outputs. While the adverse consequences of monopoly, monopsony, and monopolistic competition were all readily tackled in this abstract apparatus, the reasons why the firm emerged in the market system or the issues related to its internal organization remained unexplored.[23] Some insights can be found in the managerial models of the firm, which substantially maintain the neoclassical approach but emphasize the distinction between ownership and control, examining what happens when the enterprise behaves in the interest of the managers. They theorize that the firm does not maximize profits but pursues goals, such as the maximization of sales revenue, of capital, or of the probability of a suboptimal but satisfactory level of profit for the owners. The idea of capitalistic firm that I will consider in this stopover is different from both these views. We shall visit firms as institutions, institutions within which disparate participants (employers, workers, suppliers, etc.) are aggregated. Otherwise stated, firms here are human devices that shape human interactions for fulfilling humans wants, taking into account of the multifaceted behavioral nature of humans.

With this in mind, some questions naturally arise: What are the gains to cluster in firms? Why do humans structure their interactions through the institution of the "firm" instead of interacting directly? Or equivalently, why do they not manage their interactions in a completely decentralized manner, letting the invisible hand of the market find the solution? Since the coordinating role of the market mechanism, indeed, why did firms emerge in market systems? A path-breaking explanation of why firms exist in capitalism was offered by R. Coase in 1937, who stated that firms exist in capitalism because of the costs of transacting in a world of imperfect information [31]. Coase thus saw transaction costs as an agglomerative force. In other terms, the main reason why it is profitable to establish a firm is that there is a cost of using the market mechanism.

[23] For good or ill, the chief mission of neoclassical economics is to understand how the price system coordinates the use of scarce resources. Recall that models must necessarily be simplifications of the huge complexity of the real world.

I have already touched upon these transaction costs (TC), and this stop offers the opportunity to say more about them. Unlike the direct production costs faced by firms (e.g., wages and interest rates), TC underscore that firms necessarily operate in complex environments. If someone wants to act as an entrepreneur, she faces costs and time of creating and maintaining property rights, opening her firm, finding suppliers and customers, and negotiating and concluding a separate contract for each production and exchange transaction. Entrepreneurs need to search for and contract with people wanting to act as employees, creditors, suppliers, layers, accountants, etc. All these time-consuming, costly activities must then be repeated for every contract.

Within a firm, however, with virtually no negotiations/costs, the entrepreneur could easily find a suitable employee to execute certain tasks and punish underperformers, even firing them. According to Chandler [22], a classic example of TC-generating modern enterprises refers to the construction of the railroad system in the USA. Before the introduction of the railroad companies, the localized nature of production allowed for relatively traditional forms of organization. But the control over this new extensive infrastructure necessitated a new type of enterprise, one which was based on the division into multiple organizational units that had to be managed separately. Due to humans' insatiability and the related increasing complexity of economic systems, indeed, human aggregations typically evolve from informal to pre-formal to semi-formal to fully formal organisms. Note that, as Chandler's example shows, these evolutions are often the result of deliberate human actions rather than spontaneous order.

Financial firms such as banks and other financial institutions pop up in capitalism for similar reasons—the market alone is not able to solve all the social interactions necessary to support the life of modern humans. A digression on these firms thus permits us to add other considerations regarding the social value of the sort of aggregation we are currently traveling across. In intermediating between individuals that are demanding money—typically firms—and individuals offering money—typically households—banks shrink transaction costs. But this is not the only socially improving aspect of banks. Usually, entrepreneurs need money in larger quantities and for longer periods than does an individual saver. Moreover, there are crucial information problems—borrowers may conceal key data about the real risk involved in their endeavor so that individual savers may be unable to determine the right fundamental price (the interest rate). Specialized social aggregations such as financial and credit institutions then intermediate between the two sides of the market, shrink informational issues, reduce TC, and enhance the coordination in the system, which, accordingly, is more efficient with than without them.

Remember that private firms and markets are two distinctive elements of the concept of capitalism followed in our trip.

Transaction costs thus offer a rationale for the birth of firms in market systems. But they may also help us understand why firms persist in market systems. The basic logic is similar to that found in the Prologue—complexity of economic systems and size of TC go hand in hand. Shortly, the story goes like this. Unlike today, in the late 1700s, there were no large companies; thus, unsurprisingly, A. Smith chiefly wrote about atomistic markets. But human eagerness leads economic systems and its components—in the current case, the private firm—to become evolving entities. In more recent systems than those examined by Smith, economies of scale imply large-scale organizations, and the increasing specialization requires increasing percentages of resources to be engaged in transacting. In turn, the transaction sector tends to be an increasingly large percentage of gross national product (GNP). According to our guides, in the USA, transaction costs as a percentage of GNP rose from 24.2% in 1870 to 46.7 in 1970 [33]. In a nutshell, according to this view, as long as there are significant TC in the system, then the enterprises will remain with us.

Human hunger leads to increased system complexity, thereby raising TC, and these, in turn, lead to the birth and persistency of the firm. But the firm needs formal institutions, which makes the economic system even more complex. As the system moves from a system of zero transaction costs to one of strictly positive transaction costs, the importance of the legal system becomes immediately clear. To paraphrase in Latin—*ubi negotium ibi ius* (where there is a firm, there must be the law).

O. Williamson's findings will escort us when visiting these institutional issues. He underlined that the decision to aggregate in firm is not prompted so much by fundamental agreement on values and goals or by the desire to eliminate conflict, but, on the contrary, by the need to bring necessarily recurrent conflict into this form of organization. For our purposes, interestingly, he also stressed the role of uncertainty and behavior, in particular opportunism that, as recalled in the Prologue, he described as: "the full set of ex ante and ex post efforts to lie, cheat, steal, mislead, disguise, obfuscate, feign, distort and confuse" [34–36]. Williamson argued that a transaction includes both exchanges and contracts. Whereas the exchange is a transfer of property rights that, crucially, involves no promises or latent future responsibility, the contract promises future performance that depends on the other party's future behavior. Williamson was more interested in contracts than in exchanges, pointing out that TC is more than *search* TC (i.e., the cost of searching customers). For him transaction costs are eminently *contractual* costs, such as the costs incurred in establishing contractual relations, in making contracts enforceable by law, or by self-enforcement.

All this costly activity derives from the need to contrast the opportunism permeating social interactions, which, in turn, is incentivized by the lack of full information. The human beings examined by Williamson (the "Williamsonians") are in fact different animals with respect to Walrasians— Williamsonians are bounded rational Sapiens. Bounded rationality does not deal with unwillingness or laziness but is rather the result of Williamsonians' limited ability to process the available information in uncertain environments.

The connections between bounded rationality, uncertainty, opportunism, firm, and contractual TC can be made more explicit as follows. Uncertainty and imperfect/asymmetric information lead to bounded rationality and opportunistic behaviors because they make easier to serve one own interests rather than those of the other party to the contract. Thus, opportunism emerges as the major source of the TC involved in monitoring and enforcing contracts. Firms then allow economizing on explicit contracts, which are expensive instruments aimed to manage opportunism.

Otherwise stated, in situations where there is no uncertainty and contracts are "complete", then using the market mechanism with such complete contracts will produce the desired outcomes and internal control will be redundant. But in uncertain systems, something may happen whereby individuals have to renegotiate the contract. Uncertain events may include anything that cannot be measured ex post by a court or other mediator, since that is ultimately who would enforce any contract. This uncertain environment sustains individual bounded rationality and opportunistic behaviors and, accordingly, leads humans to behave as Williamsonians. Against this framework, Williamson eventually concludes that the cost of renegotiations is lower if the involved Williamsonians (workers, suppliers, etc.) are internal to the firm.

At this point of the sojourn, the attentive hiker may think—if firms are better than the market in dealing with TC which, moreover, are ever growing, why then do firms not replace the market in capitalistic systems? That is, why do firms not vertically integrate to internalize everything? What prevents firms from becoming giant human aggregations that manage huge amounts of inner ties? Insights come again from Williamson. Inter alia, he remarks that the size of the firm inside the economic system depends on the efficacy of legal norms. This is so because stronger legal norms imply more complete contracts, i.e., lower probability of having to renegotiate and less need to internalize.

Our guides have identified other factors that could limit the size of the firms. Among them are diseconomies of scale and scope, costs of bureaucracy, and the weakening of individual incentives. In this stopover, I limit the excursion to bureaucracy and incentives because they highlight the behavioral issues emerging within these peculiar human clusters. After some explanation of why humans aggregate into firms as well as why firms persist in market systems, indeed, the natural next step is to scout what the social life inside the enterprise could be like.

A. Smith was well aware of the potential conflicts of interest within firms (p. 990): [37] "The directors of such companies, however, being the managers rather of other people's money than of their own, it cannot well be expected, that they should watch over it with the same anxious vigilance with which the partners in a private copartnery frequently watch over their own." Williamson's job furnishes other details on the effect of incentives and bureaucracy in contrasting the pressures toward larger sizes which, in turn, leads to speak about the social life inside firms. He claimed that since procedures such as the allocation of workers to tasks could be achieved less costly through direction rather than via markets, then firms could reduce these TC by structuring human interactions and establishing a centralized hierarchical structure. But and this is the point, hierarchy and command require monitoring, enforcement, or internal incentive structures to manage the multifaceted behavioral nature of humans. Even more so in the presence of Williamsonians, who, when contracting, disclose information in a selective and distorted manner. As the frictions associated with coordination become progressively more severe and, hence, the life inside firms become increasingly difficult to manage, the recourse to market exchange becomes more attractive.

Within hierarchical entities such as firms, a canonic case of the potential need to manage opportunistic behaviors via monitoring, enforcement, or internal incentive structure concerns employers and employees. They have opposing interests in that the employee effort typically leads to benefits to the firm and costs to the employee. Incentives that possibly motivate workers to supply labor and, more in general, humans to give up agency may be by and large distinguished in coercion, compensation, and non-pecuniary reward. I shall focus on compensation and non-pecuniary reward. The former leads to voluntary exchanges in the form of *do ut des*.[24] The latter includes intrinsic rewards such as the satisfaction from doing one's duty, the enjoyment out of supplying the product, or it is linked to a sense of belonging or solidarity (firm as a family). This view clearly suggests that the level of opportunism in real-world firms may be less widespread than what was conceptualized by Williamson.[25] In fact, we shall see that opportunism is not the only behavioral reaction within firms—when addressing humans it is often better to not take extreme positions. Let us inquire a bit more into these themes.

Referring to intrafirm interactions featured by pecuniary incentives and voluntary exchanges, our guides have advanced and elaborated on the idea of efficiency wages. The rationale is as follows. In Walrasian firms, wages depend on labor productivity—by and large, the more you produce, the more you gain. In the efficiency wage vision, the perspective is inverted. Firms are willing to pay higher than Walrasian (market clearing) wages in the belief that workers' productivity depends on the wage paid—efficiency wages thus embody an incentive for workers to increase their effort. Otherwise stated, in the absence of complete contract, efficiency wages are regarded by the employer as a costly instrument of enforcement. Empirical findings show that wages above the market clearing level actually increase effort, decrease employee theft, decrease absenteeism, and decrease employee exits [38, 39]. A possible historical example is the success of H. Ford's decision to increase his workers' wages to combat rampant absenteeism. In the early 1910s, Ford introduced the moving assembly line (described by C. Chaplin in his famous movie *Modern Times*).[26] It boosted productivity but also lateness and absenteeism. In a sort of "Great Resignation" of that time, many workers quit, and the labor turnover rate skyrocketed to 370%. In January 1914, Ford announced that his company would double its workers' wages to five dollars a day conditional on meeting all of the company's requirements. Part of Ford's reasoning was that workers who were troubled by money problems at home would be distracted on the job and that greater

---

[24] In the Epilogue, I shall highlight that the *Four* are very often put in place contextually and that they can help each other.

[25] In fact, Williamson was careful to note that opportunism is not the only way in which humans behave and that human behavior is mixed. His logic sounds like "better safe than sorry"—is the inability to easily identify the Williamsonians (due again to bounded rationality) that makes guarding against the hazards of opportunism the prudent course.

[26] The moving assembly line is a way to produce subdividing assembly operations into a number of smaller tasks that are assigned to workers placed sequentially in a fixed order, and the product is moved from one worker to the other by conveyor.

wages could stimulate workers to do their new boring and mundane jobs. As I mentioned, the move was a success.

Behavioral economists have elaborated on how pecuniary incentives can affect social norms within firms. They have argued that by offering higher-than-market wages, enterprises may trigger reciprocity—workers reciprocate in their commitment to the firm and fairness—the more that employees feel the wage is fair, the more they work hard [40–42]. Our guides have also claimed that an employer can increase profits by offering a higher salary to prospective employees than is needed to attract them (i.e., the market rate for the job) because they will be grateful for the generosity and will work harder [43]. There is also evidence that monetary punishment may have adverse effects on moral norms, which again, although indirectly, sustains the positive contribution of money on the immaterial social glue existing in the firm. Economists report the following example [44]. Wanting to curb the flu outbreaks that seemed to happen with suspicious frequency just days before and after the weekend, in the early 2000s, the Boston Fire Department ended its policy of unlimited sick days. Firefighters taking more than fifteen sick days would have suffered monetary fines. The firemen responded to the new incentives: those calling in sick on Christmas and New Year's Day increased tenfold over the previous year. The Fire Commissioner retaliated by canceling their holiday bonus checks, but the firemen responded, and the following year, they more than doubled their claims of sick days. Many of the firemen, apparently angered by the new system, abused it or abandoned their previous ethic of serving the public even when injured or not feeling well. The foregoing also suggests that material incentives may affect immaterial incentives thus praise apart pecuniary and non-pecuniary stimuli may be difficult.

Examining monetary incentives, the principal–agent literature is another well-established strand of economics that can be exploited to cast an eye on the social interactions within the firm.[27] It concerns how one individual, the principal (say an employer), can design a compensation system (a contract), which motivates another individual, his agent (say an employee), to act in the principal's interests. Analyzing corporations, economists talk about the "divorce between ownership and control" [45] which occurs whenever an owner (the principal) submits a risky operation in which she has an interest to an operator (the agent, for example, or the employed manager) whose conduct he can monitor only imperfectly or with great difficulty or cost.

The basic problem for the principal is twofold. The first is that it is difficult and costly for the principal to monitor the agents (not to mention problems of privacy in developed countries). The second is that the agents often know their own business better than the principal; that is, information is asymmetric. To solve the issues

[27] As intuitable, the principal–agent problem is very widespread in social interactions whose complexity raises several kinds of issues that can be addressed from disparate standpoints. In fact, the principal–agent literature is also known as information theory, incentive theory, contract theory, or signaling theory. In this stop, I just scratch the surface of these various viewpoints.

stemming from their interaction, the principal and the agent may engage in a contract in order to regulate and divide up the gains from their interaction.

If effort is contractible, providing efficient incentives is trivial. From the firm owners' standpoint, for example, a complete contract forces managers to maximize the present value of future returns to the owners and employees to work hard and well. But typically, contracts are incomplete in the sense that they specify parties' obligations imprecisely, and business relations are riddled with informal agreements and unwritten codes of conduct. In the scene, as usual, stone guests are the complexity and uncertainty pervading modern human aggregations that permanently flank the innate compound behavior of humans. The result, of course, is the difficulty in designing complete contracts. While in modern economic systems, the ability to define complete contracts is small, the number of disputes and litigations is large [46].

Besides complexity and uncertainty, a third pervasive element in all human networks is risk which, unsurprisingly, is another element considered by our guides in analyzing the interaction between the principal and the agent. Assume then that in their interactions uncertainty is measurable. The crux is that there are instances in which the outcome of cooperation depends not only on the agent's effort, but also on events outside his control. For instance, employees are not responsible for, and have no control over, entrepreneurial risks such as technological change or demand shocks. To take a specific example, consider a landlord and a farmer. On the one hand, the former cannot observe the effort made by the latter (or prove to a court that this effort is insufficient); on the other hand, the farmer is only partially responsible for the output because of climatic or other hazards over which he has no control. Now, who should bear the risk inherent in the firm activity?

Against this framework it seems reasonable to consider the different propensity toward risk of the humans involved. Among other institutional devices, to solve this sort of coordination problem humans have concocted sharecropping, an institutional arrangement practiced worldwide and that has evolved over time for centuries. In its most basic form, sharecropping is an agreement to produce agricultural products, whereby the landowner provides the land and the sharecropper provides the labor. At the end of the agricultural cycle, the harvest is divided between the parties on a pre-agreed basis. Thus, sharecropping divides production and price risk between landlord and tenant, who act, respectively, as the principal and the agent. In other words, sharecropping is a way to deal with the trade-off between incentives and risk sharing.

At one extreme, in an attempt to make the gain for the agent a sort of "independent" variable, parties can think of fixed-wage contracts.[28] Though these agreements

[28] Thought at a very different level and within a package full of several other proposals—thus to be read in our tour cum *grano salis*—an attempt to separate the wages from business risks was made in Italy in the late 1970s. In these years (in Italy and elsewhere), inflation showed double-digit rates and, hence, it was a period of huge uncertainty. The general secretary of the most representative Italian labor union then claimed that wages could no longer be regarded as an "independent variable" (La Repubblica, Jan. 24, 1978).

totally remove production risk from the tenant, who is fully ensured, they also shrink incentives to provide effort. At the other extreme, fixed-rent contracts provide perfect incentives: the farmer pays a fixed sum (the rent) to the landowner and receives all the proceeds of his labor above this sum. But in this case, the tenant bears all the risk because her income will depend on random events. A risk-averse farmer, of course, would prefer the fixed-wage, whereas a risk-loving tenant would prefer the fixed-rent contract. In this respect, a hint may be taken from F. Knight, who argued that entrepreneurs must be less risk-averse than their employees with whom they enter into explicit contracts [47][29] (more on entrepreneurs in Sect. 5.2). But humans are complex animals living in complex environments; thus, the trade-off between incentives and risk-sharing likely involves further elements. In the late nineteenth century, for example, most African-American freedmen preferred to rent land for a fixed payment rather than receive fixed wages. It could be a case of love of risk and/or entrepreneurial spirit, but since most humans are risk averse and African-American freedmen were very numerous, it is more likely that the choice was based on the fact that former slaves did not want to submit again to supervision and harsh discipline. Humans have memories, and this may make the outcome of current interactions dependent on past ones.

As observed, there is another way to motivate workers to supply labor, one which is not based on pecuniary incentives. In Chap. 5, I will report evidence showing that, because of their passion for science, some workers accept lower wages in order to work as scientists. This viewpoint reinforces that when the employee's effort level cannot be completely specified in a formal contract, then other elements such as ethic and informal institutions may complete the missing part of that contract. Trivially, there is no need for the contract to be perfectly designed if the employee's work ethic precludes his or her shirking on the job. Formal institutions are useful to the extent that behaviors need to be managed to achieve socially useful outcomes—*ubi societas ibi ius* only if humans are not all saints. Social norms may even impact duration of the contract—disgruntled employees are likely to quit as soon as they find another job, and the firm may lose productive workers. The case of Ford's moving assembly lines may also be illustrative in this respect. In fact, many workers quit not because of lower wages but rather because skilled craftsmen, previously proud of their labor, were assigned to trivial, rote tasks. It may be figured out that in a restored ex ante situation, they would have returned to work even without extra monetary incentives.

Among the reasons why firms may choose to rely on the intrinsic value workers get from doing their jobs is that both monetary incentives and monitoring are costly. Besides monetary costs, extreme monitoring to complete the contract is also at odds with privacy and liberty (G. Orwell *docet*). On the other hand, firms may increase the effort of their workers, even reducing physical controls on the workers in the belief that they will then work harder and better for a sense of reciprocity and fairness. The

[29] Unlike employees, entrepreneurs must address problems of raising capital and bearing risk in addition to identifying and pursuing opportunity [47].

sense of fairness is created by having supervisors treat workers decently, by having impartial rules for settling disputes and determining promotions and job assignments, and the like. A general sense of fairness in turn enhances the social capital inside the firm. Creating an adequate work environment is indeed among the tools used by some firms to stimulate, via non-pecuniary stimuluses, the workers' motivation. Clues about that may be drawn by the recent attempts to measure and publicize the "best places to work" based also on elements such as culture, values, sense of belonging, and work–life balance.[30]

4.4 Other Human Aggregations: Cities, Communities, and Nations

Two historical milestones are remarkable when scouting the human aggregation called city. According to archeologists, (around) 9.000 BCE was the year in which the first city Jericho was settled. There is no agreement on that because of definitory issues. Economics does not have the monopoly on these kinds of troubles. Just to mention, if a city is defined by the number of buildings and/or individuals living together, then there is insufficient information on Jericho. The second cornerstone year for the city was 2007 CE, when, according to the data *collected* by the United Nations [48], humans became more urban than rural. The history between these two dates tells that the economic importance of this sort of human aggregation has been increasing so much that cities now account for the major fraction of the global economy. The path followed by the urbanization of humans is not linear. Actually, it became exponential only since the Industrial Revolution (cf. Chap. 6). Data show that in 1800, only 3% of the world's population lived in cities. Today, as said, humans are mostly urban dwellers, with cities providing 60% of world GDP.

Why did humans excogitate the city? Just as with other aggregations, the deep motive is the interplay between humans' insatiability, cleverness, and sociability. The city is yet another talented response to our constant will to live together, longer and better, an artificial system that enables millions of us to live in close proximity. Similar to what was said about the family, opportunities and incentives to aggregate in cities emerge for both economic and natural reasons. Human groups based on hunting are necessarily nomads, but continuously stalking the food makes life uncertain and dangerous—the opposite of the basic aspirations of humans. Moreover, it is almost impossible that each sub-aggregation (such as families) has its own spot whereby to satisfy the need for water, wood, grass, shelter, etc. Settling down to cluster in peculiar locations, namely the cities, is thus a necessity as well a good strategy.

Once the decision is made to cluster, the next choice deals with location. Especially in early stages, nature played a big role. Situations favorable for

[30] A point in case is the list elaborated by the magazine *Fortune* on "100 Best Companies to Work For."

cultivating—as with the Sumerian cities in Mesopotamia—and for defense—as with Athens with the Acropolis and Rome on seven hills—determined the location of ancient cities. When humans started long-distance trade, economic motives flanked natural ones. Cities began sprouting up because a pit-stop or caravan-to-ship port was necessary. Comprehensibly, cities were commonly located at the innermost angle of gulfs (e.g., Liverpool, Venice, and Hamburg).

Following our guides' observations, we see that other details on humans' choices behind the birth and location of cities emerge. Economists have been emphasizing how economic factors can be significant in steering humans toward the urban solution. To the extent that individuals are free to choose where to live, economists assert, then the convergence of humans in a certain zone—precisely the city—implies that cities must have some greater attraction force with respect to other places. When talking about the costs and benefits related to living together in a city, our guides refer to transportation costs and agglomeration economies [49]. A broad interpretation of transportation costs includes the difficulties in exchanging goods, people, and ideas. Keeping in mind this broad view of transportation costs, the benefits to cluster in cities—i.e., the agglomeration economies—all ultimately derive from transportation cost savings.

A look at the measures of success of a city permits us to make progress. Usually economists use wages, prices, and population to measure the success of a city and to infer the reasons why humans are attracted to them. Basically, the argument explaining the "gains from urbanizing" goes like this. To the extent that in a city (i) employers are willing to pay more for workers, that (ii) people are willing to pay more for staying there, and that (iii) more individuals are moving to that city, then the city should have some agglomeration economy.

In fact, there is evidence that the larger the city, the higher the wage. Data show that a doubling of city size is associated with a 4–8% increase in wages [50]. This phenomenon is known as the *urban wage premium*. Since standard economics suggests that wages go hand in hand with productivity, then the urban wage premium may indicate that cities are highly productivity places. According to our guides, in fact, doubling of city population is associated with a 2–5% increase in productivity [51]. If employers are willing to pay the urban wage premium, then it may signal that the city is an unusually productive site and the size of this premium may quantify, ceteris paribus, the amount of the city-related higher productivity. This is so because, among other things, living together in a city enhances labor division and specialization—and, accordingly, productivity and wages. This is yet another way to see that unity is strength.

If higher productivity may convince employers to pay the urban wage premium, why do workers ask for relatively higher wages to work in a city? Two reasons come to mind for this extra which, indeed, may reduce the probability to be hired. Employees may ask for higher wages because living in cities means either paying high rent for a central location or suffering from the discomforts of the suburbs (crime, poor amenities, etc.). In any case the point remains—the presence of the urban wage premium suggests that cities are highly productivity places.

When addressing complex dynamic social systems (that are omnipresent in our journey), some cautionary note on causal links is as necessary as instructive. Though establishing the positive correlation between city size and labor productivity is relatively easy, inferring the causal chain in their relationship is difficult. It could be that high wages reflect the fact that cities are highly productivity places, but it may also be that, for example, cities are more productive because they attract more skilled workers. This second case has evident normative fallout because it means that to maintain or improve the productivity of a city, policies must target skilled workers.

Among easier-to-establish causal chains, there is one that is particularly compelling in this trek because, on the one hand, it explains the urban choice made by poor people and, on the other hand, it helps to clear an occasionally reported non sequitur about the size of the city and poverty. Because of the large number of poor people living in a modern metropolis, indeed someone might wonder whether cities impoverish individuals. The answer is negative—urbanization does not cause poverty. Just as immigrants flow from poor nations to rich nations, cities attract—they do not create—poor individuals. Quite the contrary, cities appeal to poor people because they are aware that the city might help them fulfill their wants.

The second indicator of the success of a city is high housing prices. Although high housing prices may reflect a rigid housing supply in the city (which clearly is not a clue of the presence of agglomeration economies), they may also signal strong preferences for living in a city and/or embody agglomeration benefits. Rising levels of inequality in their nation, for example, have led wealthier humans to be willing to pay more and more to live in low-crime, high-amenity areas with significant socioeconomic vitality. High prices may then mirror the status-symbol component of living in an exclusive zone (real estate agents *docent*). Intriguingly, a similar logic seems to hold not only "horizontally" but even "vertically," with people willing to spend more to live higher up. Examining choices regarding the location within commercial skyscrapers, economists have documented that high productivity (richer) companies locate higher up, with less productive offices lower down [52].

This said, wages and housing prices could be low even in a successful city. It may happen when, for instance, supply is overabundant, so that housing prices are low. This is why a look at population dynamics may be informative on the level of success of a city. From the increase in its population one may infer, ceteris paribus, the liking for a particular city, which, in turn, indicates the existence of agglomeration economies in that city. By the same token, a shrinking population size may signal the reduction in the city's appeal. As Chicago boomed in the late nineteenth century, humans flooded in from New England and upstate New York. California's gold rush drew ambitious individuals in the 1840s; the recent Silicon Valley rush draws them again. Of course, these dynamics are not a peculiarity of the humans living in the USA. Many countries have witnessed similar developments.

Just as with families and firms, in sum, there are several reasons to explain why cities exist. But there is another common question featuring human aggregations such as families, firms, and cities. All these clusters naturally raise the question of why they are so persistent in modern economic systems. Regarding the city, the point is that the innovating activism of humans and the resulting endless innovations flow (cf. Chap. 5) are reducing transportation costs and, hence, agglomeration economies. So, why do the cities continue to be a prominent presence in technologically advanced economic systems? Economists' reasoning puts forward that, though technological progress makes transporting goods less and less costly, moving people across spaces may remain costly. A. Marshall [53] pointed out that factors hampering the spatial mobility of people are labor market pooling, sharing of specialized inputs, and knowledge spillovers (recall that transportation costs involve goods, people, and ideas).

Pooling refers to the fact that if many firms are located close to cities, then workers living in cities are better off because it is typically easier for workers to change jobs than cities. Specialized human capital may then trigger labor market pooling because specialized workers cannot readily take up another task. The empirical findings of our travel guides confirm. Jobs characterized by unique knowledge base exhibit higher levels of geographic concentration than do occupations with generic knowledge requirements [54]. Regarding knowledge spillovers, in general terms, they function via exchange of ideas among individuals. The rationale is that the higher the concentration of employees of the same specialization on a territory, the higher the possibility of idea exchange that can further lead to innovative solutions. The spillover effect emerges because our own knowledge builds on things that we learn from people around us. By looking at our neighbors, we may reduce the costs and uncertainty of exploring unfamiliar knowledge domains. Exchanging ideas leads to brand-new ideas; even brainstorming may be productive. Hence, knowledge spillovers spur agglomeration economies, and this contrasts with lower transportation costs.

Our guides have more to say about the persistence of cities in innovative economic systems. They have been studying whether the success—hence the persistence—of cities depends on whether the city is an idea-producing place rather than a good-producing place. To this end, they have compared the disparate development of a number of US cities over the last few decades, stressing the larger success of idea-producing cities like New York and Boston with respect to that recorded by good-producing cities like Cleveland and Detroit [55]. These outcomes point out that cities and technological progress can fruitfully coexist.

Finally, cities are still with us because they have the advantage of the critical mass. As easily seen, the quality and quantity of goods and services available in a big city is much larger with respect to what one can find in a village. Only large cities can afford to sustain the demand for niche products and/or the high fixed costs of cultural activities such as theater, museums, and the like. As long as humans appreciate these activities, there are reasons sustaining the urban solution. P. Krugman's job [56] helps to shed light on this stage of the excursion underlining the dynamic aspect of the matter. In order to realize scale economies while minimizing transportation costs, he argues, manufacturing firms tend to locate in the region with larger demand. But the location of demand itself depends on the distribution of manufacturing. That is, urban concentration is beneficial because the population benefits from the greater variety of goods produced (forward linkages) and may be sustained because a larger population in turn generates greater demand for those goods (backward linkages).

Thus, the economic system tends to become structurally differentiated into an industrialized core (urban sector) and an agricultural periphery.

But this is only part of the story. In a kind of relay, the intertwined development of agriculture and manufacturing triggers the birth of a third sector, one which makes urbanization even more diffuse. More evolved economic systems need banks, professional services such as engineering and medicine, government services, wholesale, and retail trade. The development of the service economy reinforces urbanization—the larger the service sector, the longer the cities exist. Basically, the argument is the following. Service industries can be roughly defined as sectors that require person-to-person delivery. While this may be too strong a view, there is no doubt that services involve a lot more face-to-face contacts than manufacturing. Gyms, retail establishments, cinemas, and the like require visits by clients, and we would expect them to be located near their customers. As mentioned in the Prologue, then, reputation may be a remarkable capital for shopkeepers, and it may be decisive for their choice to maintain their historical urban location. As a result, the city is a strong attractor for services which, in turn, sustain the urban solution.

Now that we know that the city is a useful—hence permanent—element of modern economic systems, the visit goes on, inspecting the behavioral aspects of living together inside this kind of human aggregation. Just as the decision to live in the savannah spurred the socioeconomic Big Bang, indeed the urban leap implies a drastic change for humans. This transition toward the new normal raises interesting questions for our tour. One may ask whether urbanization impinges on the behavioral attitude of humans and, if affirmative, if it pushes toward smaller or greater individualism. Perhaps due to the complexity of human beings, of economic systems, and of their intersections, the short answer is that so far there is no unanimous position with regard to these questions. What is sure is that no matter whether they live in cities or in villages, humans maintain their compound behavioral nature.

As usual, a look at some contrasting views may be fruitful for our trip's aim. R. Redfield [57] compared various kinds of human clusters in Mexico, ranging from small villages to the Yucatán capital (Mérida). He found a positive gradient between the size of the aggregation and degree of individualism of the inhabitants. In the isolated little rural village of Tusik, the economy was mainly based on agriculture and social relations were lifelong and highly interdependent—the institution of divorce did not exist, and married couples were permanently connected to their spouse's kin. In the city of Mérida, the economic system was more heterogeneous and more modern, involving structures such as commercial and manufacturing activities. With respect to Tusik, in Mérida, kin relations were less enduring as divorces and marital desertion were relatively common. Redfield posited that the different scene is induced by the greater struggle for individual status, sense of insecurity, and inner conflicts among residents in the more disperse and disorganized urban network. P.M. Greenfield [58] has then claimed that living in a city increases wealth and education, which offers greater opportunities to choose more things to do and more goods to buy, driving humans to behave more independently. Another possible explanation behind the positive correlation between urbanization and individualism is that living in economically developed aggregations such as our modern cities reduces the need to rely on a group for survival, allowing humans to prioritize individual goals and personal freedom.

While the view that concentrating in urban locations leads to greater individualism has valid justifications, the opposite standpoint sounds reasonable as well, which may explain the extant mixed evidence. When spread in large and flat spaces, for instance, humans live and work virtually alone, which may amplify their attitude toward individualism. On the other hand, it is likely that an individualistic person prefers to live not so close to others. Evidence from the USA supports this view. Individualism is diffuse in the wide and sparsely populated open spaces of the Mountain West (Arizona, Colorado, Montana, etc.) and Great Plains (Kansas, Nebraska, North and South Dakota, etc.) [59].

The positive correlation "larger city–greater individualism" is also at odds with the fact that citizens are immersed in dense social networks whereby establishing and maintaining ties is paramount (cf. Section 3.1). Just as humans must use wisely their compound behavioral nature when performing their trading businesses and forecasting others, then they must behave carefully when aggregating. We have seen aggregating issues even in special clusters as families. Very few humans like to be ostracized; many like to be popular. In modern cities proximity and social dynamism may lead humans to behave prosocially, to mix independence and interdependence in such a way as to live a peaceful existence. Every day urban Sapiens necessarily have some interaction with dozens of strangers. They use public transport, must participate in condo meetings, must share car-parking, must queue, and so on. In dense human networks such as modern cities, cooperation becomes more a necessity than a virtue. If being a citizen means to live close to each other and, hence, to have greater necessity to behave prosocially, it also enhances the skills needed to behave in that way because urban humans learn from each other. Cities spillover technological knowledge and ideas but also sociality. That citizens may be driven toward greater sociability also emerges from the evidence that becoming urban has more positive effects on cognition than on physical abilities such as physical strength [60]. In the present context, this finding can be interpreted as follows. Since unity is strength, in going ahead with our evolution as social animals, we need larger behavioral adaptability and lesser necessity to count on our body. To some extent it looks like domestication, which leads animals to have smaller overall size and strength but greater dependence upon their owner.

All of this suggests that cities may be schools for both social life and individualism. As in any human business, a balance between individualism and sociability seems necessary for urban life. If citizens must hold off excessive individualism and if sociability is important, dependence upon others must not lead to a lifestyle so soft and protected as to eliminate the essential fighting spirit that humans take from their individualism.

The final aspect of the city that I want to explore is the phenomenon of segregation. It enters into the picture considering that cities, just as other kinds of social clusters, show at the same time characteristics of differentiation and integration. Segregation is intended here as clustering and isolation among communities within the same city. Points in case are Little Italy, Chinatown, and Spanish Harlem. This is not negative per se, since it can sustain cultural and social capital within a community. Most humans populating those neighborhoods have the same foreign nationality and street names, churches, stores, eateries, music, and other manifestations of their culture and national identity. But segregation can have a detrimental effect on cities' social stability, may augment social fragmentation, and can hamper social mobility. I have already noticed that, usually, humans aggregate such that the greater the sense of belonging to a group, the weaker the relations between groups. In cities, moreover, the presence of vulnerable groups and deprived districts may instigate attribution effects and stigmatization as well as set in motion neighborhood effects, whereby segregated areas are involved in a downward spiral leading to ever-greater segregation and social exclusion. As emphasized by our guides, these neighborhoods typically suffer from multidimensional problems that reinforce each other [61]. There is also the possibility of intersections between segregation and individual preference for (possibly violent) political actions (such as demonstrations, marches, and riots). According to an empirical analysis referring to cities of the United States, in response to problems blacks show greater propensity toward political actions than whites of similar status who live in similar urban areas.[31] The reason for this greater propensity to protest to gain visibility on the part of blacks with respect to moving is their lower mobility because of segregation—if you cannot move away, you react.

The insights advanced by T. Schelling disclose further elements [62]. His model of segregation is an agent-based model that illustrates how individual incentives can lead collectively to segregation.[32] Suppose that each individual belongs to one of two groups (say, blacks and whites) and aims—has some incentive—to reside within a neighborhood where the fraction of peers (same color) is above a predefined tolerance threshold value. At the beginning, individuals are randomly assigned in the city. All those who are unhappy with their initial situation—i.e., that are above the threshold value—get up and move. This generates a chain of further movements. Assume that these adjustments converge to a stable equilibrium—i.e., a situation whereby everybody in the city is happy with her location so that there is no more incentive to move. Schelling shows that, although simple, this model posits two powerful basic messages. First, there is no need to have strongly intolerant citizens to end up with a segregated city. Even if each individual just wants a bit more than one-third of his neighbors to be its peer, segregation arises. Second, aggregate patterns occasionally are not useful for inferring about individual motives. Some

[31] Orbell J M and Uno T (1972). A Theory of Neighborhood Problem Solving: Political Action vs. Residential Mobility. American Political Science Review 66:471-489.

[32] In agent-based models (ABM) the economy consists of purposeful agents who interact in space and time and whose micro-level interactions create emergent patterns. ABM consist not of real people but of computational objects that interact according to rules. In a nutshell, they are artificial economic systems aimed to obtain positive (how systems work) and normative (how systems ought to work) hints on actual economic systems.

unexpected phenomena might emerge that are socially unsatisfactory and that most individuals did not want. Quite the opposite of the invisible hand mechanism.

Urban communities, as observed, are still alive and kicking. But there are other kinds of communities that deserve a stop on our tour. By and large, a community can be defined as individuals sharing a common location or people united by their common interests, symbols, norms, social groups, or nationalities. Community, thus, is a very human way to group—only humans may wrap up in an abstraction. Think about communities such as the European community, the Jewish community, or the scientific community. Virtual communities show then that innovating contributes to this kind of human clustering, too.

Among the many possible excursions, in this passage I want to look at how a community of humans can successfully arrange behaviors and institutions when facing a peculiar economic good. In particular, I am referring to the communities studied by E. Ostrom [63, 64], who, accordingly, will be our guide in the current tour stop. In her numerous field studies, Ostrom has extensively examined how communities succeed or fail at managing special goods and resources such as grazing land, forests, and irrigation waters. Let us call the Sapiens gathered in these communities "Ostromians." The particular objects that they have to manage are known in economics as common-pool resources or common property resources (CPRs). As Ostrom put it, "CPRs are sufficiently large that it is difficult, but not impossible, to define recognized users and exclude other users altogether. Further, each person's use of such resources subtracts benefits that others might enjoy [65]." CPRs thus involve a well-defined community of users who share an exhaustible (scarce) resource that is hardly excludable. Remember that a good is excludable if the owner can exercise private property rights and can prevent others from consuming her good. CPRs are thus different from private goods and the difficulty in achieving excludability is critical for the governance of the CPRs. In Chap. 2, we saw that the invisible hand of the market can efficiently manage easily excludable private goods (although under some conditions, cf. also Chap. 6). The problem with CPRs is that coordination via the market may suffer from problems of congestion, overuse, pollution, and potential destruction. As we shall see, Ostrom has shown that when facing CPRs, fallible, norm-adopting humans operating in complex and uncertain economic systems are nonetheless able to arrange working institutional answers to manage behavioral issues.

To better appreciate Ostrom's findings, I introduce the social dilemma first presented by W.F. Lloyd and subsequently made famous under the label of "Tragedy of the Commons" by T. Harding [66, 67]. The tragedy may be sketched as follows: the commons belongs to *us*, but it is ultimately consumed by *me*. Imagine several cattle herders sharing a common parcel of land, the commons, on which they are each entitled to let their cows graze. Assume that all herders have one cow each on the pasture and everybody gains 100$. Call this the cooperative situation. Suppose now that a herder can put another cow on the pasture. He will gain something less than 200$, since putting another cow on the pasture causes some costs. These costs may be due, for example, to the fact that each cow can now eat less grass because there are more cows on the same pasture, and, hence, each cow produces less milk.

Thus, the extra costs are shared by all. However, the non-cooperative herder gains a bit less than 200$, whereas all others gain slightly less than 100$ because they only carry the cost of the additional animal with no benefit. Under the assumption that all the herders behave in the same selfish and myopic way, everyone will add a cow and the problem arises. Free individual choices lead to the desertification of the pasture and, accordingly, to a 0$ gain for everyone. The tragedy may then be thought of as a prisoner's dilemma played by a community of players. Otherwise stated, Hardin theorized that CPRs have the deadly combination of being exhaustible and non-excludable which, coupled with myopic selfish behavior, lead humans toward tragedies.

Against this framework, Ostrom has stressed that the real problem with the commons does not lie in the nature of the CPR but in the behavior of humans and its management. The crux is that, as North put it, humans are able to devise constraints that shape human interactions. Contrary to Hardin's predictions, in fact, Ostrom was able to find empirical evidence that the tragedy is not the only possible outcome of the game if humans tackle it wisely. Specifically, she has uncovered that when natural resources are jointly used by their users, in time, rules are established for how these are to be cared for and used in a way that is both economically and ecologically sustainable. I have already noticed that what was predicted by a one-shot prisoners' dilemma cannot be the typical outcome of human interactions.

Management of CPRs can find an ally in the human natural instinct to cooperate for surviving—by facing dilemmas, humans may change the payoffs via institutions in order to improve the social outcome. A classic example of the skill of Ostromians to manage CPRs was found by Ostrom in a Swiss village where the tragedy could easily crop up. Swiss farmers had private plots for crops but shared a communal meadow to graze their cows. Ostrom discovered that problems with overgrazing were solved by a common agreement among villagers dating as back as 1517. The "economy-environment" balancing rule is that no farmer is allowed to graze more cows than she can look after during the wintertime. One of the reasons behind this kind of happy solution might be cultural. Swiss were contextually farmers—hence tendentially collectivists—and breeders—hence tendentially individualistic: a mixed solution could be expected. A last remark on this happy ending is that if the market mechanism is possibly an unintended outcome, the agreement achieved long ago in Swiss mountains surely followed deliberate actions. Of course, Ostrom's findings are not limited to the Swiss. She has documented more than 1000 similar effective examples of "governing the commons" in her research all around the globe. Ostrom's conclusions are thus robust and held in many contexts.

A general message stemming from Ostrom's works is that humans are able to avoid the tragedy of the commons without requiring top-down regulation—working as a community, Ostromians are able to coordinate their actions using self-governance. The emergence of this kind of bottom-up solution is important because, since CPRs have no private owner, they cannot be managed via the conventional governmental protection of property rights. Indeed, the lack of institutional alternatives might be another reason behind the self-governance solution. Otherwise stated, Ostrom has showed that in communities populated by Ostromians, there is (institutional) life between the private sector (the individuals) and public sector (the state).

Because of humans' behavioral multiplicity and insatiability, however, Ostromians' lives hardly proceed straightforwardly. If Ostrom has claimed that Harding's conclusion is true under very specific and limited conditions,[33] working self-governance of the commons requires the credible neutralization of opportunistic behaviors. Not a trivial task, indeed. Ostrom has summarized eight core institutional design principles for humans to live together, better, and longer in CPR communities. Basically, these principles' requirements are to ensure that local communities get equal rights and responsibilities for managing the resources, which sounds logical.

But these requirements, on the one hand, only address specific human aggregations and, on the other hand, are not as loose as one would wish. Encompassing some of them into what we have seen in our journey highlights valuable intersections. First, there must be proportional equivalence of costs and benefits; members have to earn their benefits and not just appropriate them. Fairness is not a trivial element in human interactions. Second, there must be collective choice arrangements; most members affected by the rules must be allowed to participate in modifying the rules. In this respect, recall that *most* is the discriminant word used by Acemoglu and Robertson to define inclusive nationwide institutions. Thus, wide, active participation seems to be a key factor when managing human affairs. Third, monitoring must be internal and sanctions adequate. Disruptive self-serving behaviors must be detected and punished by the participants themselves, without the intervention of external authorities. To maintain community cohesion, then, sanctions must be fast in punishing severe cases but also, as C. Beccaria claimed centuries ago [68], graduated and fair with a proportionality between the severity of violations and sanctions. This brings to mind the sense of "fair justice" that we met when exploring the tit-for-tat strategy (cf. Chap. 1).

Two final considerations on the Ostromians' solution are the following. The first is a behavioral-institutional element recursively resurfacing in our journey and, hence, worth stressing—humans are often both the problem (opportunism) and the solution (self-governance). The second refers to whether the Ostromians' solution pops up spontaneously in the community or rather needs some deus ex machina in order to kick-start and/or to be sustained. Indeed, rarely are communities totally free to manage their commons. Formally or not, public actors, international donors, etc., are often afforded a role in the governance of the commons. For instance, there is evidence that the social capital stemming from the presence of non-governmental organizations may be behind the development of communities [69].

The last excursion on humans' way to aggregate is devoted to the nation. It could be hardly different—the nation is among the most critical instances of human

[33]These conditions include that participants are fully anonymous, have no property rights to the resource system, cannot communicate, and lack long-term interests in the CPRs.

clusters. But before moving forward, a preliminary question must be addressed. Even if modern states are usually labeled nation-state because all the nationalities living in one state stand integrated into one nation, nation and state are different social entities. To proceed in our sojourn with due clarity seems thus advisable to say something on these two concepts. Basically, the state is typically understood as a political organization featured by four strictly necessary elements—population, territory, government, and sovereignty.[34] The nation, instead, is a group of people living together because of social, cultural, psychological, and political ties. These definitions submit that, unlike the state, the nation deals more with common people than with elites—as Louis XIV famously stated, instead, *l'etat c'est moi*. According to these views, then, there are states where more nationalities live—e.g., Belgium and Canada—as well as there are nations with no state—e.g., Kurds and Rohingya. I note this also to stress that common roots (culture, language, etc.) may be a stronger social glue with respect to common location; symbolic language seems to lead humans to group around abstractions more than material elements. As compressed as it is, this discussion nonetheless highlights that nations relate to institutions and behavior of ordinary people more than states. Nations thus turn out to be social aggregations that are closer to what we are examining in this chapter. Accordingly, I will concentrate on them (I will return to the state, although as meant here, in the Epilogue).

The nation is the umpteenth example of human device often taken for granted. But the nation as we know is a relatively recent institution. A little bit of etymology allows us a glimpse into the historical depth of the junctures relating to some of the human aggregations that we have explored so far. The Latin word *natio* (which may be by and large translated with birth) was typically understood to be a group of humans who belonged together because they were born in the same city and, hence, shared common language and customs. According to Cicero, specifically, the *natio* was a community of foreigners who lived in the large cities, busy ports, and colonial settlements of the Roman empire. These communities were then called *nationes*. In light of the typical socioeconomic dynamics encountered during our tour, it is understandable that in ancient times, humans did not have the same concept of nation as we have today. Those humans could not understand terms such as nationalism, and they did not consider themselves part of a nation. For millennia humans rarely left their village and knew little of what happened outside of it. Over time nations have been forming in several, sometimes unconsciously and fortuitus, ways. For example, England emerged as a result of geographic isolation, Australia as a result of emigration, and modern Turkey from the collapse of the Ottoman Empire. Differentiated by their heterogeneous genesis, a common thread of nations is to satisfy humans' wants. Accordingly, to prosper, nations need a working economic system. Formal institutions (one for all the Constitution), informal institutions, and social capital must be well-established and well-functioning in nations. As repeatedly stressed in this tour, all these ingredients are important for the *Four*.

[34] As said, in our tour the state is intended eminently as government and independent authorities.

A celebrated book by R. Putnam and associates [70] permits us to trek through the function of political institutions and social capital in fostering the prosperity of nations. Exploiting a sort of natural experiment, Putnam studied the effect of social capital in spurring the evident socioeconomic gap separating the more advanced northern regions of Italy from those of the south. In 1970, Italy's central government established fifteen new regional governments that, ideally, would have worked very similarly throughout the nation. The outcome of this natural experiment was instead that all of the southern regions showed the worst performances from both the economic and the institutional standpoints.[35] Putnam argued that the gap was due to the smaller social capital accumulated over time by the South. In fact, Putnam collected evidence of territorial differences in civic engagement like community organizational life, engagement in public affairs, community voluntarism and informal sociability, and on other possible measures of social capital.

If worse performances were ascribed to smaller social capital, Putnam attributed this to historical developments. During the Middle Age, his argument goes, the civic life of people living in the south was strictly regulated through a feudal, bureaucratic, and autocratic network whereby individual autonomy was repressed as soon as it appeared. In the North, instead, individuals were much freer to exert the *Four*. Northern people exploited their freedom to develop horizontal associations, self-government, and social capital.[36] This favorable environment led them to promote good governance by shifting preferences from particularistic interests to more group-oriented concerns. Using Putnam's terms, by developing the "I" into the "we" in the North, citizens regarded the public domain as more than a battleground for pursuing personal interests. At this point one may recall the famous J.F. Kennedy's phrase "Ask not what your country can do for you—ask what you can do for your country." Transmitted—hence maintained—generation after generation, these opposite evolutions may explain the heterogeneity in the socioeconomic conditions that can still characterize Italy today.

In view of the current stop, but also for the tour as a whole, several insights can be drawn from Putnam's analysis. First, his research points out that similar formal institutions may function differently in different social environments and that the contribution of social capital in economic systems may be significant. An intriguing point, then, is that greater individual behavioral autonomy may be associated with both larger social capital and better individual as well collective outcomes. In addition, his research reminds us that multiple equilibria are far from being rare in humans' affairs. These multiple equilibria can show up in economic systems when patterns exhibit strong positive feedbacks. Regarding the Italian case, in particular, humans living in geographical proximity may have been induced to behave uniformly, for good or ill, because everyone expected that others made the same

[35] In ruling on civil cases, for example, the judicial system is slower in the South; despite the legal system, the career path for judges and human capital are not so dissimilar.

[36] Evidence on the positive correlation between horizontal associations and social capital referring to different nations and periods is reported, among others.

move—dissimilar behavior may be very costly within social groups. This is how social norms and conventions crystallize and drive behavior within human groups. Since different groups may be attracted toward different behaviors, then informal institutions may differentiate the behavior among different clusters and this may lead toward disparate performances. Finally, the Italian experiment suggests an answer to the question of where the nationwide social capital comes from. In particular, Putnam's study allows us to stress that besides culture and nature, historical patterns may have an impact even if, of course, history itself is a blend of factors. That past events and dynamics matter are confirmed by other historical examples. For instance, while international wars have steered nations to develop both better-quality institutional settings and larger social capital, civil wars have piloted nations in the opposite direction (multiple equilibria once again). Basically, a nation historically surrounded by several potential enemies must have well-functioning bureaucracies and strong widespread social cohesion to fund warfare and to maintain national security. To survive, it has no other option. Though with due distinction, one is tempted to connect this logic to that which steered early Sapiens to cooperate in the dangerous savannah.

References

1. Solow R M (1999) Notes on social capital and economic performance. In Dasgupta P and Serageldin I (eds), Social Capital: A Multifaceted Perspective, Washington, DC: The World Bank, pp. 6–9.
2. Greif A and Tabellini G (2017) The Clan and the Corporation: Sustaining Cooperation in China and Europe. Journal of Comparative Economics 45(1): 1-35.
3. Alesina A and Giuliano P (2011) Family Ties and Political Participation. Journal of the European Economic Association 9(5): 817-839.
4. Becker G (1991) A Treatise on the Family. New York: Simon & Schuster.
5. Hess G D (2004) Marriage and Consumption Insurance: What's Love Got to Do with It? Journal of Political Economy, 112: 290–318.
6. OECD (2011), Divided we stand–why inequality keeps rising, Paris.
7. Lundberg S (1985) The Added Worker Effect. Journal of Labor Economics 3(1): 11-37.
8. Hess G D (2004) op. cit.
9. Kotlikoff L J and Spivak A (1981) The Family as an Incomplete Annuities Market. Journal of Political Economy 89:372–91.
10. Kaplan R M and Kronick R G (2006) Marital status and longevity in the United States population. Journal of Epidemiology & Community Health. 60(9): 760–765.
11. Apps P F and Rees R (1988) Taxation and the Household. Journal of Public Economics, 35: 355–69.
12. Jeanfreau M et al (2018) Financial Infidelity in Couple Relationships. Journal of Financial Therapy, 9, 1, 2.
13. Rubinstein A (1982) Perfect Equilibria in a Bargaining Model. Econometrica 50: 97-110.
14. Nelson J A (2015) Are women really more risk-averse than men? Journal of Economic Surveys, 29(3): 566-585.
15. Browning M, Chiappori P, and Weiss Y (2014) Economics of the Family. Cambridge: Cambridge University Press.
16. Bridgman B et al (2012) Accounting for Household Production in the National Accounts, 1965–2010. *Survey of Current Business* 92: 23–36.

17. Kanal D and Kornegay J T (2019) Accounting for Household Production in the National Accounts: An Update. *Survey of Current Business* 99(6).
18. Greenwood J et al (2014) Marry Your Like: Assortative Mating and Income Inequality. American Economic Review 104(5):348-53.
19. Stevenson B (2007) The Impact of Divorce Laws on Marriage of Specific Capital. Journal of Labor Economics 25(1): 75-94.
20. Ginther D K and Pollak R A (2004) Family Structure and Children's Educational Outcomes: Blended Families, Stylized Facts, and Descriptive Regressions. Demography, 41(4):671-96.
21. Duncan G J and Brooks-Gunn J (1997) Consequences of Growing Up Poor. New York: Russell Sage Foundation.
22. Goldin C and Katz L F (2002) The power of the pill: Oral contraceptives and women's career and marriage decisions. Journal of Political Economy 110(4): 730-770.
23. Wilson W J (1987) The Truly Disadvantaged: The Inner City, the Underclass, and Public Policy. Chicago, IL: University of Chicago Press.
24. [illegible] The [illegible] of gender gaps in industrialized countries [illegible] (1):405 434.
25. Pollak R A (1985) A Transaction Cost Approach to Families and Households. Journal of Economic Literature 23: 581–608.
26. Harrison L E and Huntington S P (2001) Culture Matters: How Values Shape Human Progress. Basic Books.
27. Sacerdote B (2011) Nature and Nurture Effects On Children's Outcomes: What Have We Learned From Studies of Twins And Adoptees? In Handbook of Social Economics Benhabib J, Bisin A, and Jackson M O North Holland Vol. 1, pages 1-30.
28. Bisin A, Topa G, and Verdier T (2004) Religious intermarriage and socialization in the United States. Journal of Political Economy 112:615–64.
29. Fryer R G Jr (2007) Guess Who's Been Coming to Dinner? Trends in Interracial Marriage over the 20th Century. Journal of Economic Perspectives 21(2):71–90.
30. Bisin A and Verdier T (2000) Beyond the melting pot: cultural transmission, marriage and the evolution of ethnic and religious traits. Quarterly Journal of Economics 115:955–88.
31. Coase R H (1937) The Nature of the Firm. *Economica* 4:386–405.
32. Chandler A D (1977) The Visible Hand: The Managerial Revolution in American Business. Cambridge, MA: Harvard University Press.
33. North D C and Wallis J J (1986) Measuring the Transaction Sector in the American Economy, 1870–1970. NBER Chapter in Long-Term Factors in American Economic Growth, pages 95–162, NBER, Inc. In fact, their data refer to the share of the "transaction sector" on total GNP but in our short tour it is not possible to give details.
34. Williamson O E (1980) The organization of work: A comparative institutional assessment. Journal of Economic Behavior and Organization 1: 5–38.
35. Williamson O E (1985) The Economic Institutions of Capitalism. New York: The Free Press.
36. Williamson O E (2002) The Theory of the Firm as Governance Structure: From Choice to Contract. Journal of Economic Perspectives 16(3):171–195.
37. Smith A (1776) op. cit.
38. Shapiro C, and Stiglitz J (1984). Equilibrium unemployment as a worker discipline device. American Economic Review 74: 433–444.
39. Weiss A (1985). Absenteeism and wages. Economics Letters 19: 277–279.
40. Fehr E, Kirchsteiger G, and Riedl A (1993) Does Fairness Prevent Market Clearing? An Experimental Investigation. Quarterly Journal of Economics, 108:437–59.
41. Fehr E, Gachter S, and Kirchsteiger G (1996) Reciprocal Fairness and Noncompensating Wage Differentials. Journal of Institutional and Theoretical Economics 152:608–40.
42. Fehr E, Gaechter S, and Kirschsteiger G (1997) Reciprocity as a Contract Enforcement Device. Experimental Evidence. Econometrica 65(4):833–860.
43. Akerlof G (1982) "Labor Contracts as Partial Gift Exchange. Quarterly Journal of Economics 97(4):543–569.

44. Bowles S (2016) The Moral Economy: Why Good Incentives are No Substitute for Good Citizens. Yale University Press.
45. Berle A A and Means G C (1933) The modern corporation and private property. New York: Macmillan.
46. OECD (2013), Judicial Performance and its Determinants. A Cross-Country Perspective, OECD Economic Policy Papers.
47. Knight F H (1921) Risk, Uncertainty and Profit. New York: Houghton Mifflin.
48. United Nations Secretariat, 2008, Population Division, Department of Economic and Social Affairs, 21–23 January, [UN/POP/EGM-URB/2008/01].
49. Glaeser E L (2011) Triumph of the City: How Our Greatest Invention Makes Us Richer, Smarter, Greener, Healthier, and Happier. The Penguin Press.
50. Echeverri-Carroll E L and Ayala S G (2011) Urban Wages: Does City Size Matter? Urban Studies, 48(2): 253-271.
51. Ahrend R et al (2014) What Makes Cities More Productive? Evidence on the Role of Urban Governance from Five OECD Countries. OECD Regional Development Working Papers, No. 2014/05, OECD Publishing, Paris.
52. Crocker H L, Rosenthal S S, and Strange W C (2018) The vertical city: Rent gradients, spatial structure, and agglomeration economies. Journal of Urban Economics 106:101-122.
53. Marshall A (1920) op. cit.
54. Overman H G and Puga D (2010) Labor Pooling as a Source of Agglomeration: An Empirical Investigation. NBER Chapters in: Agglomeration Economics, pages 133-150 National Bureau of Economic Research, Inc.
55. Glaeser E L and Ponzetto G A A (2007) Did the Death of Distance Hurt Detroit and Help New York? NBER Working Paper No. 13710.
56. Krugman P (1991) Increasing Returns and Economic Geography, Journal of Political Economy, 99 (3):483–99.
57. Redfield P (1941) The folk culture of Yucatán. University of Chicago Press.
58. Greenfield P M (2016) Social change, cultural evolution, and human development. Current Opinion in Psychology 8:84–92
59. Shortridge J R (1993). The Great Plains. In Cayton M K, Gorn E J, and Williams P V (eds.), Encyclopedia of American social history Vol. 2 pp. 1001-1015. New York: Scribner
60. Bacolod M B, Blum S, and Strange W C (2009) Skills in the city. Journal of Urban Economics, 65 (2):136-153
61. Fainstein N and Fainstein S (2018) The spatial dimension of poverty, in: Western Capitalism in Transition: Global Processes, Local Challenges. Andreotti A et al (eds) Manchester University Press, p. 239-255
62. Schelling T C (1978) Micromotives and Macrobehavior. New York, WW Norton.
63. Ostrom E (1990) Governing the Commons: The Evolution of Institutions for Collective Action. Cambridge: Cambridge University Press.
64. Ostrom E (1993) Design Principles in Long-Enduring Irrigation Institutions. Water Resources Research 29 (7):1907-1912.
65. Ostrom E (2008) The Challenge of Common-Pool Resources. Environment 50 (4): 9-20.
66. Lloyd F W (1833) Two Lectures on Population. Population and Development Review 6 (3): 473–496.
67. Hardin G (1968) The Tragedy of the commons. Science 162:1243–1248.
68. Beccaria C (1764) Dei delitti e delle pene. (Eng. trans. Farrer J A (1880), Crimes and Punishment, Chatto & Windus, Piccadilly, London).
69. Islam M R and Morgan W J (2012) Non-governmental organizations in Bangladesh: their contribution to social capital development and community empowerment. Community Development Journal 47 (3):369– 385.
70. Putnam R, Leonardi R, and Nanetti R (1993) Making Democracy Work. Princeton, NJ: Princeton University Press.

5 Innovating: Humans Are Ingenious Animals

5.1 Introduction

Humans are innovative animals. As evidence from biologists shows, the human being is not the only animal with this propensity. Chimpanzees use long sticks for capturing termites and ants. Crows drop stones in pitchers to raise the height of water inside. Groups of wild bottlenose dolphins have been observed while carrying marine sponges in their beaks to stir ocean-bottom sand and uncover prey [1]. As far as we know, it is even possible that our ancestors have copied some of these clever behaviors from other species. However, the innovating endeavors of humans are definitively unique. Rephrasing A. Smith, one might say that nobody ever saw a dog imagining, planning, and realizing a space lab. The uniqueness of our innovating disposition may stem from the unparalleled insatiability of humans and/or from our symbolic language. Abstractions, symbols, and ideas allow us to imagine, to figure out strategic visions; they permit the posing of questions such as "What if?" In addition, and importantly, language is critical in collective learning and cultural transmission, and both are key in making our innovating efforts so special. It permits our species to go faster than natural evolution would allow us. As I. Newton famously put it, we can stand on the shoulders of past giants to go further. This is even more so, as said, when we use the unifying language of mathematics.

It is easy to see the gains from innovating; most of us recognize the paramount role of innovating activities for both the individual well-being and systemwide performances. Those who innovate directly enjoy the fruits of their inventiveness. All others take advantage of the outcomes of these endeavors which assist them in having a better and longer life. Innovating is a crucial determinant of socioeconomic progress as well as an important support to help address global challenges such as climate change, sustainable development, and pandemics.

In general terms, the vast majority of people agree on the gains from innovating and, possibly, even on the dark side of these businesses (cf. Chap. 6). But the placidity of the situation breaks down when facing a basic question—what does innovating specifically consist of? In answering this question, the convergence of

M. Bovi, *Why and How Humans Trade, Predict, Aggregate, and Innovate*, Contributions to Economics, https://doi.org/10.1007/978-3-030-93885-7_5

opinions shrinks, calling for some definitions under the usual definitory *caveat*. In our tour, innovating is made up by innovations, innovation diffusion, inventions, and technical progress. Let us proceed step by step. According to the OECD, innovation is "a new or improved product or process (or combination thereof) that differs significantly from the unit's previous products or processes and that has been made available to potential users (product) or brought into use by the unit (process) [2]. In essence, an innovation should be something new, implemented, and ameliorative. In fact, not all innovations are completely brand new. If the innovation is based on products and processes that were already in use in other contexts (countries, regions, sectors, markets, firms, etc.), then our guides talk about innovation diffusion. Only through diffusion do innovations actually spread from their very first implementation and can have a significant economic impact. Implementation, instead, is more crucial and leads to distinguishing innovation from invention. According to J.A. Schumpeter [3], who many believe is the founding father of the economics of innovation, invention is a step before innovation, and it can be seen as a novel idea, sketch, or model for a new or improved product, process, or system. For the purposes of this tour stop, innovation is invention put into practice and both are "innovating."

The main difference between these efforts emerges, considering that working under laboratory conditions is different from working under commercial conditions. The title of a paper is rather suggestive about that: "3000 raw ideas equal 1 commercial success" [4]. Though distinct, of course, inventing and innovating are related activities. The typical situation is one whereby innovators (e.g., entrepreneurs, businesspeople, and venture capitalists) take advantage of the inventors' geniality, and the latter need the innovators' skill in financing, organizing, and marketing. H. Ford was a revolutionary innovator whose unappeasable aim was to offer "the best possible goods at the lowest possible price." The crux here is that in his innovative push toward the democratization of novel ideas, Ford exploited the invention "car." A more recent example is Apple, where S. Jobs' entrepreneurial ability generated value from S. Wozniak's ideas. In the context of this tour, Jobs' trading and aggregating activities put in place Wozniak's creativity, and their innovating efforts have made humans' lives better and perhaps even longer. If innovation is invention put into practice, then inventions are sped up by implemented technology in a sort of endless spiral. Consider the boosting effect on inventions of increasingly powerful computational or measurement tools.

Lastly, some hints on how ameliorative innovations are can be drawn by introducing the notion of technical change/progress. Following again the OECD glossary, technology can be described as the currently known ways of converting resources into outputs. Therefore, a technological *change* is a new technology that enables us to do something quicker, faster, or more precisely.

Sometimes, the outcome of innovating as meant here is so ameliorative to be path-breaking. Think about the discovery of bronze, the compass, penicillin, the light bulb, and the cell phone, which all have irreversibly and radically transformed humans' lives. Sometimes its products are "general purpose" in the sense that they are widely used across the whole economy, as in the cases of steam engines, electricity, computers, and semiconductor chips. The first steam engines, for example, were used in factories, which enabled mass production and also revolutionized transport with the railways. The recent news about the shortage of chips then stresses how diffuse these components are in several industries. But most outcomes of the activity we are currently exploring are neither so revolutionary nor critical and, luckily, it is not necessary to be a genius to make humans' lives longer, easier, and nicer.

Many innovations come from small changes, such as the use of existing things in a different way. Peanuts were known even before the late 1800, when J.H. Kellogg patented his process for making peanut butter (in fact, Ancient Aztecs were the first to crush peanuts into a paste). The Berbers in North Africa already used argan oil, but they did not use it as an ingredient in the cosmetic industry, as we do today. More recently, Dyson vacuum cleaner applied existing industrial cyclone technologies.

According to our guides, during the year 1982, over 85% of the innovations they identified from a comprehensive review of over 100 trade journals were modest improvements to existing products [5]. Economists have also found evidence that in the first 40 years of the twentieth century, general-purpose technologies contributed only 38% of US total factor productivity growth (to be defined below) [6]. All told, regardless of the size of its impact, innovating is an immanent activity in the human world.

Besides their own interlinks, inventions, innovations, diffusion, and technological change also have big bidirectional connections with the economic system. For example, Marxist theory suggests that changes in modes of production can lead to changing the type of economic system. Innovating indeed shapes our economic systems—how we produce, how we work and do business, how we trade, how we distribute goods and services, how we consume them, and how we communicate and relate to each other. But all that does not come easy. Before any endeavor is successful, there are often multiple attempts and efforts at it. Innovating proceeds through trial and error.

Apart from the intrinsic difficulty of innovating, there are other reasons that might hamper innovating or slow it down. These reasons, which again stress the connections of innovating and systems, include economic factors (e.g., high costs or lack of demand), enterprise factors (such as lack of skilled personnel or knowledge), and legal factors (regulations, tax rules, etc.). In Sect. 5.4, we shall see that rules of the game, such as intellectual property rights, impinge on innovating endeavors. Even brilliant and potentially path-breaking ideas languished for centuries before becoming really useful for the human race. Instances of inventions that become innovations with huge lags are the wheel (available since the Neolithic), Leonardo da Vinci's airplane, and the Gutenberg printing press. It may be for technological reasons, as shown by, for example, the lack of an adequate engine for the Leonardo's airplane. But it may also be that inventions are not implemented for socioeconomic reasons. A trend-breaking invention may meet strong societal resistance as it conflicts with the prevailing socio-technical regime that incumbent actors, combined with strong social networks, want to maintain. When we explore Schumpeter's insights on innovating, we shall see that innovating embodies creation but also destruction (cf. Sect. 5.3). As already observed, lastly, any commodity that cannot be sold at a profitable price will not be produced—ideas need markets to become innovations, and many do not do the leap. To stress the concept, the history of the Post-it offers a nice example. In 1977, 3M launched post-its but nobody bought them. Two years later 3M gave away the product and success materialized.

There is nothing new in all that, it is yet another example of the complex way in which behaviors and systems interact when humans perform the *Four*. It is also not a new concept—and one that is shared by all of the *Four*—that failures and difficulties have never prevented humans from creating and exploring despite the complexity and uncertainty they face. For good or ill, humans' ever-growing wants are bullet-proof and make us stubbornly stronger than any ambiguity, difficulty, and defeat that we encounter. Rather, humans often reuse failure's experience in unpredictable and fruitful ways. In addition, besides being supported by the natural predispositions of humans, since the socioeconomic Big Bang, all of the *Four* have been fueled by a variety of drivers.

Regarding innovating, in the next section, I will show the variety of its drivers, as well evidence of the dramatic transformation of humans' lives in recent times coupled with an evaluation of the knotty issue of how to quantify the role of innovating activities in these developments. The visit then will continue with the Schumpeter's view on the key role of entrepreneurs and their innovating efforts in affecting capitalist systems. In the last part of this trek, we shall inspect the delicate combination of innovating activities and property right protection. All that once again points out that innovating, just as the other businesses we are traveling through, is a social process whereby behaviors, institutions, and economic systems are essential ingredients.

5.2 Innovating: Importance, Sources, Measurement

In 1930, Keynes expressed great optimism for the economic future of the Western world [7]. He imagined that thanks to innovating, by 2030 the standard of living would be dramatically higher and that humans, liberated from basic wants, would work no more than fifteen hours a week, devoting the rest of their time to leisure and culture. This constituted an abrupt U-turn with respect to the view famously expressed by T.R. Malthus in 1798 [8]. According to the so-called Malthusian trap, in the long run, economic systems could only record a stagnant economic and demographic growth because excess population (N) due to GDP growth stops this latter because of shortage in the food supply. This trap implies the impossibility of sustained labor productivity growth as measured by the increase of the GDP/N ratio. Evidence is at odds with both views.

Unlike what was claimed by Malthus, macroeconomic data referring to Western countries over the last two centuries record large and diffuse improvements in humans' well-being, however not as large as Keynes predicted. Malthus' predictive error was to underrate the unflagging alacrity and insatiability of humans and, as far as our tour across the *Four* is concerned, to understate the importance of an inclusive view when addressing human affairs. I shall return to the Malthusian trap in the Epilogue. Regarding Keynes' forecasts, using the economists' logic, the presence of longer-than-expected working hours may be due to an income effect larger than the substitution effect—workers may have preferred to exploit their higher productivity not to work less and enjoy more leisure (the substitution effect), but to gain more (the income effect).[1] Be it as it may, that is yet another example of the difficulty of forecasting economic objects, even for exceptionally gifted humans such as Malthus and Keynes. In complex, uncertain human affairs, taking a temperate view is typically a good choice.

A look at empirical data gives a practical sense of the developments that we are journeying through. Working hours for the average worker have decreased dramatically over the last 150 years [9]. In 1870, workers in most of OECD countries worked more than 3000 hours annually (i.e., more than 60 hours each week for 50 weeks per year). Today, hours have been roughly cut in half. Less time spent working is then associated with greater purchasing power. Even more importantly, the enhancement involves not only less work and larger quantities but also better quality. These days we can choose between a spectrum of goods and services that our grandfathers could not even imagine. A bird's-eye view at the evolution of spending in the USA is illustrative of the qualitative and quantitative developments witnessed by many developed countries. According to the Bureau of Labor Statistics, in 1900 about 80% of the family budget was spent on food, clothing, and housing. One hundred years later, these basic expenditures accounted for just 50%. Besides enjoying the improved quality of food, clothing, and housing that is available now, American households are now free to spend half of their income on less basic needs, or, equivalently, to spend half of their income on their wants. They can send their children to summer camps and contribute to pension funds; they can purchase televisions, computers, vacation homes, boats, and other items which were unknown and undreamed of a century ago. The world's richest people in the early 1900s could not enjoy the colors of an HD flat TV or the utility of having a smartphone in the pockets as, thanks to the democratization of ideas, most of us can.

The improvement of quality also involves work conditions. Most of our jobs today are less risky and less physically hard than in the past. Even the products of human effort are less subjected to randomness these days. For instance, agricultural production is now less subject to uncontrolled factors such as weather and livestock diseases.

---

[1] As a matter of fact, this is particularly true for the USA. According to OECD data, for instance, in 2015 the French workers worked an average of 1482 hours a year, while American workers worked about 1790; moreover, while US workers receive about 15 days off per year their European counterparts get about 30. Besides different preferences, these choices may be due to the larger welfare state in European countries. The so-called "Great Resignation" which is occurring in the United States (people quit their jobs due to the ongoing coronavirus pandemic, which led many to re-think where, how, and why to work) might eventually make more similar European and US workers.

This great transformation naturally raises two questions in the present stop—How do we quantify the role of innovating in all that? How do ideas, innovations, and technical progress emerge? Regarding any of the human affairs under scrutiny, the answer is complex and involves disparate dimensions. In the following, I offer some indications on the second question. Though they are presented separately, they often overlap.

Fortune is immanent in human life and hence in economic systems. Thus, it comes not as a surprise that the output of innovating occasionally stems from serendipity. It is possible, for example, that Palestinian metalworkers produced brass about 3500 years ago—accidentally—in the attempt to make bronze. At that time the difference between zinc and tin was not so clear, and while brass is an alloy of copper and zinc, bronze is an alloy of copper and tin [10]. A more recent example is the microwave oven that was accidentally invented by P. Spencer [11]. He was experimenting with a magnetron, an electronic tube that emitted extremely short (or micro) radio waves, the type of tube used to generate radar waves. While running a test, Spencer noted that a candy bar in his shirt pocket melted even though he had not felt heat. He speculated that the effect might be useful in cooking. Finally, Viagra—the famous little blue pill—initially was intended to treat hypertension and angina pectoris.

It also happens that bad intentions accidentally bring out good outcomes. Innovating affairs triggered by deplorable ends, such as wars (or defense, to use a more positive term), often produce socially useful technical progress. Two points in case are canned food and the Internet. In Europe, the eighteenth century was a period of wars that highlighted the need for a stable source of food for soldiers and sailors who were spread far and wide. In the late 1700, the French Directory decided to offer a 12,000-franc prize for a breakthrough in the preservation of food. After some years of tests, N. Appert won the prize with his idea of food packed in tin cans. In the late 1960s, the first workable prototype of the Internet was born with the creation of the Advanced Research Projects Agency Network (ARPANET). ARPANET allowed multiple computers to communicate on a single network, and it was originally funded by the US Department of Defense.

In the endless innovating efforts of humans, there are even instances of opposite developments, whereby constructive inventions ended up with potentially destructive innovations. Originally developed by the Taoists for medicinal purposes, for example, gunpowder was first used for warfare in the ninth century CE.

Finally, there are cases whereby specific goals lead to the invention of general-purpose technologies. A point in case is the steam engine, which was first invented to pump water from mines; its very first name was "miners' friend." At this advanced stage of the journey the traveler should not be stunned by the recurrent presence of luck and unintended outcomes in human affairs.

If its outcome may occasionally emerge more or less accidentally, innovating may be more focused. Specifically, it may be motivated by the fragility of human nature in the face of an uncertain, wild, and dangerous environment. "Necessity is the mother of invention," an old saying goes. Since the socioeconomic Big Bang, humans have wanted to capture prey that is faster and stronger than they are; to combat natural events, such as calamities, famine, and plagues; and to overcome their natural physical limits, such as the inability to fly or to see microscopic objects or objects far away from them. Visible outcomes of these ancestral pushes to innovating vary from primeval canoes to space shuttles, from stone tips to high-powered rifles, from magnifying glasses to atomic force microscopes, and from prehistoric remedies to robotic surgery.

Monetary incentives are another strong stimulus behind innovating activities. While the rationale is straightforward to see, for our tour's aim, it can be put as follows. To the extent that a good is scarce (hence it is a socially valued, priced, economic good), then there is a monetary incentive to produce it more efficiently and/or to find a close substitute for it. The oil crises of the 1970s, for example, triggered innovating activities toward energy-saving stuffs. As Schumpeter fairly specified [12], monetary incentives are in fact linked to the *expectation* of an increase in the individual income or profits. The logic is similar to that outlined by Samuelson in his two generations model explored in Sect. 3.2. As we shall see, indeed, innovations by definition modify the existing system; thus, innovators have to be forward-looking to figure out what kind of market they will face once their innovation has been put in place. Since monetary incentives are expected, moreover, they must be discounted by the risk related to the innovating endeavor—the higher the risk, the lower the incentive. This is why, as already mentioned, businessmen are typically less risk averse than the other humans. We shall return to these themes in the next sections.

While gains from innovating may derive from material elements, there is more than that. Mirroring their innate compound behavioral nature and wide-ranging preferences (cf. Chap. 2), humans also respond to nonpecuniary incentives. These include imagination and independence, love of change, altruism, persistence in spite of failure, and a thirst for science and knowledge. In the abstract of his/her seminal white paper [13], the anonymous inventor of the Bitcoin claimed that (s)he wants to help people trading on the Internet by offering them "a purely peer-to-peer version of electronic cash (that) would allow online payments to be sent directly from one party to another without going through a financial institution." Due to the anonymity, it is hard to establish what part of her/his multifaceted behavioral nature was behind this move. Thanks to our guides, however, we have some indication on nonpecuniary incentives in other fields. Evidence about new biomedical Ph.D.'s consideration of job offers from drug firms shows that job candidates accepted a 25% salary cut for jobs that allowed them to do more academic-like science [14]. As stated by J. Rawls, humans desire "meaningful work," not just good pay. As argued by economics, the 25% salary cut may be thought of as quantifying how much these scientists are willing to pay for their "taste for science."

This excursion is brief but nonetheless enough to give the impression that innovating efforts and outcomes depend on a mixture of natural predisposition and necessities, selfishness and altruism, and material and immaterial incentives. It offers an unsurprising takeaway in our trip whereby all of the *Four* share similar varieties of pushes.

How do behavioral and institutional factors enter the scene? The picture is mixed. If individualism brings to mind pecuniary incentives behind innovating, an economic system mostly populated by individualistic people may give social status rewards to people who stand out, being a special nonpecuniary incentive for innovation that is separate from material incentive. The story told about conspicuous consumption advises that the status symbol may be among the drivers of humans' actions. Widespread collectivism, instead, may promote a wait-and-see approach instead of creative activity and may encourage conformity as well as discourage individuals from standing out.

Though this suggests that while some aspects of individualism can act as a stronger booster than collectivism when innovating, others may be detrimental. For instance, opportunism and myopic individualism hamper fruitful exchanges of ideas, shrinking innovating businesses. In this respect, collectivism could make innovating easier thanks to, for example, brainstorming or idea sharing. Shifting the focus on the contrast between inclusive and extractive institutions (cf. Chap. 1), many economists agree that inclusive institutions allow individuals to exploit the gains related to the *Four*. Regarding innovating, specifically, financial market reforms, favorable taxation of investments in R&D, etc., all are policies that, if well implemented, ease humans in the pursuit of their innovating endeavors. In addition, open-minded political institutions usually go hand in hand with open-minded inventors and innovators which, according to our guides, is just what happened before the Industrial Revolution [15]. By the same token, many economists agree that extractive institutions inhibit innovating. That said, one may ask whether inclusive institutions are strictly necessary for an economy to be innovative, but in this case, a clear-cut answer is hard to find. It suffices here to observe that some economists have remarked that extractive institutions may operate in innovative economic systems as in the case of Nazi Germany [16] and that there is evidence showing that intellectual property rights may not support, and may even discourage, innovating (cf. Section 5.3).

Other insights can be drawn by relating individual behavior to culture.[2] Think about beliefs. Just as the discouraged worker gives up (cf. Sect. 5.2), individuals regarding success as due to luck or to uncontrollable external events are more likely to have a passive, resigned, and lazy attitude toward economic activities. Conversely, if people believe that economic success is related to their deliberate choices, they are more likely to be innovative. On that, our guides have found evidence that different cultural traditions may significantly entail different propensities to innovate or take risks [17, 18]. Elaborating on these topics, economists have specifically studied the connections between innovating and religiosity. Their empirical analyses show that more-religious individuals seem to have greater social capital, which is clearly good for exerting the *Four* [19]. But data also display that greater religiosity

[2] As outlined in the Prologue, informal institutions are conventions, customs, social norms, etc.; culture involves the values, beliefs, preferences, and norms prevalent among members of a particular human aggregation.

is strongly negatively correlated with indicators of openness to innovation, such as attitudes toward science, new versus old ideas, risk propensity, and so on [20]. Though correlation does not imply causation, one cannot exclude that religion acts as the opium of the people's innovating activity. Not to mention that over history, scientific discoveries have been contrasted in the name of religion. Just to name one, G. Galileo's discovery that the Earth revolves around the sun was deemed heretical by the Catholic Church.

The wandering has finally arrived at the first question—How do we quantify the role of innovating in the above-described dramatic improvement in life standards? Just as with institutions and social capital, alas, the effects of innovating endeavors are hard to measure. Their ultimate impact deals with the satisfaction of human wants at either the individual or collective level, something that is difficult to quantify. As said, for example, Putnam tried to gain insights on social capital by comparing North and South Italy before and after a critical institutional move. To learn about capitalist versus communist systems, similarly, it is usual to contrast macroeconomic indicators (e.g., real per capita GDP), exploiting conditional "ceteris paribus" conditions such as North vs South Korea or East vs West Germany.[3]

Regarding innovating, studies of specific innovations cannot provide a bottom-line metric of the importance of innovating in the process of establishing an economy-wide living standard. To this end, a common strategy suggested by our guides is to look at aggregate productivity, which is defined and measured as the ratio of output to input (e.g., GDP/N). Simply put, the rationale is that there is a virtual chain linking the notions under scrutiny: "innovating-productivity growth-economic growth-better living standards." Abstracting for a moment from the link innovating-productivity growth, the sequence tells that productivity growth generates economic growth because, by definition, higher productivity means that the same quantity of input generates a greater output. Higher productivity and economic growth, then, bring vast benefits for the economic system's prosperity. More output stimulates business profitability, which enables firms to invest and hire more employees and/or to pay higher wages. More productive individuals can afford to choose to work less for the same income or to have a higher income working for the same amount of time. Higher productivity and economic growth, finally, have profound implications for the progress in living standards because they help to sustain private and public debts, social protection systems, and the ability of macroeconomic policies to respond to future shocks.

We will now learn how to establish a quantitative link between innovating and productivity growth. To this end, I introduce the notion of total factor productivity

[3]To be sure, our guides have been elaborating several ways to test their theories. Econometrics is branch of economics that applies statistical methods to economic data in order to give empirical content to economic relationships. Also, in our tour I talk about behavioral economics which is eminently based on experiments performed in labs. Economists have then developed randomized controlled trials, that is experiments that apply an intervention to only a randomly selected portion of the target population, so that you can compare the effects of the intervention against a group that did not receive it.

(TFP), which, for reasons to be made clear below, is also known as the *Solow residual* (from R. Solow [21], the economist who proposed the method). Insights from our guides on what this residual is and how it can be reckoned clarify what sense and to what extent TFP growth is a metric for the searched quantitative link. Growth in TFP is measured as a residual—that part of GDP growth that cannot be explained by changes in labor and capital inputs (assuming that these are the only inputs used). In simple terms, therefore, if labor and capital inputs remained unchanged between two periods, any changes in output would reflect changes in TFP. Typically, computations are made in per worker terms (GDP per capita, GDP/N, if one simplifies the connections of population and employment such that N also indicates labor input, likewise for K/N). Thus, growth in TFP is measured as a residual of the GDP/N growth. This choice is also due to the fact that, with respect to K, labor is thought of as being more dependent on sociocultural demographic factors (such as fertility rate, women's participation in the labor market, and immigration) and can be adjusted more slowly than K (the stock of capital is modified by investments and depreciation).

The connection of TFP with innovating can be explained as follows. Labor productivity (GDP/N) growth comes from three primary sources: increases in capital (i.e., investments), improvements in the quality of labor, and TFP. Capital accumulation fuels labor productivity growth through investments in machines, tools, computers, factories, infrastructure, and other items that are used to produce more output. The second source comes from greater human capital, which in turn derives from the education and training levels of the workers who operate these machines, tools, computers, etc. Rapid increases in capital accumulation and/or educational attainment can increase the GDP/N of an economy and hence potentially improve living standards. But and this is the point, over the long run, simply adding physical and/or human capital cannot drive productivity growth forever. This is so because, in economists' jargon, inputs show diminishing returns—other things being unaltered, additional input results in smaller and smaller increases in output. Equipping a worker with one computer is likely to increase his/her productivity but giving him/her two, then three, four, etc. computers is likely to increase his/her productivity less and less. By the same token, continuing to add new workers, firms hire less and less productive workers. A practical example of diminishing returns comes from the Soviet Union's central planners. In the 1950s, they invested, actually over invested,[4] in physical capital to increase output, but they were successful only for a limited time.

[4]Recall that, although under some conditions, decentralized capitalistic systems are Pareto efficient in allocating resources and that the price system contains key information on what and how much to produce and invest. A central planner, instead, has not the luxury of all this information deriving from free and deliberate individuals' choices. Over investment, then, implies under consumption because the former needs saving which is not-consumed income or postponed consumption. Since decreasing returns reduced future output, the soviets were forced to under consume both today and tomorrow—they did not eat neither the egg nor the chicken.

Since augmenting one input at time or expanding one input more than others faces diminishing returns, one may think to increase output, augmenting all inputs proportionally. This can be done via replication—GDP growth can take place without innovating through the simple replication of existing technologies. Trivially, if you are able to produce a chair with one worker and one kilogram of wood, then you can produce two chairs with two workers and two kilos of wood. In economic jargon, the production function[5] exhibits constant return to scale—if you want to n-tuple the output, you have to n-tuple the inputs. In sum, you can do more. But if the technology does not improve, you cannot do better. With only replication and without innovating, output per capita will increase only in proportion to the capital/labor ratio (K/N). A sustained exponential economic growth must therefore stem from something else, an unobservable factor that this approach reckons as TFP growth.

Changes in TFP reflect the effects of change factors such as management practices, brand names, organizational change, general knowledge, network effects, and the like. These changes are then associated with innovating. To figure out the effect of TFP on production, imagine taking the same workers and the same equipment and then changing the way those workers use that equipment to get more output—"changing the way" is innovating as supposedly quantified by TFP. Another way to relate the TFP growth to innovating—as well as to point out that both are distinct from investments—is to observe that while the accumulation of capital is linked to factors such as depreciation and propensity to save (because savings finance investment), TFP growth is connected to the accumulation of knowledge and the propensity to innovate.

Data for the USA confirm the connection of TFP growth and innovating undertakings. In the first half of the twentieth century, TFP growth contributed to labor productivity growth by about 65% [22]. This was chiefly due to innovating in sectors such as mechanical and electrical engineering, transport, and chemical. Since the 1970s, however, there has been a downward trend, and most economic growth in the USA was due to the replication of existing technologies through investment and expansion of the labor force. This slowdown in TFP growth was especially dramatic in the years 1973–1989, leading Solow to claim that in those years, paradoxically, "you see the computer age everywhere but in the productivity statistics."[6]

An exception to the productivity slowdown that started in the 1970s was the period 1995–2004 whereby TFP growth was relatively higher than the previous and subsequent years, although always smaller than that recorded in the interwar years. This was mainly due to the information and communication technology (ICT) and the diffusion of the Internet [23], occasionally referred to as the "new economy." By and large, the picture is similar for all advanced countries, which over the last

[5]The production function indicates the technologically maximum amount of output possible from an input bundle.

[6]This comment, known as the Solow Paradox, appears in R. Solow's 1987 New York Times Book Review article.

10 years have recorded a lagging TFP growth constantly below the rates witnessed in any of the decades of the last 60 years [24]. This suggests that factors that may have slowed innovating are likely to be equally structural and common in developed economies. Although the evidence is mixed, economists have indicated that among the factors slowing down the TFP growth are the aging workforce (e.g., the innovating impulse may drop with age [25]) and the waning ICT boom.

An extreme standpoint maintains that humans have simply exhausted the pool of easily attained innovations. But our journey suggests that it seems to be too extreme a view—for two reasons featuring all of the *Four*, and one specific to the activity that we are currently traveling across. The two general motives, repeatedly emphasized in our tour, are that in addressing human affairs, it is often better to take a moderated position, and second, that humans never give up. Regarding innovating, specifically, our guides [26] claim that innovations and the productivity growth that they generate do not always coincide (the Solow paradox *docet*). As a consequence, relatively newer techniques (such as blockchain and quantum computing) and new materials (such as graphene) may well shift forward the production frontier in the next few years. Remember that we are exploring the sequence "innovating-productivity growth-economic growth-better living standards" that, of course, takes time to complete and it is barely linear. Moreover, the computation of the TFP statistic has several drawbacks as a measure of innovation at the aggregate level—the benefits of the generalization come at the cost of accuracy.

As usual, no model fits all. A brief excursion to examine some of the drawbacks of the TFP statistic allows us to visit other sections of the innovating affairs of humans. To start with, many agree that the real per capita GDP omits or unsatisfactorily accounts for important contributors that make humans' standard of living better and their lives longer—income inequality, good health, environmental quality, etc. Of course, this is a problem of users rather than of the tool. S. Kuznets, the father of GDP, almost a century ago already warned that GDP was aimed to be nothing more than a measure of the value of goods and services produced. As any other model/approach, then, the TFP procedure is based on several assumptions; therefore, its reliability depends on the realism of these assumptions. Among them, all productivity growth must be due to technical change only. But the Solow residual may also contain other non-technology factors (e.g., scale and cyclical effects, variations in capacity utilization), a better institutional setting, and measurement errors. The basic point is that as a computational residual that sweeps in many things, TFP is "a measure of our ignorance," as M. Abramovitz warned about 70 years ago [27]. Last but not least, the dichotomy "innovating activities—accumulation of capital" is not so clear-cut in reality. There are types of investments that enhance innovating. Consider R&D expenditures. They are a form of capital formation, but as an investment aimed at producing new knowledge, R&D expenditures are also the source of much technical change.

This is not to say that TFP cannot be fruitfully used to account for the innovating activity. As usual, a temperate position is preferable. Though still far from being perfect, the above reported evidence is based on refined versions of the original

Solow procedure so that it conveys sufficiently valid information on the innovating undertakings of humans. Just as any other human being, economists never give up.

To recap, innovating as intended in our tour takes various forms, is typically small although but occasionally game-changing, has disparate sources, is driven by various types of incentives, is supported/hampered by inclusive/ exclusive institutions, and is affected by culture. Further, its output is more or less intentional. Despite it has also a dark side (cf. Chap. 6) innovating significantly improves both economic systems and individuals' lives, even by transforming some uncertainty in risk. With this in mind, our journey through innovating goes on with two more stopovers. In the first, we will delve into the behavior of a certain group of Sapiens (the "Schumpeterians") and the creative destruction derived from their innovating activity. In the last section, we will inquire into a formal institution particularly related to innovating—intellectual property rights.

5.3 Innovating, Entrepreneurs, and Economic Systems: The Schumpeter's view

The innovating job of humans strongly affects economic systems. In the previous section, I recalled the predictions of Keynes and Malthus, both suggesting how innovating—or the lack thereof—can dramatically improve—or freeze—the life inside economic systems. Schumpeter's view on that is in a sense even more radical. He posited that innovations would have led to change the very nature of the economic system—from capitalism to communism. Though his prediction turned out to be wrong, Schumpeter's perspective on innovating, human behavior, and economic systems is so brilliant and visionary to deserve an adequate stop in our tour.

Along with Engels and Marx, Schumpeter studied in depth the dynamic links between innovating activities and economic systems, sharing the view that innovations are key in making capitalism a dynamic system. The first two authors, probably earlier than any other economists, assigned to innovating the driving force in economic evolutions [28]—"the bourgeoisie cannot exist without constantly revolutionizing the means of production." Stressing the contribution of innovations in economic systems, Schumpeter imagined capitalism as an intrinsically dynamic system whereby changes were simply indomitable. In his words (p. 158): [29] "Whereas a stationary feudal economy would still be a feudal economy, and a stationary socialist economy would still be a socialist economy, stationary capitalism is a contradiction in terms."

Evidently, Schumpeter's view on capitalism was very different from that studied by economists such as Walras. As observed, Walras approached the market system as an intrinsically stable system with a natural tendency to rest in equilibrium (cf. Chap. 1). This point is realized via the Walras's pricing rule that ends with the equalization of supply and demand for every good so as to stop any further moves because both consumers and firms are in a Pareto optimum condition. Actually, Walras ruled out innovation from his models by assuming that the technological level is constant. In terms of our trip, Walras addressed capitalistic systems as places whereby trading was more important than innovating. Schumpeter referred to this state of affairs as a "circular flow" whereby, as said, the choices of economic agents follow a static course and take place on the basis of past experiences. The problem with the static circular flow is that it was more similar to the Malthusian world rather than to the tumultuous growth that many Western countries were recording in the nineteenth century.

Tackling this issue, the great intuition of Schumpeter was to address capitalistic systems as places whereby the most important human business is innovating. By assuming that capitalistic economies do not merely grow but evolve, he was able to explain the exponential growth of Western countries. Basically, the circular flow cannot sustain an exponential growth because, without innovations, this kind of system can grow only via replication. This limit is not binding when humans are thought of as being able to do both more *and* better. In terms of our tour, a circular flow economy is not sufficient for the insatiability and proactivity of humans—their wants increase over time, and humans never stop trying to fulfill them. Specifically, Schumpeter posited that if humans do not innovate, then (apart from shocks and erratic elements) their (Walrasian) economic system will tend to return to its steady state, a situation in which at different dates the same kinds, quantities, and qualities of goods are being produced and sold at the same costs and prices [12]. But if someone innovates—i.e., if someone produces new better stuff and/or implement new better process—then the system must adapt to the new improved economic situation (with new natural prices, new goods/processes, new markets/firms, etc.).[7] In his brilliant vision, Schumpeter correctly highlighted that the concept of decreasing returns only applies to given production functions (which mirror the current state of technology) and generally stationary conditions.

Thus, innovating is key for capitalistic systems and for the humans living therein. But why should someone innovate in the system? I have already said that Schumpeter talked about expected profits, but I should expand. In Schumpeter's world, humans innovate because of the possibility to gain above-normal profit, (i.e., the Schumpeterian rent).[8] Normal profit is the minimum reward that the entrepreneur requires in order to keep her supplying her enterprise; it just covers the entrepreneurial opportunity cost—a firm making normal profits will remain in the industry because a different choice would be costlier. Normal[9] profits (i.e., zero extra profits) are what firms earn in perfectly competitive markets, at least in the long run. The logic is that, on the one hand, the existence of extra profits in a market attracts new entrants, which increases supply, shrinks prices, and eventually, although not

[7]Recall that private property, private firms, and markets are key ingredients of capitalism.

[8]A quantitative idea of the Schumpeterian rent can be found in the pharmaceutical sector. Pfizer's patent for Viagra expired in June 2013, allowing other pharmaceutical companies to produce their own version. In the UK, prices were quickly reduced from £21.27 for a pack to £1.45.

[9]In perfectly competitive systems, there is a tendency toward normal, or long run, or equilibrium values (cf. Chap. 1).

instantaneously, exhausts the extra profits. On the other hand, firms operating with below-normal profits quickly quit the market because revenues are smaller than opportunity costs.

In Schumpeter's world, the extra profit is the premium put upon successful innovation, and it implies some market power. The extra profit, however, is temporary by nature—the Schumpeterian rent will vanish in the subsequent processes of competition and adaptation. In fact, Schumpeter distinguished between two forms of competition. The first is the standard "Walrasian" price competition that places emphasis on decentralized markets as the means to eliminate the less efficient firms and to lower prices for a given set of goods and technologies. The second is the technological competition that eliminates the less innovative firms and rewards the more innovative ones. Schumpeter claimed that (dynamic) technological competition is more crucial than (static) price competition in understanding the essence of capitalism. Technological competition and the push to do different things and/or to use improved techniques allow the system to grow to a greater extent with respect to what is possible by simply replicating under the constraint of the existing processes of production. In a nutshell, there is a sequence whereby technological competition sparks innovation and innovation boosts economic growth and life standards.

But with humans' lives, trade-offs abound. The previous sequence leads capitalism to proceed through an incessant process of "creative destruction" [30]. Over time, the argument goes, technological progress has been improving the productivity of the system and has been creating millions of new jobs and goods. But the shift of the technological frontier has also been destroying several industries and jobs as some production and skills have become redundant.[10] For example, digitalization destroyed analog devices (e.g., CD vs vinyl records), and the giant of analog photography, Kodak, retreated into bankruptcy in 2012. Then the rise of the iPhone eclipsed the Blackberry. Today, typewriters and telegraph operators are virtually extinct. The creation of automobiles has destroyed most carriage drivers' jobs, Uber has eliminated many taxi drivers' jobs, and both could be dramatically affected by the arrival of self-driving cars. To the extent that general-purpose technology, such as artificial intelligence, substitutes rather than complements humans' businesses, it may have a huge disruptive force.

Against this energetic backdrop, a further question naturally arises—who constantly fuels the unstoppable innovating flow in the market system? Or, equivalently, who are the players of the technological competition? The short answer given by Schumpeter is the "entrepreneurs," whom I will label "Schumpeterians." They are agent of change; they introduce a new good or a new method of production, open a new market, or discover a new source of supply. Since Schumpeterians upset the conventional way of doing things, and remembering that "changing the way" is innovating as quantified by TFP, one may then say that Schumpeterians enhance TFP. Schumpeterians are special Sapiens. In Schumpeter's words (p. 132) [31] "To act with confidence beyond the range of familiar beacons and to overcome that

[10] We shall sojourn in the dark side of the *Four* in the Epilogue.

[social] resistance requires aptitudes that are present only in a small fraction of the population and that define the entrepreneurial type (. . .)." When successful, Schumpeterians elicit widespread imitation. Innovating as intended here goes on through an inherently dynamic process which starts from (mostly minute) ideas, proceeds with (mostly minute) innovation, and carries on with imitation, diffusion, and accumulation.

It should not come as a surprise that Schumpeterians are different behavioral entities with respect to Walrasians. Within Walrasian (neoclassical) firms, the Walrasians acting as entrepreneurs are basically "static re-producers" who look at their predecessors rather than at new markets/technologies. Schumpeterians are much more proactive. As observed, they are agents of change who increase TFP. They are highly innovative people, extracting value mainly from ideas rather than from capital. Schumpeterians are also distinct from rentiers, people who built their fortune exploiting extractive institutions and gaining monopolistic rents. Operating under technological competition, Schumpeterians are innovators incessantly pushed to innovate in order to generate Schumpeterian rents. It should be clear that these temporary extra profits are much more socioeconomically desirable and bearable than profits stemming from (typically enduring) monopolistic rents (cf. the next section and Chap. 6). If economic inequality only reflects disparate efforts and innate human capital, then it stimulates the most gifted and proactive individuals to attempt innovating exercises, and it should be acceptable for the others who benefit from the fruits of the Schumpeterians' job.

Schumpeterians are also distinct from Keynesians. As noted, Schumpeterians are humans driven by expected profits that they are able to calculate rationally. Perceptibly, therefore, the contribution of animal spirits in Schumpeterians' decisions turns out to be smaller with respect to Keynesians. Unsurprisingly, the behavior of these two sorts of humans has different impacts on the market system. If the immanent innovating push of Schumpeterians is the unstoppable engine of economic growth, immanent uncertainty can lead the animal spirits of Keynesians to generate long-lasting crises. Finally, Schumpeterians are different from inventors and imitators.[11] According to Schumpeter, innovators are not necessarily inventors, although there are exceptions (a point in case is T.A. Edison). More specifically, in the Schumpeter's system, inventors and scientists are eminently *deus-ex-machina*, that is, humans operating outside the system whose ideas are tirelessly put in place (endogenized, if you like) by the Schumpeterians. The imitators, then, diffuse the innovation in a spiral that is permanently at work in capitalism, making this latter an inherently evolutive system. According to Schumpeter, schematically, innovating proceeds as follows: new technologies are (exogenously) incessantly invented by scientists, ceaselessly implemented by Schumpeterians, and unstoppably diffused by imitators.

---

[11] Recall that in our tour "innovating" includes invention, innovation, diffusion, and technological progress.

At the beginning of this stop, I mentioned that Schumpeter predicted that innovations would have led to change the very nature of economic system—from capitalism to communism. Before investigating why Schumpeter made this forecast and why his prediction turned out to be wrong, I have to stress two points (definitions matter). First, Schumpeter was not against capitalism, which he defined as an economic system based on private property.[12] If he argued that there was no future for capitalism, he did so with a sense of resignation and regretfully asserted: "Can capitalism survive? No. I do not think it can. [. . .] If a doctor predicts that his patient will die presently, this does not mean that he desires it" [31]. Second, Schumpeter used the terms socialism and communism as synonyms (p. 168): "I have not separately defined collectivism or communism. [. . .]. If I had to use them I should make them synonymous with socialism" [32]. According to him, capitalism would have flown into socialism/communism whereby the vast majority, if not all, economic decisions were controlled by public authorities instead of by private agents. Why did Schumpeter predict such an unhappy destiny for capitalism? In light of our journey, I sketch that part of Schumpeter's arguments which highlight the intersections of innovating and aggregating by looking at the predicted involution of Schumpeterians and their innovative firms that, in turn, marks the ties of behaviors and systems.

The key position attributed by Schumpeter to entrepreneurs turns out to be a point of both strength and weakness of capitalism. The rationale is that as Schumpeterians innovate, production expands, and capitalism evolves, new forms of economic organization emerge. These new forms of human aggregations tend to be large firms—they have more incentive to innovate because they can sell innovative products to more people and reap greater rewards more quickly.[13] But the larger the firms, the greater the level of bureaucracy inside them. Schumpeter described largest-scale business as a (p. 113) [31] "petrified form of capitalism in which restrictive practices, price rigidities, exclusive attention to the conservation of existing capital values, and so on are naturally inherent." This transformation of firms does not pertain only to size and monopolistic bureaucratic methods, but also to the life inside them. During the process, Schumpeterians are increasingly substituted by depersonalized R&D departments, and the functions of ownership and control gradually tend to diverge more and more. Once routinizing becomes more important than innovating, Schumpeterians tend to become—and to behave as—salaried employees. Eventually the firms' owners become totally detached from key capitalistic institutions such as private ownership. In Schumpeter's words (pages 141 and 156) [31] "From the logic of his position he acquires something of the psychology of the salaried employee working in a bureaucratic organization. Whether a stockholder or not, his will to fight and to hold on is not and cannot be

[12]"Capitalism is that form of private property economy in which innovations are carried out by means of borrowed money."

[13]In fact, Schumpeter expressed this view in his 1942 book whereas in his 1911 (much more inspired) book he viewed small entrepreneurial ventures as the chief engine of innovations.

what it was with the man who knew ownership and its responsibilities in the fullblooded sense of those words. [...] the modern corporation, although the product of the capitalist process, socializes the bourgeois mind; it relentlessly narrows the scope of capitalist motivation; not only that, it will eventually kill its roots." Otherwise stated, Schumpeter theorized that the inexorably evolutionary path followed by capitalism would have changed the behavior of its key agents and the nature of its key producing units—the Schumpeterians and their enterprises—depleting its primary source of dynamism so as to necessarily mature in a different, less individual-based, economic system.

Interestingly, for our tour's aim, Schumpeter's idea about the dynamic path leading to the end of capitalism also involves another human aggregation, the family (p. 160) [31] "for the efficiency of the capitalist engine of production we need only recall that the family and the family home used to be the mainspring of the typically bourgeois kind of profit motive. [...] the man [...] works and saves primarily for wife and children. As soon as these fade out from the moral vision of the businessman, we have a different kind of homo oeconomicus." Once innovations lose those individual-level pushes related to entrepreneurship and family, then the market system embarks on the one-way road to self-destruction. Unlike Marx, Schumpeter forecasted the disappearance of capitalism and the emergence of socialism through involution rather than revolution, through implosion rather than explosion. In view of our journey, it is also worth noting that in this process toward a command economy, both Marx and Schumpeter figured out a significant change in the multifaceted behavioral nature of humans. Whereas Schumpeter forecasted the fading of the individualistic spirit of Schumpeterians, Marx posited that (p. 147) [33] "All human history is nothing but a continuous transformation of human nature."

Needless to say, our guides have worked hard on Schumpeter's path-breaking views. Among other considerations, economists have tried to explain why Schumpeter's forecast on the ineluctable transition of capitalism toward communism proved wrong.

A first predictive error deals with the vanishing of Schumpeterians in capitalistic systems. Schumpeter was wrong to imagine a depersonalized system whereby the individual does not count and what really counts is large enterprises; he underestimated the unstoppable proactivity of humans as well their innate share of individualism. To credit Schumpeter, until the 1960s, large corporations dominated the economic landscape. In his 1977 book, A. Chandler talked about "The Managerial Revolution in American Business," pointing out that these large firms were controlled by a hierarchy of salaried executives rather than owners. But a nontrivial number of humans dislike the routine (Ford's story *docet*). As Mandeville already warned in the early 1700s, humans have a (p. 196) [34] "violent Fondness for change, and greater Eagerness after Novelties."

Because of humans' equally innate and unstoppable spirit behind the *Four*, consumers ask for changes, firms must innovate, and markets evolve. This indomitable vitality stimulates a widespread entrepreneurial activity which keeps alive and kicking the Schumpeterians even in mature capitalism. According to the data compiled for the USA by the Kaufmann Foundation, for example, since 1996 (the earliest year available), the percentage of adults transitioning into entrepreneurship (the "new entrepreneurs") has kept stable at around 300 out of 100,000, with only minor small oscillations.[14] Our guides also affirm that high growth young firms are an especially significant contributor to job, output, and productivity growth [35]. It is hard to deny that innovating is at the heart of small firms such as startups and that these latter are not marginal in the innovating efforts implemented in modern market systems. Just to mention, startups have generated new industries such as xerography and cable television.

Innovating, then, is self-sustaining and preserves Schumpeterians in the sense that developments like the Internet and crowdfunding platforms support the ventures of innovative individuals. As can be read in the site innocentive.com, for instance, "InnoCentive's Open Innovation Marketplace connects organizations seeking solutions to important challenges they face with an unrivaled network of expert problem solvers—both experts from within your industry, but more importantly experts from outside of your industry that can offer diverse perspectives and fresh insight." Somewhat ironically, all of that is congruent with another prediction made by Schumpeter—humans will never stop innovating.

Economists [36] have then highlighted that Schumpeter did not ponder the possibility that centralized institutions might be incapable of putting into practice an effective management of the system. According to this strand of the literature, that is, Schumpeter mistakenly takes for granted that communism was more able than capitalism to assess and reward innovating. Quite the opposite, the logic goes, capitalism is more robust and flexible than command economies exactly in those dynamic environments featured by creative destruction because it is a more distributed network; that is, it does not depend on the behavior of few nodes. More or less spontaneously, the order of competitive markets decentralizes and disperses the task of producing new knowledge to an open class of as yet unknown entrepreneurs; it seeks to generate the broadest possible network of potential innovators. The crux is that economic systems are complex and uncertain. Thus, a frame whereby information flows bottom-up and individuals are free to follow incentives and preferences seems to be a better candidate than centralized top-down systems to manage efficiently that sort of environment. To reiterate, although far from being perfect and conditional to several conditions, the market system is an efficient coordinating tool whereas each economic unit is itself an information processor.

Apart from the resilience of Schumpeterians' attitudes in human behavior and the difficulty for the system of taking alternative routes, it must be recalled that capitalism as intended in our tour is a dynamic entity, as its components are. This standpoint suggests searching other insights on why capitalism survives by looking at peculiar evolutions of markets and firms that have been going on differently from what Schumpeter imagined.

---

[14] Data available at https://indicators.kauffman.org/indicator/rate-of-new-entrepreneurs

In Chap. 4, we have seen that innovating triggered the Service Revolution. This structural modification of the system has intensified the ties connecting customers and firms in such a way that in their social interactions, much attention is put on serving the consumer rather than transforming material goods and selling the resulting output. In functioning post-industrial capitalistic systems, the customer is a paramount figure, to not mention sovereign. The central element of the system is the human being rather than the product; maximizing customer satisfaction is not less crucial than optimizing production. Modern corporations are engaged in personalization and values based on loyalty program insights. As synthetized by the Amazon boss J. Bezos, customers are loyal until somebody else offers them a better service. Hence, modern businesses tend to be as personal as possible, and large firms have not evolved into Soviet Union-style production oriented planning bureaus. In a functioning market system, this happens not by chance but by necessity. Regardless of their size, if companies want to survive, they must foster lasting relationships with customers instead of ripping them off. According to survey data gathered in 2015 [37], half of companies innovate to satisfy customer needs. Amazon showed little profit for years but is thriving now because of this kind of long-run view.

Besides giving customers due regard, in several markets modern corporations must pay attention to their potential competitors as well. Competition is not necessarily killed by the presence of large corporations whose behavior and practices have some constraints. According to our guides, one of the reasons why even large firms must necessarily behave as proactively and carefully as they can is because they compete in contestable markets [38]. In these markets, competitive pressures from potential entrants exercise strong constraints on the behavior of incumbent suppliers. It should be clear, thus, that the lower the barriers to entry and exit, the more contestable the market. Otherwise stated, in a competitive market, efficiency is typically maintained by the presence of a great number of small units operating in it.

In contestable markets, the number and size of firms actually operating is not relevant for efficiency because the presence of potential entrants is sufficient to oblige incumbent firms to operate efficiently. Instances of contestable markets are electricity and gas suppliers, Internet service providers, and low-cost airlines. Ryanair, Vueling, and other innovative low-cost airlines were able to enter the market by operating from less central airports with relatively cheap landing slots. Likewise, competition from generics has been eroding the profits of the so-called big pharma industries [39]. All these are dynamic industries that have been making customers better off. Surely, then, the FAANG (Facebook, Amazon, Apple, Netflix, Google) are big corporations, but it is hard to think about the FAANG enterprises as the petrified entities imagined by Schumpeter. Moreover, the presence of firms such as the FAANG also suggests that if Schumpeterians have evolved, they are not extinct—the large internet companies have spawned hundreds of startups. Surely the FAANG raises problems of market power (cf. the next section and Chap. 6). For instance, there could be lock-in concerns that may hamper competition (it is easy for me to switch to a different social network, but how to coordinate with all of my friends to switch with me at the same time?). But these are different problems from those feared by Schumpeter and, however, they are treatable within capitalism as intended here. Moreover, even considering that Facebook is a giant in social networks; other smaller specialist companies such as LinkedIn, Twitter, and Pinterest also compete in this area. To not mention that if each FAANG company has its historical core competencies (for instance Amazon in shopping, Apple in mobile devices, etc.), there are several areas where these companies compete through pricing, product design, and innovative services. Just to mention, Apple, Amazon, Google, and Microsoft all provide operating systems. This competition keeps these firms dynamic and efficient, in the knowledge that if they slacken even briefly, they will be pushed out. Moreover, modern large firms face institutional constraints—in, well-functioning capitalist systems, the state must effectively prevent unfair, deceptive, and fraudulent business practices. For example, regulators may force incumbents to open up their infrastructure to potential entrants, or to share technology—as in the case of broadband operators being allowed to use British Telecom (BT Openreach) infrastructure (more on that in Epilogue).

All told, there are several reasons hampering the birth and the survival of Soviet-style enterprises in modern capitalism. A look at the annual list published by *Fortune* magazine reporting the 500 largest corporations in the USA may give an impression of the dynamism of the system. Comparing the first (1955) and the last (2021) list, there are only 52 companies that appear in both lists. Fifty-two percent of the Fortune 500 companies from the year 2000 are now extinct.

To recap, while Schumpeter shifted the focus from price competition to technological competition, modern economists point out that the market system turns out to have other ways of maintaining efficiency. Large or not, firms must be dynamic and run skillfully with an eye to customers and the other to potential competitors. They must also respect regulations. Moreover, customer wants are constantly changing. Humans are never satisfied and have a bulletproof willingness to prove new things. Innovating is thus essential for firms to survive because, otherwise, firms end up on the wrong side of the creative-destruction process, a process which is still alive and kicking even in mature capitalism. Managing the peculiarity of human behavior and sustained by inclusive institutions, markets are just as ruthless as nature in eliminating uncreative and unfit static operators. Once again, the happy ending of the *Four* is a matter of managing behaviors via adequate rules of the game. When tackling innovating, for example, intellectual property rights are key rules of the game that, therefore, deserve a specific tour stop.

5.4 Innovating and Intellectual Property Rights

In this stopover, we will inspect other details of the innovating activity with the main aim to cast an eye on the problems related to the enforcement of intellectual property rights (IPR) in capitalistic systems. According to the OECD glossary, IPR is the general term for the assignment of property rights through patents, copyrights, and trademarks. A patent is a right granted by a government to an inventor in exchange for the publication of the invention (say, a new type of engine); it entitles the inventor to prevent any third party from using the invention in any way, for an agreed period (lasting, usually, several years). While patents protect ideas, copyright protects expressions in a fixed form (copyrighted materials can be movies, songs, software codes, etc.), and trademarks protect names or signs so as to allow the identification of goods and services (Coca-Cola is a point in case).

IPR are different from what was intended before the WWII. Despite his evident interest in innovating, for example, Schumpeter only briefly mentioned patents and never mentioned other IPR such as trademarks or copyrights. This is an excusable omission because in the 1940s, trademarks and copyrights were not as important as today. These latter, indeed, became a salient element in market systems only after innovations such as photocopying and software computer programs—capitalism is an evolving entity from both the technological standpoint and the institutional one.

Though they have appeared at various times in the human's world, all IPR share the common feature of being property rights because they grant exclusive rights to individual agents as a tool to internalize their actions (cf. Section 2.3). But all of them are also peculiar property rights because all give the holder the monopoly on the use of the item, which raises a critical question: Why should the state intervene in the market system establishing rules of the game such as IPR? Or equivalently, why should private firms operating in capitalistic systems be allowed by law to gain, although temporarily, the monopolistic profits stemming from their innovative affairs? Possibly because of the subtlety surrounding IPR, our guides' position is not unanimous.

To get a first impression of the sensitiveness of the situation, note that if these rights protect socially useful innovating efforts, they do that by allowing individuals to block competitive products and dissuade potential competitors—do you interpret this sentence as embodying an advantage for individuals only, for the economy as a whole, or both? Even the OECD glossary, which weights disparate sources, after defining IPR hesitantly states: "By restricting imitation and duplication, monopoly power is conferred, but the social costs of monopoly power may be offset by the social benefits of higher levels of creative activity encouraged by the monopoly earnings." The use of "may be" is suggestive of the underlying *caveat* and calls for an examination of this controversy. A recent example of this sort of tension refers to the anti-COVID vaccine. In the late 2020. India, South Africa. and other developing nations proposed to the World Trade Organization that the patents on vaccinations and other COVID-related items should be waived. Their point was that an exceptional pandemic required an exceptional answer. The recipe for the life-saving jabs should be then made widely available so they could be produced locally in bulk by other manufacturers. Pharmaceutical companies forcefully disagreed.

That said, the visit continues, inquiring into the potential advantages and drawbacks of IPR in light of the key role of innovating in helping humans to fulfill their desiderata. Innovating is a risky—to not say uncertain—endeavor and as economists taught, higher risk requires higher expected returns. F. Knight argued that if there were no risk or uncertainty, there would be no extra profit earned by businesses, only normal returns. There must be then some monetary incentive for profit-seeking entrepreneurs to undertake the risks and costs related to R&D

expenditures and/or innovative projects. But ideas, innovations, and technologies may be appropriated by competitors. Lacking enforceable IPR, businesspeople may not be confident that their property rights would be respected and may hold back their innovating efforts. Some people may then shrink their creative activity while others may be pushed to behave opportunistically—i.e., to copy—and more in general, the lack of IPR may spread a wait-and-see approach. Inventions and innovations could then be underproduced, which, as everybody agrees, is critically bad for the system.

IPR, moreover, are counted as an asset when determining the value of a company and can even be used as collateral for a loan which, as learned when ranging over private property rights (cf. Chap. 2), may be helpful for both the owner and the system. In a nutshell, if trading is helped by factors such as private property and contract enforceability, innovating may be enhanced by the institutionalization and enforcement of rules of the game such as IPR. However, as I shall reiterate below, it may be, or it may not be.

P. Romer's work offers insights on why IPR may be a working device in capitalistic systems and his view [40, 41] can also shed light on the black box containing the Solow residual and, hence, on the connections of innovating and living standards (via economic growth). Romer's research stimulated a vast and still-ongoing literature on economic growth, but here I concentrate on the role of IPR in the sequence of the events connecting innovating and the exponential economic growth that I have previously described.

Within the existing tradition, Romer assumed that entrepreneurs are mainly motivated by the expected profits from their innovating efforts.[15] Departing from the standard view of dividing inputs into capital, labor, etc., instead, he proposed to dichotomize the factors of production into ideas (instructions, recipes, designs, and blueprints, which accumulate as stock of knowledge), and everything else (capital, labor, land, etc., which Romer labels "objects"). In Romer's world, ideas are thus an explicit factor of production although, as said, they are different from other inputs. While objects are private goods—hence rivalrous, excludable,[16] and Pareto-efficiently tradeable in Walrasian systems—ideas and knowledge are special goods because they are nonrival and partially excludable, and this makes them in need of special institutions to thrive in market systems.

To start with, let us concentrate on rivalry, which, as noted, is connected to scarcity. Labor is rival because a worker cannot be in two places at the same time nor can she, regardless of her skill, solve too many problems at once. Though new ideas are scarce in that humans are always willing to pay for better ideas, *existing* ideas, instead, are neither scarce nor rivalrous. The idea used to produce a vaccine, a

[15] Romer recognizes that not everyone who contributes to technological change is motivated by market incentives. An academic scientist who is supported by government grants may be totally insulated from them.

[16] As said in Chap. 2, rivalry means that the good can only be used or consumed by one party at a time. Excludable means that the owner of the good can prevent others from using or consuming it.

blueprint, etc., does not become increasingly scarce as more people use it; the same idea can be used several times. Nonrivalry then implies that it is not necessary to replicate productive ideas to produce more. If the same unit of labor or capital cannot be used by multiple producers, the same idea can be used by many, potentially increasing everybody's productivity. Note also that the fact that ideas never die implies that ideas can be accumulated (the stock of knowledge can grow) without bound on a per capita basis. Instead, of course, human capital cannot be accumulated without bound because humans, unlike their ideas, sooner or later die. All that magnifies how ideas can spur economic growth and higher living standards beyond what objects can do.

The fact that ideas are the engine of growth and can generate extra profits is not sufficient for the economic growth to materialize in Romer's world. If, when innovating, humans have in mind expected profits, then they must be sure that their current costly efforts will be sufficiently repaid in future. Like other goods, ideas are produced by profit-maximizing firms only if it is profitable. This is why IPR, as well as their related issues, enter the scene.

It may be instructive to restate the tension between individual behavior, institutions, and economic system within the current framework. Due to its nonrivalry, once the idea is realized—and the costs of producing it are accounted for—it can be used over and over again at no additional cost (the marginal cost is zero). Existing ideas should thus be shared free of charge because zero is what it costs to produce the last unit. By and large, since existing ideas cost zero but are productive, then they should thus be made freely available because that will maximize their benefit for the system as a whole. But sharing means that the single innovator does not get all the benefits so that the incentive to innovate is reduced. IPR are then a way to allow entrepreneurs to appropriate the return of their innovating efforts by giving them some market power. In sum, on the one hand, the system wants high prices to motivate individuals toward innovating adventures; on the other hand, it wants low prices to diffuse efficiently the outcomes of those innovating adventures.

The partial excludability of ideas permits progress. Basically, competitive markets do not allow innovating humans to gain extra profits because ideas are not excludable and spill over the system, quickly becoming common knowledge. But the diffusion and accumulation of ideas have a social value because they make all future inventions easier. Existing knowledge is fundamental for humans to produce new ideas—ideas very seldom come out of the blue (Newton's giants *docent*). Against this backdrop, the partial excludability of ideas theorized by Romer indicates an exit strategy.

More in detail, he highlights that the excludability of a good depends on technology but also on the legal system. For instance, the code for a computer program can be made excludable by means of encryption or by means of a legal system that prohibits copying or copy protection schemes. This suggests that the legal system may make a good partially excludable, and this is what happens with patented ideas. IPR make my idea excludable because as a holder of IPR, I can prevent others from using my idea. But what is protected is only my *exact* new invention. Once my patented idea has become common knowledge, other humans can learn from my idea and/or be inspired by it; they can use the existing knowledge as an idea for their own invention. Moreover, they can do that for free. In other words, the excludable part of the idea creates an incentive for individuals to put in place innovating; the non-excludable part of the idea embodies a spillover effect that contributes to the innovating efforts in the system as a whole, spurring faster economic growth, and hence, higher living standards.

As anticipated, the utility of IPR as a booster of innovating has been questioned. To start with, assume that imposing these legal monopolies is a necessary evil. The issue in this case is that IPR should be wisely designed, which may prove uneasy. An indication of the difficulty may be inferred by the fact that capitalistic countries have still not agreed upon a unique way to address IPR. Infringement decisions for similar types of patents, for example, sometimes differ in the European Union with respect to the USA because they have established different guidelines and definitions. In addition, IPR may refer to disparate products or processes, each of which may require different IPR so that there is no one-IPR-fits-all scheme. Inter alia, policymakers must solve an important question—what is the optimal duration of the temporary rent? That is, which is the minimum size of extra profit necessary to incentivize innovating endeavors? There are then situations whereby IPR have little momentum. It may happen in quickly changing environments where multiyear patent protection may be of little value because inventions quickly become obsolete as is typical in the ICT industry. Also, should a company with a large technology advantage over its rivals receive the same IPR protection as a company with a more limited advantage?

Apart from the difficulty of designing IPR, the simple presence of IPR may be counterproductive. I have noted that IPR may hamper opportunism. But they may also magnify this because the opportunity to obtain monopoly power *ex lege* may stimulate firms to influence governments to extract advantages. This is a general issue emerging when the impersonal forces of the market are substituted by personal forces—it opens the Pandora's box of lobbyism, corruption, rent-seeking, state capture, etc. Taking this perspective one may say that IPR persist in capitalistic systems not because of their economic efficiency but because of the action of pressure groups. Some IPR may then adversely hamper innovating efforts.

A point in case is patents because they can be obtained only for practical applications of ideas. According to US patent law, for example, the patent is granted upon a new machine, manufacture, etc., and not upon the idea or suggestion of a new machine.[17] The laws of nature, physical phenomena, and abstract ideas are thus not patentable subject matter. It may lead to underweighted abstract and theoretical research, which is clearly key for applied research. It should also be taken into account that the innovating outcome of an individual is also due to the earlier

[17] Cf. The United States Patent and Trademark Office (USPTO) https://www.uspto.gov/patents/basics

fundamental research financed by the government. In this respect IPR could be seen, although in part, as an example of "privatizing profits and socializing costs."

Several hints come then from the jobs of M. Boldrin and D.K. Levine. For instance, they document many cases whereby the financial incentives generated by intellectual property monopoly do not significantly fuel innovation. More in general, their long-lasting research led them to conclude that patents and copyrights turn out to be more detrimental than useless in stimulating innovating affairs and, hence, for the enhancement of living standard [42–44]. Interestingly for our journey, they have innovating-related insights on both behaviors and systems. Boldrin and Levine hold that extra profits are available for innovative firms even if they operate in perfectly competitive markets. It may happen because innovating humans have the first-time mover advantage, that is, the temporary monopoly that results from being first to offer a product, which economists call "competitive rents."

A related remark is that ideas may not spill over as freely as assumed in the literature sustaining IPR. There are many occasions whereby imitating is a significantly time-demanding and costly activity. Most of the times, imitation requires purchasing either some products or some teaching services from the original innovator, meaning that most spillovers are priced rather than free. It may hamper imitators from quickly entering the market, leaving competitive rents to first-time movers. Boldrin and Levine report dozens of anecdotes and cases demonstrating that this generates an advantage which is sufficient financial motivation for innovating. Among them, they recall the case of Apple (p. 10): [45] "The first iPhone was released on June 29, 2007. The first serious competitor, the HTC Dream (using the Android operating system), was released on October 22, 2008. By that time, over five million iPhones had been sold, and sales soared to over 25 million units during the subsequent year, while total sales of all Android-based phones were less than seven million. In the tablet market, the iPad has no serious competitor as of late 2012 despite having been introduced on April 10, 2010."

Boldrin and Levine observe then that there are other means to reap market success from innovating besides first-mover advantages—collateral sales, reputational effects, public prizes, subsidies, etc. They also note that the safety of the income granted by the copyright may induce once creative humans to rest on their laurels. Apart from inducing laziness, income safety may also transform Schumpeterians into ordinary Sapiens, bringing to the surface the typical risk aversion of humans, dampening risky innovating adventures featured by expected returns. Among the cases of creators discouraged by the safety built into the copyright, the authors cite an example found in F. Scherer's works [46, 47]. Scherer reported that the Italian composer G. Verdi, after having earned substantial income from score sales and performance fees, started to compose at a less frantic pace. Focusing on patents, Boldrin and Levine assert that there is no study showing that innovation increases as a result of the strengthening of patent protection in USA. They have conducted a metastudy, gathering 24 studies dated 2006 that examined whether introducing or strengthening patent protection leads to greater innovation, and have found weak or no evidence that strengthening patent regimes increases innovation. Rather, evidence points to the opposite, with markets that flourished because of the absence of patent systems. A point in case is chemical and pharmaceutical industries that, until the end of WWII, developed essentially without patentability for their products.

These authors also stress that patents can trigger welfare-reducing behaviors. Several patents are used by the owners not to finance R&D but to reduce competition, creating barriers to entry. This is especially true in the case of firms operating in a dynamic market and under the pressure exerted by potential competitors. Boldrin and Levine recall how Texas Instruments and Apple behaved years ago. The former had problems adapting to the personal computers revolution and for a while tried to survive by suing the newcomers. Regarding the latter, in the smartphone market, Apple had a much larger patent portfolio than Google, at that time a new firm in the market. With the sole scope of delaying Google's entry into the market, Apple used its patents to take Google to court in a series of ridiculous patent lawsuits. Our guides stress that if it was possible for Apple lawyers to tie up for years in the courts a giant such as Google, then the barriers to entry for smaller firms may prove insurmountable. In addition, Boldrin and Levine point out that the continuous strengthening of IPR witnessed in recent times is not causing a surge in the innovation rate, but rather, it is just generating ever-increasing rent-seeking behaviors and transaction costs (due to more patents, more lawsuits, etc.) that reduce the innovating activity. In fact, there are several cases where just the simple preliminary review process takes many years. To the extent that IPR makes innovating more a matter for lawyers than Schumpeterians, the achievement of significant economic growth is at risk. Finally, history teaches that governments may successfully use different tools. As happened in 1800s, for example, policymakers sustained innovating by not taxing away the rents produced by successful innovations.

To conclude, as far as innovating (but not only), competition is demanding for individuals but it is often effective in maintaining efficient and dynamic the system. Innovating, then may induce economic inequality. The state, therefore must tackle technological competition and innovating activities (as well as all of the *Four*) with due diligence, competence, honesty, etc. Much easier to say than to do. We will visit these themes in the Epilogue.

References

1. Patterson E and Mann J (2011) The Ecological Conditions That Favor Tool Use and Innovation in Wild Bottlenose Dolphins (Tursiops sp.). PloS One, 6,7.
2. OECD (2018) Oslo Manual, Paris, 4th edition. The generic term "unit" describes the actor responsible for innovations and it refers to any institutional unit (firms, households, and their individual members, etc.).
3. Schumpeter J A (1911) The theory of economic development. English version in 1934 Cambridge, MA: Harvard University Press.
4. Stevens G A and Burley J (1997) 3,000 raw ideas equal 1 commercial success! Journal of Research-Technology Management, 40(3):16-27.
5. Acs Z J and Audretsch D B (1990) Innovation and Small Firms. Cambridge, MA: MIT Press.
6. Bakker G, Crafts N, and Woltjer P (2019) The sources of growth in a technologically progressive economy: the United States, 1899–1941. Economic Journal, 129: 2267–2294
7. Keynes J M (1930) op. cit.

8. Malthus T R (1798) Essay on the Principle of Population. J. Johnson, London.
9. Giattino C and Ortiz-Ospina E (2000) Are we working more than ever? https://ourworldindata.org/working-more-than-ever.
10. Carlisle R (1984) Scientific American Inventions and Discoveries: All the Milestones in Ingenuity from the Discovery of Fire to the Invention of the Microwave Oven. Wiley.
11. Carlisle R (1984) op. cit.
12. Schumpeter J A (1911) op. cit.
13. Satoshi N (2008) Bitcoin: A Peer-to-Peer Electronic Cash System, Satoshi Nakamoto Institute. Available at https://nakamotoinstitute.org/bitcoin/
14. Stern S (2004) Do scientists pay to be scientists? Management Science 50:835–853.
15. Mokyr J (2010) The Enlightened Economy–An Economic History of Britain 1700-1850. New Haven: Yale University Press.
16. Boldrin M, Levine D K, and Modica S (2012) A Review of Acemoglu and Robinson's Why Nations Fail, downloadable: http://www.dklevine.com/general/aandrreview.pdf.
17. [illegible] Accumulation, Cultural Diffusion and the Origin of the Wealth of Nations. CEPR Discussion Paper No. DP6444.
18. Doepke M and Zilibotti F (2008) Occupational Choice and the Spirit of Capitalism. Quarterly Journal of Economics, 123(2): 747-793.
19. Guiso L, Sapienza P, and Zingales L (2003) People's Opium? Religion and Economic Attitudes. Journal of Monetary Economics 50(1): 225-282.
20. Benabou R, Ticchi D, and Vindigni A (2015) Religion and Innovation. American Economic Review Papers and Proceedings 105(5): 346–351.
21. Solow R J (1957) Technical Change and the Aggregate Production Function. Review of Economics and Statistics 39: 312-20.
22. Gerben B, Crafts N, and Woltjer P (2019) The Sources of Growth in a Technologically Progressive Economy: The United States, 1899–1941. The Economic Journal 129(622): 2267–2294.
23. Shackleton R (2013) Total Factor Productivity Growth in Historical Perspective. Working Paper Series, Congressional Budget Office, Washington, DC.
24. Adler G et al (2017) Gone with the Headwinds: Global Productivity. IMF Staff Discussion Notes N. 17/04.
25. Aksoy Y et al (2019) Demographic Structure and Macroeconomic Trends. American Economic Journal: Macroeconomics 11(1):193–222.
26. Brynjolfsson E, Rock D, and Syverson C (2021) The Productivity J-Curve: How Intangibles Complement General Purpose Technologies. American Economic Journal: Macroeconomics, 13 (1): 333-72.
27. Abramovitz M (1956) Resource and output trends in the United States since 1870. American Economic Review 46(2): 5–23.
28. Marx K and Engels F (1848) The Communist manifesto. London.
29. Schumpeter J A (1951) Capitalism in the postwar world. In: Clemence R V (ed) Reprinted in Essays of J A Schumpeter Addison-Wesley, Cambridge, MA.
30. Schumpeter J A (1942) Capitalism, Socialism and Democracy. London: Routledge.
31. Schumpeter J A (1942) op. cit.
32. Schumpeter J. A (1942) op. cit. It is perhaps worth stressing that this tour does not aim to learn whether Schumpeter was socialist or the like.
33. Marx K (1963) The Poverty of Philosophy. Translated from the 1847 French edition New York, International Publishers Co., Inc.
34. Mandeville B (1732) The Fable of the Bees: Or Private Vices, Publick Benefits, London: Penguin Books, 1989.
35. Haltiwanger J et al (2016) High Growth Young Firms: Contribution to Job, Output, and Productivity Growth. In Measuring Entrepreneurial Businesses: Current Knowledge and Challenges. University of Chicago Press.

36. Gintis H (1990) Why Schumpeter got it Wrong in Capitalism, Socialism, and Democracy. Challenge Magazine 34: 27-33.
37. Deloitte (2015) "The Deloitte Innovation Survey." Available at www2.deloitte.com/content/dam/Deloitte/lu/Documents/about-deloitte/lu-en-innovations-survey-25032015.pdf
38. Baumol W J and Willig R D (1986) Contestability: Developments since the book. Oxford Economic Papers 38: 9-36.
39. Frank R G (2007) The ongoing regulation of generic drugs. New England Journal of Medicine, 357: 1993-1996.
40. Romer P M (1990) Endogenous Technological Change. Journal of Political Economy 98, 5: S71–S102.
41. Paul Romer (1993) Idea Gaps and Object Gaps in Economic Development. Journal of Monetary Economics 32:543–573
42. Boldrin M and Levine D K (2008) Against Intellectual Monopoly. Cambridge University Press.
43. M Boldrin and Levine D K (2013) The Case against Patents. Journal of Economic Perspectives, 27 (1): 3-22.
44. M Boldrin and Levine D K (2015) Intellectual Property. In Kosslyn S M (ed), Emerging trends in the social and behavioral sciences: an interdisciplinary, searchable, and linkable resource, Wiley.
45. Boldrin M and Levine D K (2013) op. cit.
46. Scherer F M (2012) Quarter Notes and Bank Notes: The Economics of Music Composition in the Eighteenth and Nineteenth Centuries. Princeton University Press.
47. F M Scherer (2001) The Evolution of Free-Lance Music Composition, 1650-1900. Journal of Cultural Economics (11): 307-319.

Epilogue

6

6.1 The *Four* Are Connected and Can Reinforce Each Other: The Industrial Revolution

Since the socioeconomic Big Bang, humans started to be and to behave as individualistic social animals whose basic ceaseless aim is to live together, better, and longer. Since then, problems and solutions have been chasing each other in a groundwork whereby rules of the game, culture, incentives, opportunities, and social capital have been emerging, disappearing, and interweaving. Both humans and economic systems have been surfacing as adaptive, uncertain complex entities, with the latter aimed to manage the behavioral complexity of the former. If humans display both individualism and collectivism, systems show both integration and differentiation.

Against this intricate behavioral and institutional backdrop, trading, forecasting, aggregating, and innovating have been manifesting as immanent and critical affairs for humans. In one way or another, all of the *Four* impinge on the growth and equilibrium of economic systems.[1] Even if the *Four* are distinct endeavors, during the journey we have also observed that they are connected and put in place contextually. As noticed in the Prologue, for instance, since the outset of our species, traded materials have led to the development and diffusion of innovative tools. These days, global trade spreads innovation, and this sustains in turn trading, putting downward pressure on prices. In light of our journey, collecting and making explicit some of these interlinks is important because it can offer, through the lens of the *Four*, a narrative of the Industrial Revolution, possibly among the most critical juncture in human history (and surely the most in our tour). Taking stock of what we have learned so far, then how the *Four* can reinforce each other and their role in the Industrial Revolution are the two topics that the present stopover is devoted to.

[1] Equilibrium and growth are not antithetic. A system may show a steady state growth—a rate of growth that the economy would converge to in the absence of new shocks.

M. Bovi, *Why and How Humans Trade, Predict, Aggregate, and Innovate*,
Contributions to Economics, https://doi.org/10.1007/978-3-030-93885-7_6

Trading and aggregating activities are connected. Locations favoring trade—such as natural harbors, rivers, and valleys—tend to attract more people. Aggregating via marriages may create or sustain trading opportunities. In underdeveloped economic systems, the trading activity outside the family is limited because households mainly produce for their own use whatever is wanted. But when these households become more productive in some production activity, thanks to specialization and/or innovating, they start producing for sales rather than for intra-household use only.

Humans' eagerness then triggers them to concoct more refined ways to produce, inducing them to cluster in firms which, in turn, trigger exchanges as enterprises need to buy inputs and to sell the output. Firms are also tightly related to cities via trading. Remember, cities sustain firms' production because citizens are relatively rich (thanks to the urban wage premium) and specialized; hence, they have both the resources and the need to trade. Aggregating and trading, then, promote innovating facilitating fruitful exchanges of goods, information and ideas. The need of genial innovating humans is smaller if normally gifted researchers work in pool. Aggregating in cities, as one of our guides summarizes, makes us smarter [1].

Innovating impinges on aggregating in other ways, too. The mechanization of agriculture led to urbanization and the success, and persistence of cities may depend on whether the city is an idea-producing place rather than a good-producing place. Developments in reproductive technologies (e.g., in vitro fertilization, surrogate motherhood, and artificial insemination) and various medical forms of birth control (e.g., oral contraceptives, the intrauterine device, the diaphragm, and vasectomy) may affect the choice to live together in families. At the nationwide level, innovation reduces physical distances and can make culture more uniform within social clusters, possibly making it easier to live together. For instance, Italy is a relatively young nation featuring disparate local long histories whereby the diffusion of television helped Italian to emerge as the national language (replacing, although partially, local dialects) and to spread nationwide cultural models.[2]

Population and economic activities are often spatially concentrated, and innovation is even more spatially concentrated. Trading enters the scene, stimulating inventors and innovators to be close to each other and to customers in order to extract value from ideas. Innovating and trading are closely intertwined. Trading is stimulated by innovating because the latter makes available new goods and services as well as raises the purchasing power of consumers. For instance, innovating is crucial in enlarging the service sector and in making women more active consumers. In addition, innovating makes available network goods (such as cellphones), which spurs trading because without buying them, people would remain marginalized. Before ocean travel became feasible, smaller countries were poorer (Tasmanians'

[2]Several works point at an important contribution of television for the diffusion of cultural models that, once adopted, may have significant and persistent effects on individual behavior. There is evidence supporting the contribution of TV to women empowerment in India. On the negative side, R. Putnam blames light entertainment TV shows for civic dis-engagement in the USA during the postwar period while others argue that exposure to soap operas reduces fertility and increases divorce rates in Brazil.

docent). Once innovating made ocean travel feasible, poorer countries could exploit the gains from trade. If for these gains to emerge exchanges must be fair, deliberate and played according to well-established and enforceable rules, thanks to trading poor/uninspired countries also became more technologically advanced.

The outcome of innovating determines which kinds of products are developed, thereby influencing the future path of trading. But at the same time, the willingness to buy determines whether that outcome successfully enters and remains in the market. Further, innovating makes available new ways to propose products to consumers. Digital technologies support "two-sided markets" like eBay and Airbnb, which match individuals who can mutually benefit from exchanges.

All these businesses involve forecasting, too. Firms typically enter the market only if they think they will be able to trade their products for profit. This is even more so when firms aim to launch new goods—the behavior of Schumpeterians is driven by expected profits. Technologically, a watch with the Apple Watch functionality has been possible for a while. But firms may have waited either because they were unsure if it could become a success, or they have expected more profits by waiting.

Firms are not the sole human clusters that forecast. Households must look forward to addressing their future necessities. When trading in financial markets, firms and families need to forecast both economic subjects and objects. Aggregating in densely populated cities increases the need to forecast economic subjects. Last but not least, innovating endeavors (i.e., inventions, innovations, diffusion, and technical progress) naturally involve some forecasting exercise.

What has been said so far suggests that there could be periods in which the four activities we are traveling across reinforce each other, periods where the sum of the gains stemming from each of the *Four* boosts mankind toward big achievements. A prominent point in case is the Industrial Revolution, which started in England in the second half of the eighteenth century. By definition, it was the period in which humans became more industrialized than agricultural, but the Industrial Revolution is more than this and, indeed, is paramount in human history. Focusing on our tour's main aim and following the usual bird's-eye approach, in this stop, I will just highlight how during the Industrial Revolution, all the *Four* were sustained and that they pushed some economic systems to be increasingly innovative, urbanized, and exchange-oriented in a globalized way (as said, forecasting has connections with all the other three activities). If the term "Industrial" is suggestive of the transformation of agrarian and handicraft economies to one dominated by industry and machine manufacturing, the term "Revolution" highlights how sudden and dramatic the shift was for humans. Until three centuries ago, indeed, all economies in the world were not dramatically different from one another as they became since then. Besides remaining mostly agricultural, recorded living standards proceeded more or less steadily over time. The following figures show the huge leap in the economic growth and structural transformation that, starting with Britain, quickly spread to other economies (Figs. 6.1 and 6.2).

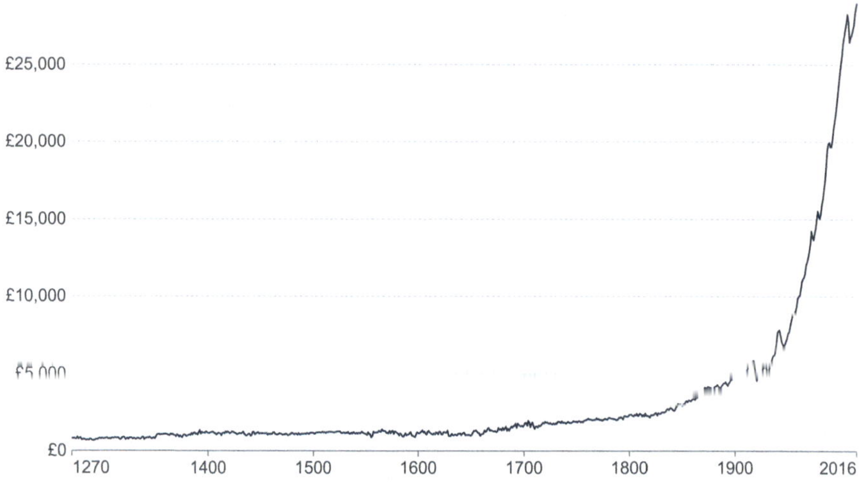

Fig. 6.1 GDP per capita in England. Source: Ourworldindata.org

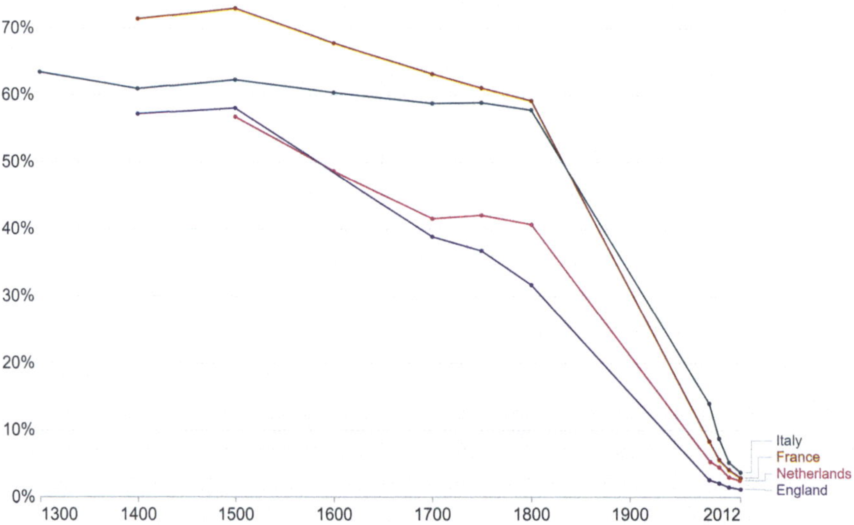

Fig. 6.2 Share of the labor force working in agricolture. Source: Ourworldindata.org

Pushing in the direction of economic growth, the *Four* actively contributed to the revolutionary transformations of the period. The classic narratives of the British Industrial Revolution [2][3] put at the core of the event a set of innovating businesses that were quickly emerging (notably, cotton manufacturing and pottery) and diffusing across firms belonging to industries such as mining, metals production, and engineering. Geographical aggregation then followed because most of the innovations required that machinery be centrally located where sources of power were available. The changes brought about by the Industrial Revolution would be unimaginable in the absence of cities and productive aggregations such as enterprises. Britain was traditionally engaged in producing yarn, cloth, and clothing. But prior to the Industrial Revolution, these products were homemade or limited to cottage industry and unavoidably small scale. Since then, however, innovating allowed production to become massive and it was increasingly located in factories. The mechanization of production made necessary urbanization.

Innovating and trading were tightly intertwined, too. Most of the innovations of the period popped up because of the presence of large trading markets. Industries such as cotton and pottery would not have grown to a large scale without the existence of the system of intercontinental seaborne trade relations that had developed since the latter part of the fifteenth century. The innovative products stemming from the British Industrial Revolution quickly invaded foreign markets, reshaping international trade.

At the national level, the period witnessed innovations in the way of trading. Marketing and advertising are points in case. Marshall summarized this fast-developing revolutionary process as follows (p. 7) [3]: "towards the end of the eighteenth century, the changes, which had so far been slow and gradual, suddenly became rapid and violent. Mechanical inventions, the concentration of industries, and a system of manufacturing on a large scale for distant markets broke up the old traditions of industry, and left everyone to bargain for himself as best he might; and at the same time they stimulated an increase of population [. . .]."

In a sense, the new normal brought about by the Industrial Revolution may have also induced different forecasting attitudes. When, as shown in Fig. 6.1, things tend to move slowly for long periods as in a static "circular flow," one is tempted to give great weight to the past when imagining the future. But when dynamics are bubbling, when one is living in the "Age of Invention" [4], when the present is so different from the past, then inertia and experience may contribute less to forecasting.[4] In the next section, we shall learn that entering a new era (be it true or only perceived) may modify humans' way of forecasting (Shiller *docet*). That is, the quick and apparently unstoppable transformation of the economic system may have led humans to look at themselves no longer as creatures of their past but as creators of their future; it may

[3]Unsurprisingly, many books have been devoted to this revolutionary period. Just to mention a few, Mokyr J (2010) op. cit.

[4]There are convincing indications that in predicting individuals tend to overweight what they experienced during their lifetimes.

have made humans more forward-looking than ever. Possibly for the first time in human history, the future was systematically weighted more than the past. The contribution of forecasting may also be somewhat inferred from the fact that, as observed in Chap. 3, sustained system-wide growth cannot coexist with systematic system-wide prediction errors.

Some data permit us to gain a quantitative impression of what was going on in each of the *Four*. Until 1800, more than 90% of the population of all nations lived in rural areas. One century later, in the industrialized economies of Europe and the USA, almost half of the inhabitants were urbanized. The dynamic patterns relative to innovating and trading activities are similar. Economists show that during the Industrial Revolution, there was a strong acceleration of patents and patentable inventions per person [5]. They have also collected data displaying that until 1800, there was a long period characterized by persistently low international trade [6]. The ratio of total trade, exports plus imports, to global GDP never exceeded 10%. Then this ratio quickly tripled, reaching 30% just before the WWI. All that permitted humans to escape from the Malthusian trap. The increase in the food supply contributed to the rapid growth of population in England and Wales, from 5.5 million in 1700 to over nine million by 1801. When in the nineteenth century domestic production gave way increasingly to food imports, the population more than tripled to over 32 million. The following sequence of figures offers a glimpse into these impressive dynamics (Figs. 6.3, 6.4, 6.5, and 6.6).

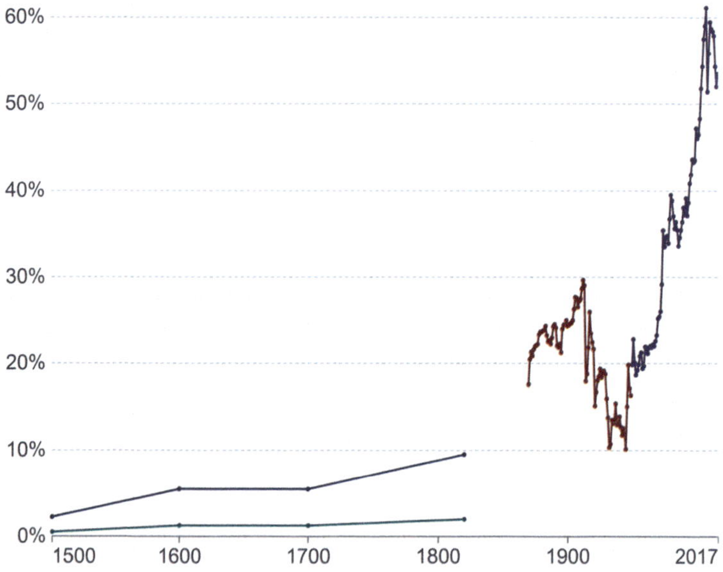

Fig. 6.3 Trading (trade openness index). Shown is the "trade openness index." This index is defined as the sum of world exports and imports, divided by world GDP. Each series corresponds to a different source. Source: Ourworldindata.org

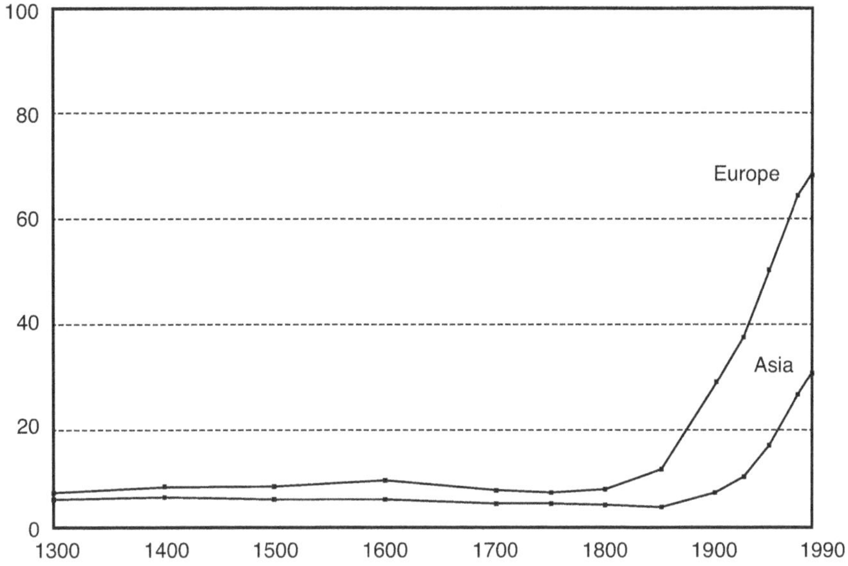

Fig. 6.4 Aggegrating (share of urban population on total, %). United Nations (1977). *Population Bulletin of the United Nations, No. 8. 1976.* New York

The Industrial Revolution was not related to a revolution in the human behavior behind the *Four*. The average human being remained more or less anchored to the same ancestral mix of individualism and collectivism explored in the Prologue. As for pre-Industrial Revolution periods, in the Prologue, we learned that in the 1600s through the 1700s, leading thinkers such as A. Smith and J. Locke pointed out the compound nature of human behavior. Another acute observer of that time, D. Hume, held a similar position [7].

According to our guides, instead, an important contribution came from the economic system which functioned as an accompanying factor or at least as a favorable background operating behind the *Four*. Marshall states (p. 7) [3], "Much of modern economics might indeed have been anticipated in the towns of the Middle Ages, in which an intelligent and daring spirit was for the first time combined with patient industry. But they were not left to work out their career in peace; and the world had to wait for the dawn of the new economic era till a whole nation was ready for the ordeal of economic freedom. England especially was gradually prepared for the task (. . .)."

Taking the viewpoint of Acemoglu and Robinson, in England the *Four* were helped by inclusive institutions because the parliamentary monarchy and the distribution of political power gave England that right degree of distributed centralism, allowing the country to establish the needed major changes to economic institutions. A counterexample is France, where the Industrial Revolution took off years later because of the French strong centralized monarchy.

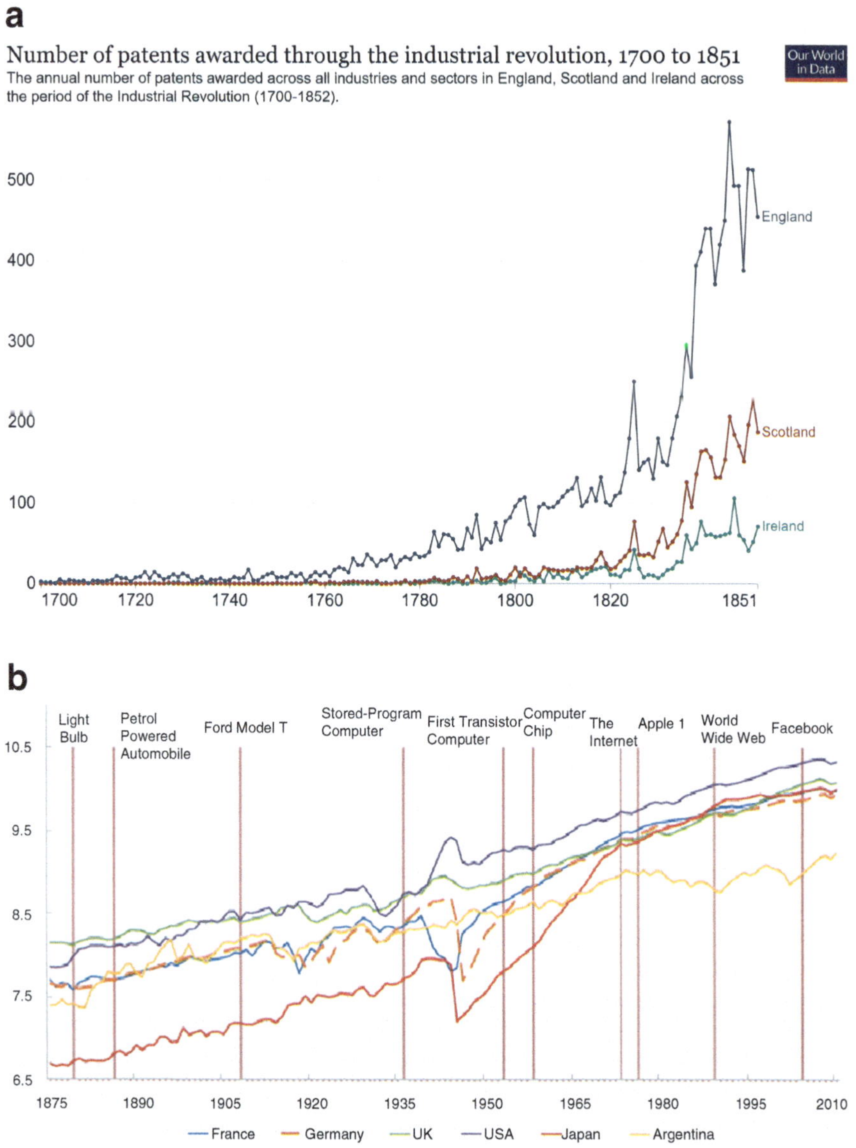

Fig. 6.5 (**a**) Innovating. (**b**) Innovating and Economic Growth (GDP per capita, 1990 International dollars (which would buy in the cited country a comparable amount of goods and services a U.S. dollar would buy in the United States), logarithms) Source: Peralta-Alva A., A. Roitman 2018, Technology and the Future of Work, IMF Working Paper No. 18/207

Thanks to the Marshallian "new economic era" and/or the inclusive institutional setting and/or whatever other driver was behind the Industrial Revolution, for our tour's aim the following point remains. The *Four* have pushed toward the same right direction and have actively contributed to the revolution.

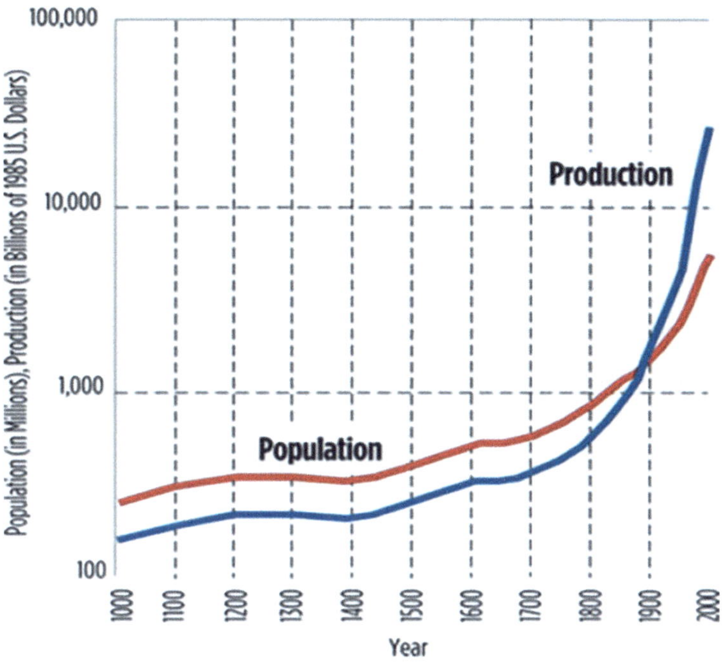

Fig. 6.6 Economic and Demographic Growth. Source: Lucas, Jr. R.E. (2004). World Population and Production

6.2 The Dark Side of the *Four* and How Humans Manage it

So far, we have explored the significant gains from trade, the critical advantages of effective forecasting at both the individual and system-wide level, the rewards of living together in various social clusters, and the accumulating enhancements made by innovating. We have seen that when all the *Four* push in the same right direction, they permit mankind to flourish. But we have also learned that an apparent iron-clad law in human actions is that they open up opportunities but also produce concerns. Maybe human efforts have a dark side because nature makes humans insatiable but also protects itself by putting counterbalancing effects on human insatiability. For good or ill, what is sure is that the *Four* are not an exception to this rule. When humans trade, forecast, aggregate, and innovate, undesirable consequences emerge. We have already met some of these issues in our wandering, but it is now time to focus explicitly on them—our short tour has arrived at the dark side of the *Four* and the way humans manage it.

As for trading, coercion is harmful for some. But the dark side of trading may materialize even in performing the bilateral and deliberate (hence, market) exchanges we are focusing on in our trip. Troubles in trading efforts may surface when in the exchange contract, there is a weak side. In these cases, market exchanges are less efficient with respect to the ideal situation whereby only fully informed/rational Walrasians trade. Some examples suggest how some consumers may trade less efficiently and be less sovereign than is supposed in Walrasian systems. First, a truly welfare-enhancing exchange should be performed by conscious-minded traders. But in various instances, one of the trading partners may lack the necessary information and/or knowledge to perform a really reasoned and thoughtful choice.

We have already noticed that occasionally, there are reasons to stop trading, such as when minors are involved (cf. Sect. 2.4). But even an adult buyer may not know how dangerous a drug or another product might be or may not be enough of an expert to avoid being cheated. In insurance and financial markets, likewise, for most individuals, it is practically unfeasible to continuously monitor the level of risk of the firms where their money is, nor is easy for them to choose among the many available types of mortgages (those with fixed vs variable interest rates, for example). Finally, customers could pay higher-than-necessary prices and/or buy low-quality products when their providers have market power.[5]

Concerns about the trading activity are not exclusively related to objective factors such as lack of knowledge or information. Our guides highlight that the dark side of trading may also stem from various psychological weakness and reasoning anomalies featuring the typical human being. We met some of them in the tour stop on forecasting (Chap. 3), but there are others that are more closely related to the flip side of trading. Walrasians are very smart humans, and among their trading skills, there is the ability to change their mind in a coherent way. They behave as expert systems (or, better, vice versa). When things go south or when their original strategy goes wrong, they recuperate, adjust, and calibrate the strategy to fit the new data. If a rational cost-benefit analysis advises exiting from an endeavor, individuals are better off doing that.

Unlike Walrasians, some humans suffer from the so-called *sunk cost fallacy*. It materializes when someone wrongly continues a behavior or endeavor because of previously invested resources (time, money, or effort) despite the fact these resources are sunk (i.e., already definitively lost). For instance, after having bought too much food, some people overeat just to "get their money's worth." Our guides sum up the situation saying that humans often throw good money after bad. Humans can then become victims of themselves, making inconsistent, short-sighted choices. That is, they tend to procrastinate endeavors with net benefits just because the costs come after the gains. Classic instances of these delayed trading decisions refer to when they start buying healthier food and investing for retirement or stop consuming spirits and cigarettes. For example, smokers just consider the current benefit of smoking while disregarding the high tobacco-related health costs that sooner or later, but surely, they will face. It is not a matter of information—they are aware of that. The point is that it is super hard for many of us to maintain the focus on the

[5] Since market power belongs to firm-related issues we will visit it in the excursion on the flip side of aggregating.

future when the present is so satisfying. As O. Wilde nicely put it, "I can resist everything except temptation." Likewise, many humans these days are aware that "diet always begins tomorrow."

Our guides, who like/need to venture in measurements, show that humans typically procrastinate for an average of 2.3 months before canceling their self-renewing membership. The average amount lost is nearly $70 against canceling at the first moment that attendance stops [8]. Needless to say, all these kinds of "non-Walrasian" trading have both individual and societal costs. The flip side of trading arises in international trade, too. Although it may produce psychological consequences, here the causes do not stem from psychology. Rather, the point lies in the fact that the presence of gains from trade does not imply that everyone in the nation will gain from trade. In fact, most extant models elaborated upon by our guides conclude that at least some groups end up worse off.[6] Points in case are employees of import-competing industries, or unskilled workers in a country that has a comparatively abundant number of skilled workers. I have highlighted similar issues in Chap. 2.

What we have been discussing calls for managing trading endeavors. We have seen some of the possible solutions during the tour, stressing that, for example, reputation is important in market exchanges, which may support the weaker side of the contract. Humans then occasionally solve temptation-related problems via pre-commitment, which is a way to impose coherence between the current and future selves. In short, humans take an earlier and easier action that makes it easier to perform the harder, yet still desirable, action later on. The stratagem is much like that of Ulysses, who wanted to listen to the bewitching song of the Sirens without dying and thus asked to be tied to a pole in order to achieve both results. Modern instances of this strategy that protects "time inconsistent" humans against their own errors include paying for an annual gym membership instead of paying day by day, signing up and paying in advance for a personal nutritionist, and setting up a monthly automatic withdrawal from one's own paycheck into a pension fund. Though, as has been said, the strategy occasionally turns out to be ineffective, these attempts suggest that there is a bit of Ulysses in many of us.

Also note the complexity of what is going on—some humans are able to solve rationally a problem stemming from their own irrationality. As strange as it may appear, even groups of humans use precommitments in order to deal with the impulsiveness which drives procrastination. A point in case is the European agreements signed at Maastricht that, inter alia, constrain the public budgets of the members in order to limit excessive indebtedness.[7] Too often, in fact, policymakers

[6]Elaborating on the Ricardo's principle of comparative advantage, e.g., the Stolper–Samuelson theorem says that opening up to trade benefits the factor of production that is relatively abundant and hurts the scarce factor. Globalization then increases income inequality because it keeps domestic wages down while allowing profits to grow. But, of course, the solution cannot be to stop the international trade. The *Four* must be managed, not stopped.

[7]Besides formal precommitments, in fact, policymakers consider fundamental reputation and trustworthiness, too. This was explored in sect. 3.1 referring to Central Banks.

are overly generous agents who use public debt to procrastinate necessary reforms.[8] But sooner or later, someone must repay the public debt and reforms must be implemented (of course, the later the costlier). Tying their hands may thus be useful for the economic system: even policymakers, after all, are humans. Accordingly, their mixed behavior must be somehow constrained by institutions.

To protect the weak side of the contract, humans have elaborated on other formal institutions. Among them, laws on informed consent, regulatory standards (e.g., ISO Certificates), passive (e.g., unemployment benefits) and active (e.g., training) labor market policies for unskilled workers, borrower protection from oppressive and opaque contracts, consumer protection from misleading advertising, and the like. To promote "healthy living" among non-Walrasian consumers, governments try then to discourage the consumption and the production of goods with negative health impacts (alcoholics, tobacco, sugar-sweetened beverages, foods high in salt, etc.) through taxation or other price policies, such as minimum pricing or prohibition to sell. In European countries 50% of the retail selling price of tobacco is due to taxes [9]. Though taxes on health-related commodities can be a powerful tool for health promotion (and to raise public funds), it requires careful consideration by policymakers. Even putting aside the reaction of producers of taxed items (which opens the already recalled Pandora's box of lobbyism, state capture, etc.) and not considering that legal prohibitions and taxes on spirits or tobacco may incentivize parallel trade and smuggling, look at the following story [10]. Suppose the intended target of making it illegal to sell spirits to minors is to affect the behavior of this group in order to reduce alcohol-related health risks. Now, if youngsters drink because they like the sense of risk and/or rebellion inherent in drinking alcohol, then making drinking illegal would make it even more a risky rebellious choice. A new incentive to drink emerges. Policymakers should carefully search for the deep causes. Not easy but essential. But there is even more. If the policy turns out to be really effective the minors will find other ways to satisfy their particular attitude toward risk, which may give rise to further social issues. An example from Hollywood is the "chickie-run" played by James Dean in the famous movie whose title is illuminating: *Rebel without a Cause.* This kind of difficulty is not limited to the management of trading. As we have seen and as we shall see, due to complexity, uncertainty, opportunism, etc., the state face big problems in managing every activity included in the *Four.*

Turning our attention to forecasting, in Chap. 3, we visited the psychological biases featuring human predictions. There, we learned that heuristics offer an exit strategy in uncertain environments and may occasionally work sufficiently well. But rules of thumb may also lead Kahnemanians to suffer from avoidable losses in that identifying a first flip side of forecasting. From the aggregate standpoint, we have seen that in economic systems populated by Walrasians, who form RE and operate in

[8]Evidently, politicians may have strong incentives to look more closely at current problems than future problems generating higher costs than benefits for the system. It is yet another instance of the issues triggered by situation whereas individual interests and collective interests are misaligned.

self-regulating and quickly equilibrium-reverting markets, there is little to fear about the dark side of forecasting. But our guides suggest that real-world things may take different, less reassuring, routes. The guides that I have selected to escort the traveler across the system-wide dark effects of forecasting are R. Shiller and H. Minsky.

H. Minsky shows how the forecasting activity of Keynesians may pilot stable capitalistic systems toward unstable and uncertain paths [11–13]. In terms of our trip, the flip side of forecasting is triggered by the stability of economic systems, manifests itself in behaviors featured by growing risk propension, and eventually produces system instability. The endogenous process shifting the market system from stability to instability, and eventually crisis, involves three steps that can be summarized as follows. Think of a Goldilocks capitalistic system that, as such, proceeds with a steady economic expansion. It leads many firms to be more confident and to develop a greater willingness to borrow. This state of affairs implies committing a rising portion of expected gross profits to servicing debt. The other Keynesians populating the system are watching the same movie: households operate in rosy real estate markets and enjoy strong labor markets; banks work in quiet financial markets with virtually no risk of failure. Hence, they too form optimistic expectations and nonchalantly participate in this increasingly indebted economy. If actual profits continually match and sustain expectations, it is easy to service debt. This hedge phase, as Minsky calls it, can comfortably proceed.

But an increasingly indebted system populated by Keynesians with expanding appetites for risk sooner or later enters the second stage, which Minsky labels the speculative phase. In this situation, debtors can cover only interest payments and cannot amortize the principal. Obviously, in this new phase, the risk becomes higher and more diffuse. The speculative content of borrowers' expectations is escalating, and this is due to the dark side of forecasting. In fact, borrowers are betting on the idea that the interest rate will not go up and the value of the collateral will not decline. As W. Buffett nicely observes, nothing sedates rationality like large doses of effortless money. These dynamics may then conduct the system to the ultra-speculative phase, whereby borrowers can cover neither interest nor the principal. Unlike in the speculative stage, in this last situation, the only way to keep the borrowers afloat is to have endless rising asset prices (or operating profit margin for private equity firms). To avoid problems, that is, prices and profits cannot just stay flat or not decline; they have to go up. Despite the self-evident hazardous nature of the situation, the dark side of forecasting drives Keynesians to expect further increments in prices and profits.

The flip side of forecasting enters the scene in another way, too. In the ultra-speculative stage, people are actually also betting that future buyers will buy these overvalued assets from them, assuming more new buyers will buy the same assets at even higher prices from future buyers. It is a Ponzi pyramidal scheme escalation of buying high and selling even higher.[9] In this ultra-speculative Ponzi phase, the dark

[9]Similar to a pyramid scheme in a Ponzi scheme (from C. Ponzi) in the ultra-speculative phase money from new investors is paid to earlier ones, and the chain works as long as there are enough new investors.

side of forecasting assumes the shape of a self-fulfilling prophecy—as more people enter the market and become speculators, prices actually rise. It is easy to imagine what can go wrong in this vulnerable system. Optimistic expectations may fail to realize because, for example, policies boost interest rates or some kind of adverse shock materializes. Just as it magically appears, then, optimism can vanish. Whatever the cause, when something eventually goes wrong, the above-mentioned spiral rides in the opposite direction. Once expectations are not matched by reality, Keynesians begin to be unable to pay back their debts. Households and firms try to sell their assets, but this depresses quotations and reduces the value of the collaterals. Because of mounting risks, interest rates rise and eventually banks start rationing the credit because even high interest rates cannot pay for the booming risks. Credit, financial, and housing markets crash. The system reaches the so called Minsky moment, and the crisis begins involving the real[10] side of the system: production and employment plummet. This is not an uncommon story in human affairs. Neglecting risks and alternating under- and over-optimism, humans not rarely put themselves in situations in which the result of their behavior is mainly dependent on luck for success.

The dark side of forecasting can be explored from another, actually not dramatically different, standpoint. I am referring to R. Shiller's view that argues that the predictive exercises performed by humans are featured by a nontrivial amount of *irrational exuberance* [14]. This latter is a state of mania among (clearly not Walrasians) traders who are so confident that the price of an asset (stock, commodity, currency, house) will keep going up that they lose sight of its fundamental value. Shiller's research, therefore, offers a look into speculative bubbles, which, in this trek, I see as another manifestation of the flip side of forecasting. As noticed in Chap. 3, basically, a large misalignment between market prices and fundamental prices is indicative of the presence of a bubble and has huge bad consequences for the system. The rationale is that how we value real and financial assets influences major economic and social policy decisions that affect not only investors but also society at large. For instance, the present and future value of the stock market must be balanced in order to avoid investing too much in some sector while underinvesting in others, not to mention the macroeconomic effects following the bubble burst. Two points in case are the dotcom bubble and the real estate bubble. As observed, market prices are a great source of information, but, clearly, usefulness strictly depends on correctness. Shiller posits various reasons contributing to the psychology behind the presence of speculative bubbles. Some of these factors operate in the background of the market. Among them are the ICT revolution, the political shift in support of business, the demographics of the Baby Boom (to save for their eventual retirement, many Boomers competed against each other to buy stocks inducing high price-earnings ratios), and low and stable inflation (which is favorable to stock markets).

[10] Real here is in the sense of distinct from financial, not distinct from nominal.

This flip side of forecasting may also emerge from elements that work in the foreground and shape the changing culture of investment—the mutual funds explosion; the expanding volume of trade; and the feeling, amplified by the mass media, that the economy has moved into a brighter "new era." Examining the individual-level side of the matter, then, Shiller recalls the findings of psychologists. Specifically, he elaborates on the herd behavior and anchoring that we have already met in, respectively, Chapters 2 and 3. As for the latter, I add that Shiller claims that if people's expectations are not anchored to economic fundamentals, then agents may use anchors stemming from psychology, which may bring out the dark side of forecasting.

Humans have worked out various devices to tackle the flip side of forecasting. As for that which leads to bubbles, humans have established authorities such as the US Securities and Exchange Commission. To prevent extreme events it, inter alia, occasionally restrains trade in financial markets. Another way to intervene is to enlarge the available information and to improve the degree of financial literacy among the general public. Governments typically aim to make financial information and data more easily accessible. They sustain financial literacy programs that explain the benefits of diversification and long-run investing, as well as the dangers of extrapolating recent returns into the future. These programs and the advice that "past performance is no guarantee of future results" can help to reduce personal failures and system-wide concerns. But, just as writing "smoking kills" on cigarettes packs is not sufficient (according to "*The Lancet*", the number of smokers worldwide has increased to 1.1 billion in 2019), these policies can barely transform all humans into Walrasians—the dark side of the *Four* is hard to tackle.

Turning our attention to the Minskian flip side of forecasting, our guides have suggested to "throw sand in the wheels" of speculative markets. J. Tobin, for example, proposed that the speculative price movements in the market for foreign currencies be restrained by levying a transaction tax on them. This so-called *Tobin tax* is recurrently re-proposed over time—especially, and unsurprisingly, amid turbulent times. Minsky's insights on the fact that complex financial derivative products contribute to and accelerate the destabilizing process suggest another way to intervene. In his words (p. 319) [15], "Bankers are merchants of debt who strive to innovate in the assets they acquire and the liabilities they market." Indeed, before the financial crisis (too) many humans were downplaying the evident risks related to opaque instruments such as CDOs (collateralized debt obligations) and other kinds of derivatives. Five years before the 2007 financial crisis, W. Buffett gave a warning describing these tools as "financial weapons of mass destruction."[11] The normative insight is easily taken. In order to tackle the dark side of forecasting, policymakers

[11] A derivative is a financial security whose fundamental value is reliant upon or derived from an underlying asset or group of assets (stocks, bonds, commodities). Though it that can be fruitfully used to hedge a position, speculate on the directional movement of an underlying asset, or give leverage to holdings, it is difficult to value correctly a single asset let alone value instruments whose price derives from a group of assets. Not to mention that most derivatives are also sensitive to changes in the amount of time to expiration, the cost of holding the underlying asset, and interest

should carefully monitor and regulate the innovating activity that leads to both new instruments and new operators in financial markets and credit markets. Since financial markets are extremely globalized and fluid, financial watchdogs must operate at the international level. In fact, this is what happened in the sequence of international agreements signed at Basel.

Unity is strength, but aggregating is neither costless nor easy. Aggregative tensions (i.e., the dark face of aggregating) are widespread. Communal living offers many types of discomfort because of the presence of various discords and conflicts among members. Even within the smallest and most cohesive social cluster—the family. Homophily, divorce, stereotypes, segregation, and foreign communities in cities are visible expressions of the aggregating issues that we have so far met in our trip. We have also observed that tensions become larger as aggregation becomes wider, and that the greater the internal identity, the weaker the social capital between the groups. All in all, unity does not imply uniformity—humans are individualistic social animals.

In view of our bird's-eye journey, in this break I will limit the visit to the dark face of aggregating to just two kinds of human clusters, cities and firms.

Density can have considerable downsides, which may be part of the reason why humans live both in cities and countryside, even these days. In human affairs, several forces typically drive toward hybrid solutions. Studying urban scaling laws, our guides [16] have shown that although production, innovating, and efficiency in energy consumption rise with the size of a city to a power that is slightly greater than 1, so do negative attributes such as crime, disease, and pollution. During these pandemic days, we have learned how density spreads diseases and not only ideas [17]. The increasing concentration of people in cities presents other kinds of challenges. When situations are repeated and each participant is observed by the others, benefits to cooperate may be larger than costs because deviants may be detected and punished. But this monitoring becomes less effective as the size of the city grows. In the anonymity of a big city, it is not easy to unmask and punish deviants often enough to deter cheating. To not waste the vast benefits of living together in modern cities, the downsides of aggregating must be managed. Even if it were possible, a significant regression to the countryside would be even worse than aggregating in cities. Moreover, history teaches that humans are smart problem solvers and that managing cities is feasible.

To remain concentrated on health affairs, in the nineteenth century, the USA was plagued by three cholera epidemics. Ultimately, cholera played a significant role in forcing that country to adopt important public health reforms like sewer systems, access to clean water, and clean streets [18]. Our guides recall that just as huge investments in massive waterworks were needed those days to curb the spread of cholera and yellow fever, huge investments in policing were needed to reduce crime in the 1990s [1]. On the other hand, humans are adaptative animals, and if a large

rates. In sum, there are many (in some case excessive) difficulties to perfectly match the value of a derivative with the underlying assets facilitating the emergence of bubbles.

public sector to combat the dark side of aggregating in large cities is needed, then they could eventually accept it. This may explain why, for example, people in New York are so much fonder of big government than people in rural Kansas [1].

Managing cities is thus feasible, but it is also difficult. As said, anonymity may be an ally of the dark side of aggregating because it tends to reduce cooperation and to raise opportunism. Thus, we may use CCTV cameras, policemen, facial recognition, and the like, but all that is costly and induces narrowed privacy and enlarged bureaucracy. There is then the general need for public interventions to be functional, but, as every citizen knows, it cannot be taken for granted. I will say more about that in the next section and in the following excursion, which is devoted to the flip side of aggregating related to the enterprise. In particular, we will examine market power, negative production externalities, and the relative institutional responses excogitated by humans.

What then is market power, and in what sense is it a flip side of aggregating? We have briefly met it in Chap. 5, and it is now time to inquire into it more explicitly. Following the OECD, market power refers to the ability of a firm (or group of firms) to raise and maintain price above the normal level that would prevail under perfect competition, and it is also referred to as monopoly power (the power to set prices). Remember that if a Walrasian system satisfies all the required assumptions (perfect competition, no externalities, etc.), then equilibrium prices, equating demand and supply, solve the allocation problem efficiently—the competitive equilibrium is Pareto optimal (cf. Chap. 1). Fixing prices at higher-than-normal levels, monopoly thus implies that supply and demand match each other out of the competitive equilibrium, which, in turn, produces an inefficient allocation of resources: there is at least another solution whereby it is possible to make anyone better off without making someone else worse off.

In the monopolistic solution, firms are unduly better off with respect to consumers. When a firm has no (actual or potential) competitors, then consumers desiring that good have no choice but to buy from the monopoly (which, in fact, in Greek means "single seller"), paying a higher price. There are then consumers who are willing to pay for the good at a competitive price—hence, they would benefit from buying it—but they will not get it. Besides the inefficiency stemming from charging prices above competitive market rates, monopoly power also leads firms to produce inferior-quality goods knowing that consumers have no alternatives. By the same token, market power implies reduced innovating efforts because there is no incentive either to find better ways to produce or to provide new goods. With respect to perfect competition, in sum, monopoly power means higher prices and lower quality/quantity of the goods available for the collectivity.

But market power also implies greater income and wealth inequality because few people gain monopolistic rents and persistently accumulate them, whereas in perfect competition, extra profits tend to vanish over time. Market power has various sources, but in this stopover, I shall linger on those which are more closely related to individual behavior and institutions as well as their interplay. A. Smith was aware of this potential flip side of enterprises and that human behavior often leads to situations whereby small groups cooperate at the expense of large groups (p. 99

and p. 183) [19]: "Masters are always and everywhere in a sort of tacit, but constant and uniform combination, not to raise the wages of labour above their actual rate. [...] Masters, too, sometimes enter into particular combinations to sink the wages of labour even below this rate." [...] "People of the same trade seldom meet together, even for merriment and diversion, but the conversation ends in a conspiracy against the public, or in some contrivance to raise prices [...]." Though in the 1700s, most firms were small producers and the economic system a relatively competitive arena, A. Smith also feared the possibility that even policymakers' behaviors could change the rules of the game in such a way to limit competition by creating large firms with great market power. A point in case is the East India Company. The state may then produce market power affecting the free entry/exit from the market.

When in modern capitalistic economies some banks or industrial firms are considered too big/strategic to fail, for example, they are often bailed out by governments when they might otherwise have failed. It gives these corporations the opportunity to behave less efficiently/innovatively with respect to a competitive firm; thus, their costumers' welfare suffers (not to mention that of taxpayers). In generating and sustaining market power, the behavior of entrepreneurs and policymakers is closely intertwined. M. Weber talked about *political capitalism* which he defined as (p. 164) [20] "exploitation of the politically oriented events and processes which open up opportunities for profit." In the Prologue, we have then observed how elites typically press politicians to maintain their privileges, such as market power, via lobbyism, corruption, state capture, etc. In Sect. 5.3, lastly, we have explored the technical and political difficulties to legalize market power via IPR. All that, as usual, need to be considered when the state addresses this part of the dark side of firms.

At the aggregate level, humans have been responding to these individual pushes toward market power, establishing rules such as antitrust law or antitrust policy. Their establishment is yet another instance of the sequence "behavior-hence-institution." The names of these institutions are a reminder that the constituents of social capital are instruments and, as such, may be used by humans for good or ill. For the sake of example, in a famous antitrust case, the US Department of Justice accused Microsoft of behaving anti-competitively by "bundling" its own Internet Explorer web browser with its Windows operating system. These days, a coalition of state attorneys general have launched a new antitrust lawsuit against Google, accusing it of abusing its control of the Android app store.

As observed, large corporations fight to maintain their privileged position, and in modern capitalistic economies, the game "market powered entities vs anti-market power rulers" has complex dynamics and increasing stakes. In the USA, big corporations regularly hire former lawmakers or ex-regulators to shape government policy. According to data compiled by OpenSecrets.org since 2000, the total spending on lobbying in that country has gone from $1.56 billion to $3.53 billion. In capitalistic systems, the solution is to have regulators and other authorities who are as independent as possible from political power, but the game is far from being over. The awkwardness of tackling this sort of issues reaches its maximum in international settings. In fighting international cartels such as the OPEC cartel, for instance, which *deus-ex-machina* has the political power to contrast such opportunistic agreement and to enforce antitrust policies?

The second element of the flip side of aggregating in firms that I want to explore is externalities. Before seeing why externalities are a flip side, a definition is necessary. According to the OECD glossary, externalities emerge when the effect of production or consumption of goods and services imposes on third parties' costs or benefits which are not reflected in (i.e., remain "external" to) the prices charged for the goods and services being provided. Externalities may thus refer to consumption and production, and their effect on third parties may be either positive or negative. In our trip, we saw a case of negative production externality in Chap. 2 whereby a railroad spread sparks igniting fires in a wheat field near the tracks. As for consumption externality, going to university brings positive externalities because more educated people tend to show greater civic engagement and to be more enterprising, which brings greater economic value to society.[12] Since this trek deals with the flip side of enterprises, I concentrate on negative production externalities. If, as said, collusive behaviors may contribute appreciably to create market power, the role of the market system becomes more central when dealing with externalities.

More specifically, we have learned that if Walrasian systems satisfy all the required assumptions, then the invisible hand mechanism coordinates behaviors so as to materialize the Pareto optimality. But this efficient allocation only considers private effects; that is, efficiency only refers to people *directly* involved in the transactions while indirect effects are simply not accounted for. Thus, social—i.e., direct plus indirect—effects are only partially priced in. In this sense, it is not a matter of collusive behavior, but it is a "technical" failure of the market system. Externalities pop up even in competitive markets because these markets cannot internalize them, and this generates inefficiencies. Otherwise stated, regardless of the presence of market power, externalities lead equilibrium prices to fail to reflect the true social costs and benefits of the interaction; thus, the allocation turns out to be Pareto inefficient. It should clarify why externalities are a flip side of the firm.

To visit more in detail this flip side I consider one of the most-watched example of negative production externality, pollution. As it should be clear, a firm that pollutes the environment creates costs to society, but those costs are not priced into the final good it produces. From its individual viewpoint, the private firm behaves as expected—it produces optimally, and it does that only considering its private costs. These costs do not include the pollution of air and water because these latter have no market prices; thus, the firm can treat air and water as free goods. Lacking pecuniary constraints, then private firms will tend to overconsume air and water (i.e., to over pollute). But from the system viewpoint, production goes hand in hand with pollution, which encompasses social costs. The decisions of polluting firms,

[12]Education, e.g., has positive externalities because more educated citizens are typically better informed and more socially engaged but that is not accounted for by private firms that, accordingly, underprovide it. To be sure note that although education makes workers more productive, this benefit is partly internalized because markets reward education with higher wages.

accordingly, are suboptimal for society because the market solution leads to overproduction—taking account of the social cost of pollution, the firms' optimal production should be lower. Otherwise stated, this part of the flip side of enterprises is epitomized in the overproduction of *bads* that is, in the current case, pollution.[13]

It is easy to see the dramatic importance of this dark side of aggregating for the current and future welfare of humans. The majority of us agree that global warming is among the most lethal *bads* produced by humans and that its impacts are felt by everyone all over the globe. To address pollution (but the basic logic is valid for other sorts of negative externalities), it is typical to use one particular approach and two specific policy tools. Their common intent is to align individual and system-wide interests. The approach consists in what our guides refer to as the "polluter pays principle," which can be applied, for example, to greenhouse gas emitters. The rationale is to force emitters to internalize the cost of pollution in order to yield the market outcome that would have prevailed with adequate internalization of all costs by polluters. To induce the polluter to pay, one of the two policy instruments is a price-based mechanism in the form of a carbon tax, whereby the price of pollution is determined by the rate of the tax for each ton of greenhouse gas emitted. Trivially, suppose that every unit produced generates a negative externality in the form of dirty air quantifiable in 1$. The government could then place a 1$ tax on each unit produced to ensure that the firm pays the actual cost of production. As a result of the higher cost of production, the firm will reduce its production, thus reducing the level of pollution [21].[14] In principle, taxes are preferred by policymakers because they increase public finance, whereas regulations are costly (they need authorities, monitoring, etc.). But empirical evidence from several European countries suggests that addressing pollution via taxation is not easy—the tax revenue is less than half of the total estimated external costs (not to mention the difficulty of estimating external costs).

The second institutional tool exploits the trading spirit of humans, the market mechanism, and the general argument that most externalities result from the lack of property rights. Governments may introduce property rights that, creating pollution markets, help internalize the externality.[15] More specifically, the policy instrument takes the form of a quota-based system, often referred to as a cap-and-trade or emissions trading system. A cap is set on the total amount of certain greenhouse gases that can be emitted by the firms covered by the system. In passing, note that this is a first advantage with respect to taxation—the total amount of emissions is established by the state (which should carefully follow the suggestions of scientists but, as the experience of the current pandemic shows, the state can fail in several

[13]In passing, notice that just as negative externalities lead the market to overproduce *bads*, goods providing positive externalities are less than optimally produced by markets. That is, for instance, the market solution provides less education than optimal from the social viewpoint.

[14]In passing, note that A.C. Pigou has been tackling these "ecological" issues since the early 1900s. He introduced the concept of externality and suggested addressing negative externalities via what is now known as Pigouvian tax [21].

[15]Recall that in capitalistic markets the exchanged object is a property right (Sect. 2.3).

ways). Within the cap, firms buy or receive emissions allowances or permits that give firms a legal right to pollute a certain amount (e.g., 100 units of carbon dioxide per year). Firms can and trade these rights with one another because some firms find it easier or cheaper to reduce emissions than others and can thus sell permits to firms whose cost for reducing emissions is higher. Therefore, the trading in pollution markets takes place between high-cost and low-cost polluters, thereby determining the price of a polluting permit. The polluters pay to ensure they have enough permits to cover the volume of emissions they have emitted for the given year. After each year, in fact, each firm must surrender enough allowances to cover fully its emissions; otherwise, fines are imposed. Note that the presence of pollution markets fixes a positive price to a public good (the atmosphere) whose price, from the private standpoint, would otherwise be zero (and, hence, would be overconsumed).

Evidence shows that the cap-and-trade approach has proven to be an effective tool in driving emissions reductions cost. According to the EU Emissions Trading System, for example, in Europe, emissions have been reduced by about 35% between 2005 and 2019. Other observations are worth stressing for our tour's aim. First, the cap-and-trade approach is yet another instance of the positive connections of trading and aggregating—the former may help to manage the latter. Second, note the complex tight ties between state and market within the market system and how the state may fruitfully exploit the market—a market failure is tackled by the state, which eases the birth of a new market via an institution, and then leaves the market mechanism to solve the interaction in a socially acceptable way. Third, the circumstance that human behavior is less central here with respect to the described situation referring to market power possibly eases the solution of the game between firms and state—it is easier to fix a technical failure than a behavioral failure because behavioral issues affect all humans, no matter if they are private agents or policymakers. Fourth, someone may see pollution markets and the right to pollute that are exchanged therein as an immoral way to proceed. They may suggest using "moral suasion" to incentivize firms to internalize the cost of pollution voluntarily and/or consumers to pay higher prices to buy less environmentally damaging items. Though these strategies may surely accompany cap and trade and be possibly useful in the long run, cap and trade is significantly more effective as immediate tool. Moral hazard (i.e., behaving in ways that are harmful to others when we are not going to be held fully responsible) is typically stronger than moral suasion. As repeatedly stated, the economic system (in this case via the ingredients of capitalism) should aim to arrange scarce resources (in this case the atmosphere) managing mixed behaviors, and it should do that taking as given the inherently compound nature of human behaviors. The essential point is that with the current conditions of technology, human wants, and human behaviors, we cannot eliminate either firm production or pollution. As usual, a temperate position is preferable to extreme ones, and cap and trade is coherent with this view—it is a working approach to incentivize firms to reduce pollution as efficiently as possible.

In Chap. 5, we explored the paramount contribution of innovating in improving both the individual well-being and the performances of the economic system as a whole. What can then be the dark side of ideas, innovations, technical progress, and their diffusion? A first indication could refer to the fact that, as has been said, innovating may aim to bad ends and/or its outcome may be used for good or ill. Innovating may then produce mixed effects. During the journey, we have observed that the diffusion of television may both integrate and polarize societies. In visiting Minsky's viewpoint, we saw how innovation in financial markets may produce instruments such as asset-backed securities or CDO. They can destabilize the system, inducing uncertainty because of the difficulty of computing the fundamentals of such complex tools and favoring very risky behaviors. Innovating may raise moral issues, too. Among them are, the reduction in privacy (as in the case of video cameras, data retention, tracking of mobile phones, facial recognition, or telephone tapping) and the exigency to find the extent to which scientists can venture in "playing God" (as in the cases of human cloning, genetically modified organisms, or sentients humanoid).

Following the insights offered by our guides, in this stopover, I want to examine the flip side of innovating from another standpoint. Marx predicted a world in which technical innovation would increasingly devalue and impoverish workers. Keynes talked about "technological unemployment" to mean that the ability of humans in innovating often outruns that of creating new jobs, although generating only a "temporary phase of maladjustment" [22]. Schumpeter highlighted that innovating makes the market system inherently dynamic; thus, capitalism is virtually always in a transitional state between old and new equilibria. But even if the recent historical experience tells that over time the balance is positive, during the transition phase, innovating may badly affect part of the population; for someone, that is, it may be more destructive than creative or, in our tour's jargon, darker than brighter. These days, UBER displaces cab drivers, robots displace workers, Amazon displaces physical shops, and Booking.com displaces travel agencies. This parallels the mentioned fact that for some people international trade has a dark side.

Obsolete machinery can be junked, but what about the losers of the transition phase? As for jobs and wages, then, innovating may unevenly affect the humans populating innovative market systems. A point in case is when innovating has disparate effects across different birth cohorts. Since the transition period may be long-lasting, in fact, older workers might never experience the higher wages and employment allowed by innovating. During the Industrial Revolution, for example, real wages began to rise continually only from the 1830s. Not to mention that older workers could justifiably be less prone to invest in their human capital and be less flexible in adopting the new technologies than youngsters. For some of them, thus, the bright side of innovating could be obscured by its dark side. Notice that because technical change in modern systems is endless, there will always be some sort of generational digital divide—it is the demographic dark side of the creative destruction.

Negative fallout is not limited to demography. Technological change may reduce the demand for unskilled workers, decreasing their employment and wages. Since, on the contrary, innovating increases the wages of skilled workers, it gives rise to phenomena such as the *wage college gap*, that is, the wage gap between workers with a college education and those without. Now, skill-biased innovation could be welfare enhancing if the gains of the skilled workers are more than sufficient to compensate for the losses of the unskilled workers. But while the skilled workers could compensate for the unskilled workers, such compensation seldom occurs triggering the flip side of innovating. Additionally, in many advanced industrial countries, those who suffer more during the transition period are often humans at the bottom of income distribution; thus, innovating can contribute to raise poverty (at least in relative terms).

Against this backdrop, it is unsurprising that among the most discussed themes dealing with the flip side of innovating are, on the one hand, the associations between innovations and income/wealth inequality and, on the other hand, the contraposition between humans and robots. Addressing the former, economists [23] observe that in the ranking of the wealthiest individuals in the USA compiled by *Forbes Magazine*, 11 out of 50 are listed as inventors of a US patent and many more manage or own firms that patent. They then remark that the increase in top income inequality has been pervasive across occupations, but it has particularly affected occupations that are closely related to innovating—entrepreneurs, engineers, scientists, and managers. They also report causal relationships: an increase of 1% in the number of patents increases the top 1% income share by 0.2%. Last but not least, they stress that patenting and top income inequality go hand in hand even outside the USA.

In light of what has been said, inspecting Schumpeter's view, it comes not as a surprise that many rich humans are Schumpeterians—they are the most dynamic and value-producing agents in the market system. To the extent that income/wealth inequality derives from "deserved" Schumpeterian rents, the issue for the state is to preserve incentives while avoiding socially and/or morally excessive disparity. But as remarked in Sect. 5.3, problems are even greater than this because it is hard to discern patents protecting genuine Schumpeterian rents from those protecting monopolistic rents. It is also the case that some patents turn out to be unnecessary or harmful. Last but not least, one must consider the race to ensure monopolistic rents.

Elaborating on the fact that greater social mobility limits inequality, some economists have shown that innovation is positively associated with social mobility but less so in local areas with more intense lobbying activities [24]. Others have claimed that interest groups put pressure on policymakers in order to maintain their privileged positions through blocking the potential for technological innovations [25]. The problem is not peculiar to capitalistic economies, although elsewhere, the game is played somewhat differently. These days, for example, China's large tech corporations such as Alibaba, Tencent, and Xiaomi are investing billions into Chinese President Xi's vision of "common prosperity." It is a case of "share otherwise I intervene" policy: Chinese corporations are "invited" to be "altruist" in order to avoid strict regulations.

Turning our attention to the second topic, economists have been studying the specific impact of robots on labor markets [26, 27]. Empirical evidence from aggregate data for the USA shows that one more robot per thousand workers reduces wages by 0.42% and the employment-to-population ratio by 0.2 percentage points, or, equivalently, one new robot reduces employment by about 3.3 workers. The crux is that as the cost of robots continues to fall while their capabilities go up, robotization will continue to grow for the time being. As usual, definitions matter, and in this case, they also offer hints on the winners and losers of robotization. The International Federation of Robotics [28] defines an industrial robot as "an automatically controlled, reprogrammable, and multipurpose [machine]." Thus, textile looms, elevators, cranes, or transportation bands are not robots, since they have a unique purpose, cannot be reprogrammed to perform other tasks, and/or require a human operator. Taking advantage of this standpoint, our guides [29] have argued that the dark side of innovating turns out to be pertaining not to the usually considered skill of workers but, rather, to their tasks. Bookkeepers, clerks, and certain assembly-line workers are relatively easy to routinize (H. Ford *docet*): thus, they are the most likely to get displaced by automation and robots. In contrast, high skill jobs that use problem-solving capabilities, intuition, and creativity (e.g., engineers and architects), as well as low-skill jobs that require situational adaptability and in-person interactions, are less easy to routinize. Instances of the latter are babysitting or elderly care, which, in fact, do not suffer from the flip side of innovating (indeed, quite the reverse).

The takeaway from what we have been discussing is that the gains from innovating can be unevenly distributed and may imply deep, painful structural adjustments. Policymakers must then alleviate the social impact of the dark side of innovating. They can manage it by spreading the gains from innovating as widely as possible. The state must design an education system enhancing the comparative advantages of humans with respect to robots. As per those already in the labor market, one way is to implement redistributive policies favoring the losers via, for example, differentiated income tax cuts. Other relevant policies include stronger social safety nets centered on empowering and protecting technological displaced workers. Likewise, interventions promoting the investment in human capital made by low-skilled workers help to reap the gains of technological change. Since low-income households may have problems in accessing credit markets to finance investments in human capital, governments may also intervene by directly financing them.

Needless to say, all these policies need taxation and all affect the functioning of markets.[16] For example, employment protection legislation (dismissal and hiring regulations) may increase job security, and the greater enforceability of job contracts may increase workers' investment in innovative activities. But it also increases firms' adjustment costs, which may lead to underinvestment in activities, such as innovations, that require adjustment. Besides stressing the pros of protecting vulnerable groups, our guides report evidence pointing out that job dismissal regulation may lengthen the duration of unemployment and that the employment protection

[16] Taxes are said to be neutral if they do not cause inefficiency by distorting the structure of incentives. Neutrality is often proposed as a desirable property of a tax system. Poll taxes and lump-sum taxes on economic rents are neutral, but it is hard to find any other examples.

legislation induces significantly lower innovation intensity in industries with higher job layoff propensity [30, 31]. Unfortunately, it is not trivial to stress that policies must tackle the flip side of the *Four* while not shrinking its bright side, which, admittedly, is a hard task. Consider for instance the political pressure faced by policymakers. The push exerted by the losers of innovating is great because they are usually a well-defined and well-organized cluster of individuals, fired employees, for example. In contrast, the bright side of innovating is shared by all the consumers who are a vast but sparse network. Employees and owners of firms affected by the dark side of innovating (as well as those affected by globalization) then try to survive by asking for subsidies, tariff protection, and bailouts. The negative side of this kind of state intervention is that the survival of unproductive firms and jobs generates unfair competition and lowers the efficiency of the system as a whole. This has some similarities with the too-big/too-strategic to fail story. In sum, behaviors and institutions intersect in complex ways when humans perform the *Four*.

6.3 Speculating on the Future

We have so far journeyed across the *Four,* exploring several topics, highlighting the role of behaviors and economic systems, and offering a narration of some historical passages. The idea of this last stopover is to take stock of what we have learned so far to envisage some possible near-future scenarios—say from now to 2050, to use an eye-catching year. As you have noticed, forecasting is a hard task. It is even more so when dealing with human affairs that proceed along highly nonlinear trajectories that make it misleading to expect that analogies are identical, that history repeats itself exactly. Hence, even what will happen in the few decades ahead may turn out to be not a simple projection of the past. This said, the knowledge gained by looking into to the *Four* turns out to be fruitful for accumulating insights on both past and future patterns. Although immersed in a permanently evolving, complex, and uncertain socioeconomic environment, in fact, some of the elements emerging from our tour will likely remain with us. Even the definitory *caveat* is among these constants. Just to mention, if in its infancy, artificial intelligence (AI) was seen as a very specific set of search-based techniques, currently AI is thought of as including several subfields such as robotics, natural language processing, computer vision, and machine learning (along with all of its variations, including deep learning, reinforcement learning, imitation learning). Other recognizable time-invariant features in our trip are the insatiability of human beings and their multifaceted behavior, the presence of the *Four*, the behavioral problems and institutional solutions that these social interactions create, and the contextual permanence of integrating and disintegrating forces. For in the next few decades, at least, I do not expect humans to give into natural limits, and I believe they will continue to chase their wants implementing the *Four*, behaving with collaborative spirit but also with inexorable opportunism.

Where all that will take us mainly depends on us. The ambiguity and complexity of human life and the immanent role of fortune must not lead us to conclude that our lives are totally predestined or out of our control. As it has been emerging in our journey across human affairs, uncertainty is widespread, and luck is important in breaking existing schemes. But from then on, humans have been the architects of their destiny, and I do not see clues of changes. It may be for better or worse, and all we hope that Sapiens will behave as wisely as its name suggests.[17] The stories narrated in this tour are encouraging and disclose that in human affairs, it is often advisable to not take extreme views. Several challenges have repeatedly tested the resilience and adaptability of humans and their systems, and they often have overwhelmed the capacity of existing systems and models; however, humans have never passively faced them, and they always have found a solution. Despite their insatiable appetite and mixed behavior, humans are still alive and kicking. I do not foresee major changes in these behavioral attitudes of humans, and I do not see any dystopic scenario in front of us.

Against this general backdrop, in the following I will speculate about, always through the lens of the *Four*, the near-future patterns that could move along some existing trends, emphasizing the behavioral and institutional aspects of the matter. The trends I will examine are those stemming from innovating efforts dealing with ICT industries, digital technologies, and the like. The rationale goes like this. Just as many other outcomes of innovating, these developments involve individuals, markets, firms, the technical and social relations within and between them, as well as the other three businesses under scrutiny. As we are witnessing day after day, in fact, innovating is making the other three *Four* ever more "digital" (in broad terms) and "digitalization" is a central aspect of the other three human endeavors, being both part of the problem and part of the solution. While I frame the discussion trying to separate these human endeavors, overlapping is evident. On the positive side, it is in line with what we learned through our journey—the *Four* are highly intertwined and I speculate they will continue to be so.

In looking toward the foreseeable future, the main points that I want to emphasize are the following. I daresay that innovating will lead to a number of hybrid solutions in the social interactions we are traveling across. Innovating is creating a sort of digital mirror of the physical world, one with its own activities, behaviors and institutions that are flanking those offline. Since I believe that humans will maintain their compound behavior, I expect a greater role for the state because the need for it will be larger than in the past. There is nothing new in that—as pointed out in our excursions, usually solutions are balanced in human societies which typically become growingly institutionalized, passing from informal to formal organisms, and I believe this will continue.

Concentrating on trading, just as the service revolution has increasingly dematerialized the traded object, so innovating is transforming traditional services in virtual exchanges. On the Internet, we can already find services to write letters to

[17] Homo Sapiens literally means *wise man*. The conflict of interest is crystal clear: Sapiens is the name that the human being has given to himself. It would be nice to know how the other animals call us (especially the endangered ones).

friends and to mail holiday cards; we have online services such as banking, legal and health services, education, and customer care. But humans are insatiable, consumers are voracious sovereigns, random events happen, and opportunities abound. The current pandemic is yet another element supporting the search for new ways/goods to trade, and, in fact, tech companies are providing essential online services and are proactively placing new bets. The blockchain technology, for example, is potentially revolutionary in helping humans to solve the traditional challenges posed by trading, such as trust, risks, efficiency, and transaction costs. Likewise, AI can fully automate the process of matching and pricing a truck to a load, drastically reducing time and costs with respect to phone or email. AI can also automate customer care services; many call center and help desk services are already "staffed" by virtual agents whose skills and tasks are growing (think about language skills). Amid all these frantic changes occurring in how humans trade, it seems interesting to note that if new forms of money are appearing (cryptocurrencies and digital currencies), forms of barter are resurfacing. If we use Facebook, for example, we have the service. But it is not a free lunch; we pay by giving Facebook our data and our attention.

Gains from trade will in fact be extracted ever more from goods (in the sense of Marshall) such as access, data, attention, and information. New goods and new ways of trading evidently call for updating legal and regulatory frameworks. Just as in old times, the first trading efforts outside families and villages steered the enlargement of the institutional set; the same boost arises these days when we venture into virtual markets. If the state must still inform and protect the weaker side of markets, such as credit, health, and financial markets, for example, it must now also inform and protect the countless users of eBay, Amazon, and other online trading platforms. If users are allowed to manage permissions, indeed, these permissions are hard for common people to use, understand, and control, not to mention that privacy policies can change—sometimes dramatically—after a user creates an account. As noticed for health messages on the packaging of tobacco products, individuals very seldom read the "instructions;" they just "tag" what is needed to continue, and the state must account for that. Likewise, there is nothing new in the evolutive path that led oil to be the new gold and now data to be the new oil. The point, rather, is that data is a different kind of good with respect to oil and gold. Specifically, its non-rival nature implies that data can have many owners and, as learnt through our trip, the non-private nature of goods requires the attention of the state.

If the current race to digitalization reduces the physical limits of the traded goods and permits us to overcome the issues related to physical distance between suppliers and customers, it does not mean that traditional face-to-face exchanges of material stuff will disappear. Our tour suggests that in human businesses, balanced views are often preferable to extreme ones. Technological problems as well as natural and cultural attitudes push toward hybrid solutions in trading. As for technology, online systems have trouble telling shoppers exactly what looks fresh, what they might like, and what other options exist. In fact, these days, Internet buying accounted for a tiny fraction of overall grocery sales. Even central bankers have been arguing that digital currencies simply will complement, rather than replace, current forms of money.[18]

There are then some aspects of human nature and cultural sociality that prevent the complete digitalization of trading in the near future—if humans have disengaged from some material necessities, some others will likely remain with them. Regarding physical shops, just as supermarkets superseded but not eliminated the traditional retail markets sector because of the benefits embedded in personal exchanges, so e-commerce will reduce but will not eliminate physical commerce because of a mix of socio-psychological factors working at individual, group, and societal levels. Among them there is the merit that humans seem to attach to face-to-face contact. As remarked in our tour, an obvious benefit of in-person exchanges is that they support social capital. Trading is a social interaction, and consumers also derive cultural and social benefits from direct contact with sellers. Consider the advantages that many humans attach to the physical markets operating either in small towns or in the communities living in cities. The presence of these markets has accompanied humans for thousands of years, and it seems hard to imagine a near future whereby those human aggregations have no physical shops, street markets, or farmers' markets. A blended solution is forecastable for trading in the entertainment industry, too. Despite all efforts by powerful streaming platforms such as Netflix, a significant share of humans still enjoys physically clustering to watch movies, operas, and shows. The purpose, of course, is also to socialize to meet new people. The physical contact argument seems to apply even to material goods. Think about the ongoing presence of physical books and the resurgence in the demand for vinyl or physical photographic films. There is always a share of humans wanting it. In any case, as typically happens when executing the *Four,* it seems likely that even digitalization will lead both to integrating and differentiating humans.

During our stop devoted to how humans forecast economic subjects, we learned that beliefs and informal institutions are critical. As noticed in Chap. 3, then, humans also use all five senses when forecasting economic subjects. With more or less awareness, likewise, they also take advantage of the body language. Until recently, social interactions have been eminently physical, and this is the typical way in which humans have been using senses and learning how to form and use beliefs and informal institutions to predict the behavior of the others.

In the near future, however, it might be harder for individuals to forecast economic subjects. Social networking portals or sites have several uses and can be helpful in many aspects of life, but virtual social life may present drawbacks to humans' skill in predicting the behavior of others. Just as innovating is dematerializing trading, so it is depersonalizing communications and relationships among humans—from penmanship to typewriting, from face-to-face discussions to

---

[18]The present and future of money in the digital age, Lecture by Fabio Panetta, Member of the Executive Board of the ECB (Dec 2021) https://www.ecb.europa.eu/press/key/date/2021/html/ecb.sp211210~09b6887f8b.en.html. Money and Payments: The U.S. Dollar in the Age of Digital Transformation, Jan 2022, Board of Governors of the Federal Reserve.

telephones, from physical communities to virtual groups, and from offices to remote working.

Our social interactions are held increasingly online, perhaps too quickly. Sooner or later most humans will adapt to this new normal as well as they eventually will be able to predict the behavior of the others even in virtual social interactions. But adapting takes time, and in the meantime, problems emerge—depersonalization must not end up with dehumanization. It would be really sad if most of the smiles that we exchange were emoticons or emoji. Sad and unhealthy—we do know that smiling comes with some psycho-physical benefit. As for the skill of forecasting economic subjects, if virtual social networks result in the degeneration, individualization, and isolation of humans, these latter would be deprived of the foundations for the sufficient understanding of social relations. On the other hand, innovating should support pre-existing social networks, not enlarge them just because it is technically feasible.

This new normal is particularly dangerous for youngsters. As we have seen in our tour, humans have long, distinct periods of childhood and adolescence that enable us to learn, play, socialize, and absorb important experiences. We have also seen that Aristotle viewed family as a gymnasium whereby the young learn to live in larger groups. Modern scientists have discovered that most people do not reach full psycho-physical maturity until the age 25. Before this age young people are still learning about intimacy, friendship, family, self-expression, and political and social awareness, and so deserve adequate support and protection. These days, however, youngsters interact more frequently online than in the real world. This leads teenagers to face two problems in their learning about how to approach others. On the one side, the unstoppable innovation in the digital world deteriorates the already tumultuous parent-child relationship, enlarging the distance between "digital immigrant" parents and "digital-native/addicted" children. Making the generational gap larger, virtual social networks are thus making harder to attain the advantageous vertical transmission of culture. On the other side, the stronger peer-to-peer contamination among youngsters cannot substitute the reduced role of parents in training children to learn about how to forecast economic subjects. Even more so if horizontal transmission occurs mainly in the virtual world. Indeed, having many virtual friends often means maintaining superficial relationships from which it is difficult to infer behaviors. Not to mention that behaviors in real life and on virtual sites are different and that the latter may be less authentic because, just as we noticed for large cities, cheating is easier in the anonymity of virtual worlds. Just for the sake of example, from April to June 2021, Facebook removed more than 1.7 billion fake accounts from its site. One dramatic consequence of that is that young humans may become highly vulnerable to cybercrime and cyberwarfare. Some people, in fact, may feel more secure in the traditional physical world where one's behaviors and beliefs are more protected in the sense of being less exposed to became common knowledge (because, e.g., of hackers or acts of revenge by former friends). This is less the case for youngsters, who tend to be more confident in the Internet and social media, making public central personal life issues. But if Latins wisely adverted that *verba volant, scripta manent* (spoken words fly away, written words remain), the Internet has infinite memory.

All that evidently calls for a careful monitoring by the state—social platforms were not designed for security but for openness and information sharing. Among others, socializing in virtual sites has raised the issue of the "right to be forgotten," which enables individuals to request information to be removed from the indexes of major search engines.[19] Although the visibility of the information is significantly limited, however in practice, it is not removed from the open web. The basic point is that innovating should help real social life, neither deteriorate, nor complicate nor substitute for it.

All considered, I guess that the dangers of virtualization along with the difficulties to manage it, on the institutional side, and the need of some control and face to face contact, on the behavioral side, will prevent digital social interactions from substituting for real-world ones. Eventually, humans will learn to perform hybrid forecasting exercises that allow them to live together, better, and longer in both worlds.

If innovating might force humans to refine their ability to forecast economic subjects, it makes it easier for certain groups of humans to perform these sorts of predictions. Innovations, for example, are allowing us to put into practice the old idea of "basic emotions," which claims that emotions can be recognized based on facial "microexpressions."[20] The emotion recognition technology (ERT) uses AI to analyze facial expressions, body language, and voice to identify people's feelings or their level of attention. ERT is a big industry, and it is getting bigger. The global emotion detection and recognition market size is projected to grow from USD 19.5 billion in 2020 to USD 37.1 billion by 2026.[21] Applications are indeed vast and fruitful. ERT may be used to predict psychotic disorders, monitor moods and attention of employees and drivers, reveal engagement in online learning, and prevent and detect crime.

But there is no need to be an Orwell fan to see how potentially dangerous ERT can be. First, these technologies are still far from being perfect. According to information gathered by the Association for Psychological Science in 2019, there is no scientific support for the assumption that a person's emotional state can be readily inferred from her facial movements. Thus ERT, acting as a sort of digitally induced stereotype, may produce misleading forecasts and social polarization. ERT then requires the mass collection of personal data to track, monitor, and profile individuals, often in real time, which may be at odds with individuals' dignity,

[19] For instance, this right was established by the Court of Justice of the European Union in 2014 as a way to protect users' rights to privacy and data protection. Its interpretation and implementation have however created a worrisome tension with the right to freedom of expression and information.

[20] Emotion recognition technology is based on the 1970s theory by psychologist P. Ekman, called the basic emotion theory which, in turn, is based on 1897 Darwin's paper titled "The Expression of the Emotions in Man and Animal."

[21] https://www.marketsandmarkets.com/Market-Reports/emotion-detection-recognition-market-23376176.html

privacy, and freedom of opinion. It is perhaps unsurprising that certain innovations have captured the attention of governments in centralized economic systems, China being a point in case. Recently, the government of this country has been implementing a social credit rating system. It works somewhat like a penalty point system for drivers—data are collected from multiple public and government sources to create a social profile of an individual citizen. Each individual starts with 1000 points, with points added for being a "positive member of society" and deducted if they do not contribute as positively. There is no need to underline the potential danger nested in these practices (re-education camps *docent*). This said, even in systems whereby the individual is given more weight, things must be taken under tight control. For big data to be a legitimate tool, the system needs checks and balances.

Among the themes emerging from these issues, there is the possible worsening in the relationship between consumers and private firms, which may require state regulations. Large enterprises are progressively exploiting big data to profile potential consumers by summarizing data which include their shopping habits, lifestyles, income level, preferences, etc. Even not considering the issues of privacy, etc., other dangers can arise from the availability of such detailed personal data. To the extent that customers will face informatic engineers and data scientists rather than traditional sellers, for example, their sovereignty and gains from trade may be at risk. Consider the case when the knowledge of emotions reveals a vulnerable emotional state. It can be used to mentally force people to perform actions they would not do otherwise—for example, buying goods they do not need. Recall that when one of the trading partners is in some sense weaker than the other, then the flip side of trading is likely to occur.

Two practices that are already widely implemented and that are currently under the radar of the state are price steering and personalized pricing [32]. The latter is a form of price discrimination whereby the firm tailors the prices of products based on individuals' willingness to pay. This willingness is estimated by gathering information on consumers' conduct or characteristics using tools such as big data analytics. For example, Zalando and Amazon use their consumer data to implement different prices for different consumers. While this practice may permit low-end consumers to buy at lower prices, it could be negative for those customers who are willing to pay more. The point is that since they do not know exactly how much consumers are willing to pay, firms charge all customers the same price; thus, there are consumers who pay less than they are willing to pay. With personalized pricing, however, these consumers pay more.

If this sort of *divide et impera* exercise may end up with a mere redistribution of money from customers to firms, there could be bigger social perils stemming from it. Despite the availability of big data and advanced technology, in practice, personalized pricing cannot be implemented at the individual level and is typically based on groups of consumers who exhibit similar traits and behaviors. But this cluster-level microtargeting may lead to price discrimination based on factors like race, religion, age, health, gender, or national origin, which is something to be monitored closely. In Chap. 2, we noticed that if private health insurance companies could discriminate between individuals on the basis of, for example, genetic data, some individuals could not obtain medical insurance at an affordable price.

Personalization on e-commerce sites, possibly disadvantaging the users, may then be obtained by manipulating the products shown to them. This is what the second mentioned practice—price steering—does. It consists of manipulating the results of an Internet search according to some consumers' features, preferences, and behavior in order to display more expensive products to consumers with higher willingness to pay. Unbeknownst to users, for example, the travel website Orbitz "steered" Apple users toward more expensive hotels in select locations by placing them at higher ranks in search results. As easily seen, there is nothing substantially new in these practices—sellers always want buyers to spend as much money as possible. In physical supermarkets, for example, there are similar forms of subtle conditioning, although they are based on psychology. In these supermarkets, indeed, fresh scented colored produce (fruits, vegetables, flowers, etc.) is the first thing one sees because the seller expects that the vibrant colors and fragrances put the (non Walrasian) customer in a good mood, and the happier the client, the more he is likely to spend.[22]

If from the behavioral viewpoint price steering is just an updated version of the traditional game played by the same kind of players, the institutional answers will differ. To reiterate, our trip leads us to presume that in implementing the *Four,* the naturally mixed behavior of humans remains substantially unchanged while the economic system evolves. It is easier and quicker to implement institutions than to wait or to try to induce changes in innate behaviors. If price discrimination often benefits consumers by increasing trade and driving firms to compete, without well-designed antitrust and consumer protection laws, these practices may become exploitative, distortionary, and exclusionary with respect to customers and other firms. In this job, as usual, formal institutions are and will continue to be flanked by social capital and informal institutions. These pricing strategies, for instance, trigger the horizontal transmission of information. When consumers find out that they are paying more than their friends for the same product, overall trust in the retailer may drop. As learned through our trip, moreover, fairness must not be neglected in human affairs—many consumers may feel that a high variation of prices is unfair. In the early 2000s, some Amazon customers made public that by deleting cookies they could buy the same good and spend less. Amazon's boss J. Bezos said the price difference was part of a company test offering random prices to determine an optimal price for products. This notwithstanding, Amazon gave thousands of customers refunds, and Bezos apologized. In 2012, the mentioned Orbitz's practice was made public by a *The Wall Street Journal* article. Readers posted hundreds of comments saying that they would never use Orbitz again, and Orbitz stopped this practice. Just as physical nightclubs have doormen to protect their customers and

[22] In our excursion on forecasting economic subject (Sect. 3.1), we have learned that humans react to smells and other sensorial conditioning.

business, virtual platforms attentively hamper the access to undesirable parties—they want to send the message that they are a safe place to perform social interactions. These days customers can exploit social networks to monitor the situation and can rapidly spread information. Word of mouth has always been a powerful tool for customers. Even more so in our modern systems where word spread in a digital manner—through viral tweets, hashtags, and the like.

Turning our attention to life inside firms, innovating will continue to change it, leading to a different role for humans in the workplace of the future. I am specifically referring to the recent developments dealing with remote working and robots, which can alter how humans aggregate in firms. Big data and machine learning will make it possible to automate many tasks that were difficult to automate in the past. AI unlocks entirely new capabilities for robots, making the latter less rigid and more responsive to the world around them. As observed during the excursion in innovating, robots may substitute for humans in the performance of several tasks; thus, in the near future, life inside firms may be even more automated.

Innovating, however, will not lead to the dehumanization of work. Besides robots, humans have been creating the so-called cobots—robots created to collaborate with humans. Cobots help humans in assembly, dispensing, finishing, welding, material removal, quality inspections, and more. Typically, the operator takes care of the precision work, while the cobot handles the more dangerous, repetitive, and heavier task. A point in case is material handling, which often consists of repetitive tasks and is one of the most dangerous jobs in manufacturing. According to Markets and Markets, the cobot is projected to skyrocket from USD 1.2 billion in 2021 to USD 10.5 billion by 2027. Therefore, humans and robots will be complementary in firms, and a blended solution is likely to emerge.

Similar hybrid solutions may also pop up in offices with the diffusion of telecommuting.[23] In recent years, the demand for a better work–life balance contextually able to preserve productivity has been among the drivers behind the search for new ways to work. In the ranking mentioned in Chap. 4, we have seen that firms try to attract workers by offering them the "best workplace," which involves several dimensions, including work–life balance. These days peculiar intersections of technological, cultural, and natural elements are pushing toward remote working. Thanks to innovating, the economic system will be more able to move the result of work rather than workers. If nature is behind the current pandemic, the cultural shift that has been set in motion by lockdowns has then speeded up that technological evolution, putting remote working under the spotlight. In the near future, thus, the principal–agent relationship between employers and employees should focus more on workers' results than on workers' presence.

Will these recent shifts keep humans out of offices? In the short- to mid-term, it will happen, but only partially. At the system-wide level these pandemic days have shown that there are jobs that can easily and efficiently be performed remotely (e.g.,

[23] Needless to say, these evolutions strongly affect other kinds of human aggregations such as families and cities, too. But in our short trip I will limit reflections to enterprises only.

in white-collar industries), while others strictly need physical presence (e.g., services with face-to-face interactions). Of course, then, there are many intermediate cases, even within the same firm. In the system, innovating and aggregating are going to add yet another dichotomy in jobs besides blue/white collar, low/high skills, etc.—"remotizable" vs. not remotizable.

At the individual level, several factors emerge, some steering toward telecommuting and some favoring the traditional workplace which, again, pushes toward the mixed solution. Among the drawbacks limiting remote working, there are the following. Some firms may have problems of coordination, monitoring, cybersecurity, tracking tasks, and productivity. Some remote workers may instead find it more difficult to build relationships with colleagues, may miss the daily habit to lunch with their work clique, or may suffer from reduced mutual aid and synergies. Humans typically like, if not need, face-to-face contact to build social capital and social relations. After all, not long ago, facilitating collaboration was a main motive behind creating open spaces in offices, and humans have not dramatically changed since then. Lastly, individuals working from home may experience practical technological issues because of less-than-ideal furniture, space, and IT equipment.

This said, both firms and workers may gain by aggregating in this blended way. Remote work offers employees flexibility and firms agility and resilience. It may give workers the necessary continuity of income and firms the operational continuity when the next shock (due to extreme weather, terrorism, pandemic, or whatever Taleb's "black swan") inevitably will hit the system. There are indications that working from home can enhance productivity and make workers happier (even in pre-pandemic days [33]). Firms may then offer lower wages that employees may accept because they may save transport time and costs and/or they prefer to stay at home. Some big tech companies, including Microsoft, Google, Facebook, and Twitter, have already started to offer less pay for employees based in locations where it is more inexpensive to live. But smaller firms such as Reddit and Zillow have announced that they will pay the same no matter where employees are based, saying that this improves diversity.

The state should not intervene directly in the bargaining between workers/unions and private firms because imposing detailed laws is likely to reduce the flexibility that is among the advantages of these new forms of organization. The state must instead promptly intervene to help firms and workers find a socially functioning equilibrium because it can affect both the costs and benefits of telecommuting. For instance, the state can step in to enhance the speed and stability of connections, reduce the digital divide, keep balanced the bargaining power,[24] and ensure effective formal institutions for the new normal.

[24] Notice that imbalanced power among trading partners entails the flip side of trading that the state must tackle.

Ultimately, efficient telecommuting is more a question of socioeconomic progress than technological progress. Consider the gig economy.[25] Innovating can sustain and enlarge it. But to the extent that it induces physical immigration of unskilled workers (people engaged, for example, in personal transport or food delivery or cleaning), the state must address issues involving immigration, social welfare, public finance, and employment regulation. Possibly this complex political backdrop may explain why gig economy workers have been—and still are—suffering from several problems (independent contractor misclassification, job insecurity, lack of occupational health protections, and the like). Diverse socioeconomic issues from telecommuting, which yet again call for implementing uneasy policies, may then emerge in some nations. Among the platform works that have been developing recently,[26] for example, some could magnify the immaterial emigration of specific highly skilled employees. As the traveler might note, this situation is the opposite of what has been said about the gig economy and is currently less under the spotlight with respect to other work-related themes, possibly because the individuals involved are not among the most disadvantaged workers.

But the topic is not trivial for the system as a whole. The crux is that the opportunity to work from home may induce specialists and professionals to continue to live in countries where the cost of life is lower and to work for firms that, being located in nations where the cost of life is higher, can afford to give them higher wages. If both firms and workers gain from this situation, the system loses highly skilled workers because of a curtailed workforce (not to mention the loss of the money spent to train those professionals). The state should therefore intervene to hamper this costly outflow.

If firms gather data and information on customers, the flow also operates the other way around. I have already recalled the cases of Amazon and Orbitz. This perspective highlights a number of intersections possibly involving the *Four* in the next few decades. Specifically, it is suggestive of how innovating may counterbalance what human aggregations such as large enterprises can actually do in their trading efforts. These days technological progress allows information to move borderless and to reach most humans very quickly. This puts large enterprises under the spotlight—several sectors of the economic system are now able to constantly monitor them on disparate collective themes. Big Pharma is under pressure to lower the prices of life-saving medicines and to hand over intellectual property for the coronavirus vaccines. The oil industry companies are increasingly pressured to reduce their carbon emissions and shift toward more sustainable energy sources. Social networks are often called on to be more aggressive in preventing personal information leakages, for being more neutral intermediaries, and for convincingly contrasting the diffusion

[25] The gig economy is an economy in which digital technologies enable teams to be assembled around a given project while platforms seamlessly connect buyers with sellers. A point in case in food delivery is Deliveroo.

[26] Platform work is an employment form in which organizations or individuals use an online platform to access other organizations or individuals to solve specific problems or to provide specific services in exchange for payment.

of falsehoods and fake news. Banks have been facing the Occupy Wall Street protest movement and the birth of cryptocurrencies (cf. Chap. 5). There is then the possibility of hackers' attacks that could be seen as the virtual version of what Greenpeace's activists are doing in the physical world.

Some big companies even report pressures from insiders. When Google withdrew from a US government program to develop AI for military purposes, it signaled that its employees' objections were more important than the interests of a large, lucrative client. F. Haugen, a former Facebook employee, revealed that Facebook executives had been aware of how badly the company's algorithms fail to protect users, public health, and democracy, but that the firm put profits above everything else. In sum, public opinion is increasingly informed and increasingly points the finger of blame on large corporations when referring to questions relating to fairness, (mis) information, common health, inequality, and environment.

Notice that this does not contrast with the behavioral continuity that I expect to hold in the near future. The fact that individuals are now sensitive to global threats like climate change, deforestation, pandemics, and the like does not necessarily mean that the degree of collectivism is significantly increasing. At least in the forecastable future, our species will maintain its multifaceted behavior. Humans can adapt their innate mixed behavior but do not—perhaps just cannot—change it definitively. Our wandering through the *Four* gives several hints on how humans have solved misalignments between individual and collective interests without evolving in a behaviorally different animal. If the socioeconomic Big Bang led humans to cooperate, it did not erase their individualism. If Ostromians successfully tackled their environmental issues, they did so by constraining their inexorable individualism. Typically, markets and effective rules of the game have evolved over time to manage, not to modify structurally, the compound behavior of humans. Probably, it is so because of self-awareness—humans know their weaknesses, hence they tie their hands (North *docet*). On the other hand, if many humans these days address collective topics, it may be for individualistic motives. Not to mention that if everyone is against global warming, most of us still behave as it is a matter for the others; the NIMBY (Not In My Back Yard) attitude is far from being defunct. In a nutshell, cooperative behavior will continue to face free riding, moral hazard, and opportunism in social interactions for the near future, at least.

By the same token, private firms will still pursue individualistic goals. Thus, for example, their pro-environmental acts and declarations are not (and will likely not be) induced by other-regarding impulses of their managers and/or owners. Just as enterprises became sensitive to "energy saving" eminently to maximize their profits in the aftermath of the oil crises of the 1970s, there is no green soul behind the recent decisions of oil companies to invest in renewable energy. The crux is, rather, that in the pursuit of profits, private firms must increasingly consider other human aggregations—stakeholders, customers (actual and potential), employees, and local and global communities.

Like never before, firms will compete to show a convincing civic engagement, trustworthiness, etc.—i.e., to gain social capital—because their profits will also depend on that and on how efficiently they align their interests with those of other human aggregations. In other words, firms' profit maximization efforts will face inner and external constraints stemming from both technology and society. In the near future, at least, it seems unrealistic that a significant, persistent decoupling among the interests of individuals, the state, private firms, and other aggregations do not trigger some kind of error correction mechanism in the market system.

What is the role of the state in all that? The short answer is—ever more critical. The previous discussion should have emphasized enough that recent trends are affecting the market system in such a way as to magnify the role of the state. Due to their delicate role as information spreader, for example, the state must closely monitor podcasts and social media platforms, fine-tuning between freedom of opinion and falsehood. Just as with the market mechanism and the market price, even the Internet is a useful source of information and coordination only under some conditions, which brings into play the state. Similar indications derive from the fact that the new "seven sisters" (Microsoft, Apple, Amazon, Google, Facebook, Tencent, and Alibaba) are Internet-based firms that currently constitute two-thirds of total market value worldwide.[27] The introduction of a countervailing power to balance this sort of private firms is essential and can only be done through government oversight. More generally and even more crucially, public goods are becoming progressively more essential as well as troubles ever more global and intertwined—cybersecurity, supply chains continuity, climate change, immigration, biodiversity, financial markets, tax heavens, etc. All these issues involve a blurring of public and private vulnerabilities. If the other ingredients of capitalism remain essential, thus they will need a greater input from the state for the *Four*-inspired humans to live together, better, and longer.

Further, as has been said, I believe in the substantial continuity of behaviors, at least in the short to medium term. That is, I do not believe that global threats will lead humans to shift toward a level of collectivism sufficient to allow them to tackle climate change, immigration, biodiversity, etc., with civic engagement or willingness to cooperate only. In the management of the *Four*, therefore, if an enlarged social capital may help, it cannot substitute for, formal, enforceable rules. In other words, the common background system behind the *Four* that we have been exploring in our tour—private firms, markets, state, informal institutions, and social capital—is likely to become more dependent on the state. In the forecastable future, the state must interface more intensely with both the private sector and other states to create the inclusive institutional setting which is necessary to implement the *Four* with due efficiency and sustainability. There is nothing new in all that, it is the usual positive correlation between the increasing evolution and greater formalization of the system that we have been seeing on our tour. But to the extent that this movement will materialize, it casts some shadow on near-future developments.

[27] The seven sisters of the twentieth century, which dominated the world oil industry from the 1920s to the 1970s, were Standard Oil Company (Exxon since 1972), Mobil, Chevron, Texaco, Gulf Oil Company, British Petroleum, and Shell.

The first tension stems from the fact that the state impinges on several elements of the economic system, which results in a careful and uneasy modulation of its moves. As observed, in addressing the *Four,* the state must ensure equal opportunities without reducing individual incentives and fighting spirit—imposing ex post equality means imposing ex ante lack of incentives and may create state-addicted individuals. If the state must both enable and restrict individual behaviors, then its policies should also keep a sufficient internal coherence. A recent example is that energy prices are very high these days, inducing some policymakers to adopt measures to calm them. While interventions may alleviate the situation of low-income individuals, they nonetheless disincentivize energy-saving behaviors, making them at odds with pro-environmental policies. State-individual relationships are intricate and subtle even as far as the linkages between state and social capital. As seen on our four systems that usually resort to formal institutions to manage the *Four* diminish the opportunity for humans to form and develop social capital, which, in turn, calls for even more formal institutions because this is the way individuals are used to solving their interactions. Then, if the state may foster social capital easing the connections between and the alignment of the interests of the various economic agents, it can obtain good results only acting as an honest and efficient facilitator. In a nutshell, the state must operate with sufficient competence, information and integrity in the economy; otherwise, it may create even bigger problems.

This steers the discussion toward the second worry, which is related to the predicted behavioral continuity. If the state must still face free riding, opportunism and the like by individuals, and state capture, rent-seeking, etc. by firms, I do not see enough motives to expect that policymakers will become more virtuous, prompt, informed, and competent than they have been in the last several years. The concerns thus lie in the fact that in light of the increasing role of the state, there will still be the usual burdens—demagogism, delays, state capture, corruption, lack of information, ineffectiveness, inefficiency, etc. If private firms need some counterbalancing power, then the same can be said for governments, which need of incentives and accountability. Only if policymakers were always virtuous, farsighted, competent, etc., there would be no need for checks and balances; but recent trends do not bode well.

In a nontrivial number of countries, for example, populist politicians present overly simplistic answers to complex questions in a highly emotional manner and/or by behaving opportunistically. These voter-maximizing strategies are unlikely to be welfare maximizing for society at large, and it is even certain that they cannot help most humans to efficiently implement the *Four*. If cheap and speedy communication makes it easier for citizens to monitor the performance of their government, then, the fabric of fake news is still not under control and policymakers do not seem extraneous to this situation. Individuals thus often end up confused and concerned about the reality on the ground. In these environments, then, private firms are induced to lobby policymakers even more than usual. All that impoverishes social capital and polarizes the system, which, in turn, makes it harder to align the interests of the economic agents.

Just as we saw with private firms, actually, there seems to be the necessity for policymakers to enlarge their social capital, as data confirm. According to Pew

Research Center,[28] in the 1960s, more than 70% of Americans trusted the government in Washington; in 2021, only 24% say that they do. The OECD has warned that only 45% of citizens trusted their governments in 2019. On that it is worth recalling that our tour suggests that *most* people must actively participate for the system to function well; that part of the social capital involving civic engagement is key. An expanding state calls for the civil society (community groups, labor unions, professional and trade associations, NGOs, etc.) to check over it.

Two other potential inconveniences for the state are growing public debts and the need to cooperate at international level. Regarding the former, if the current pandemic has highlighted the benefits of accumulating "extra" public debt amid deep recessions, the increasing worldwide tendency to finance the state via public debts has high costs. Higher public debts today hamper a more adequate managing of the *Four* in the coming periods/shocks and may crowd out private sector investments. Policymakers must then effectively spend public money but as recalled, this faces several technical, political, and behavioral difficulties. As already observed, for example, the US Congressional Budget Office has recently forecasted that in 2050, the debt will be twice the GDP. Otherwise stated, public debt is expected to run faster than GDP. Likewise, European fiscal commitments are under revision. If flexibility is good, it also weakens commitments—credibility is essential. As Latins warned, *pacta sunt servanda* (agreements must be kept). These days the macroeconomic situation is improving—will governments be able to repay the debt, or diet always begins tomorrow? Currently, then interest rates are nearly zero which is yet another push for financing policies using debt rather than taxation. But eventually higher public debt will exert tension on its cost and, hence, on its sustainability.[29] The sovereign debt crises of Latin America in the 1980s and that of Greece in the 2010s remind us that public debts must be carefully managed to avoid more painful adjustments (not to mention that, of course, sovereign debt crises for larger economies would be much more devastating).

The call for international cooperation emerges considering that global problems need to be managed globally. There is no technical way in which issues related to climate change, pandemics, the Internet, and the like can be solved at the national level. The point is that international agreements face behavioral and institutional troubles. From the behavioral standpoint, nationalism is far from being extinct; from the institutional standpoint, there is no *deus-ex-machina* to enforce international agreements and, of course, rules are as good as how they can be enforced. As the recent confrontation between Russia and Ukraine teaches, states that sign international cyber norms may simultaneously conduct large-scale cyber-operations against their adversaries. Another kind of issue is that it may be objectively hard to align interests at national and international level. Just to mention, climate change is not a *bad* produced today—how today's nations may overtake it? As free trade

[28] https://www.pewresearch.org/politics/2021/05/17/public-trust-in-government-1958-2021/

[29] Inflation may help indebted countries. But it raises further issues.

among nations is effective only under some conditions, so climate regulations need to take into account of the disparate histories behind the current situation.

This said, our tour suggests that balanced views are often more valid than extreme ones. Regarding climate change, for instance, I believe that a solution will eventually be found. International norms typically appear to be developing slowly but steadily, over the course of several years if not decades. It will likely be not the best solution but only a compromise solution that, nonetheless, will work somehow. As usual, moreover, this is not because of a change in behavior but rather because of nationalism. In the USA, for instance, intelligence and defense advisors warn that climate change will increasingly exacerbate a number of risks to US national security interests.[30] Likewise the Federal Reserve has recently created the Supervision Climate Committee and the Financial Stability Climate Committee which view climate-related financial risks as an emerging threat to the financial stability of the USA.

It is time for concluding remarks. Although systematically engulfed by several worries and featured by a ceaseless run-in between solved issues and new ones, our journey suggests that eventually humans succeed in finding solutions to their affairs. Solutions that will likely be not extreme. Although keeping virtually unchanged their traditional mixed behavioral paradigm, even at international level humans will find a way to cooperate, reaching some consensus. Accordingly, I daresay that in the near future, the *Four* will still help humans have reasonably higher average living standards, that these businesses will continue to be implemented in an evolving mid-range system without infamies and without louvres far from both anarchy and pure command economies, and that behaviors will still remain multifaceted and stuck in an endless fight between self-centeredness and concern for and commitment to others.

References

1. Glaeser E L (2011) op. cit.
2. Allen R C (2007) The Industrial Revolution: A Very Short Introduction. Oxford: Oxford University Press.
3. Marshall A (1890) op. cit.
4. Sullivan R J (1989) England's "Age of invention": The acceleration of patents and patentable invention during the industrial revolution. Explorations in Economic History 26(4): 424-452.
5. Sullivan R J (1989) op. cit.
6. Ortiz-Ospina E and Beltekian D (2018) Trade and globalization. Our World in Data.
7. Hume D (1739) op. cit.
8. Della Vigna S and Malmendier U (2006) Paying not to go to the gym. American Economic Review 96(3): 694-719.

[30] National Intelligence Council's National Intelligence Estimate on Climate Change available at: https://www.dni.gov/files/ODNI/documents/assessments/NIE_Climate_Change_and_National_Security.pdf

9. Sassi F, Belloni A, and Capobianco C (2013) The Role of Fiscal Policies in Health Promotion. OECD Health Working Papers 66.
10. Bisin A (2011) Introduction to economic analysis, Dept. of Economics, NYU.
11. Minsky H P (1975) John Maynard Keynes. Columbia University Press NY.
12. Minsky H P (1977) The Financial Instability Hypothesis: An Interpretation of Keynes and an Alternative to 'Standard' Theory. Nebraska Journal of Economics and Business 16 (1): 5–16.
13. Minsky H P (1986) Stabilizing an Unstable Economy. New Haven, CT: Yale University Press.
14. Shiller R J (2000) Irrational Exuberance, Princeton University Press. Princeton, NJ. The phrase "irrational exuberance" was coined by former Federal Reserve Chairman Alan Greenspan in 1996.
15. Minsky H (1994) Financial Instability Hypothesis. In Arestis P and Sawyer M (ed), The Eglar Companion to Radical Political Economy, Aldershot, Edward Elgar.
16. Bettencourt L M A et al (2007) Growth, innovation, scaling, and the pace of life in cities. Proceedings of the National Academy of Sciences 104 (17): 7301-7306.
17. Eilersen A and Sneppen K (2021) SARS-CoV-2 superspreading in cities vs the countryside. APMIS–Journal of Pathology, Microbiology and Immunology, February.
18. Ferrie JP and Troesken W (2008) Water and Chicago's Mortality Transition. 1850-1925. Explorations in Economic History 45(1): 1-16.
19. Smith A (1776) op. cit.
20. Weber M (1921) Economy and society. University of California Press, Berkeley (1978).
21. Pigou A C (1920) The Economics of Welfare. London: Macmillan.
22. Keynes J M (1930) op. cit.
23. Aghion P et al (2019) Innovation and Top Income Inequality. *The Review of Economic Studies* 86(1):1-45.
24. Aghion P et al (2019) op. cit.
25. Mokyr J (2000) Innovation and its enemies: the economic and political roots of technological inertia. In: Olson M and Kähkönen S (ed) A Not-So-Dismal Science. Oxford University Press, New York.
26. Autor D H and Dorn D (2013) The Growth of Low-Skill Service Jobs and the Polarization of the U.S. Labor Market. American Economic Review, 103(5): 1553–97.
27. Acemoglu D and Restrepo P (2020) Robots and Jobs: Evidence from US Labor Markets. Journal of Political Economy 128(6): 2188-2244.
28. International Federation of Robotics (2014). World Robotics: Industrial Robots. Technical report, International Federation of Robotics, Frankfurt.
29. Acemoglu D and Restrepo P (2020), op. cit.
30. OECD (2020) OECD Employment outlook 2020, OECD publishing, Paris.
31. Murphy G, Siedschlag I and McQuinn J (2017) Employment protection and industry innovation. Industrial and Corporate Change, 26(3): 379–398.
32. OECD (2018) Personalised Pricing in the Digital Era. DAF/COMP(2018)13.
33. Bloom N et al (2015) Does Working from Home Work? Evidence from a Chinese Experiment. Quarterly Journal of Economics 130(1):165–218.

The manufacturer's authorised representative in the EU is Springer Nature Customer Service Centre GmbH, Europaplatz 3, 69115 Heidelberg, Germany. If you have any concerns regarding our products, please contact ProductSafety@springernature.com

Printed and bound by CPI Group (UK) Ltd, Croydon, CR0 4YY
30/09/2026
02225462-0001